AN AMERICAN REQUIEM

God, My Father, and the
War that Came Between Us

James Carroll

A Mariner Book
HOUGHTON MIFFLIN COMPANY
BOSTON • NEW YORK

For information about permission to reproduce selections
from this book, write to Permissions, Houghton Mifflin Company,
215 Park Avenue South, New York, New York 10003.

For information about this and other Houghton Mifflin trade
and reference books and multimedia products, visit
The Bookstore at Houghton Mifflin on the World Wide Web
at http://www.hmco.com/trade/.

Library of Congress Cataloging-in-Publication Data
Carroll, James, date.
An American requiem : God, my father, and the war that came
between us / James Carroll.
p.   cm.
ISBN 0-395-77926-X
ISBN 0-395-85993-X (pbk)
1. Carroll, James, 1943–   — Family.   2. Novelists — 20th cen-
tury — Family relationships.   3. Ex-priests, Catholic — United States —
Family relationships.   4. Vietnamese Conflict, 1961–1975 — Protest
movements — United States.   5. Fathers and sons — United States —
Biography.   6. Catholics — United States — Biography.   I. Title.
PS3553.A764Z464   1996   95-52125 CIP
813'.54 — dc20

Printed in the United States of America

Book design by Robert Overholtzer

QUM 10 9 8 7 6 5 4 3 2 1

The author is grateful for permission to quote from the following:
Lines from "Vapor Trail Reflected in the Frog Pond," from *Body Rags* by
Galway Kinnell. Copyright © 1965, 1966, 1967 by Galway Kinnell. Reprinted
by permission of Houghton Mifflin Company. All rights reserved.
Lines from "Vietnamese," from *Growing into Love* by X. J. Kennedy. Reprinted
by permission of Curtis Brown Ltd. Copyright © 1969 by X. J. Kennedy.
Lines from "Death of Little Boys" from *Poems: 1922–1947* by Allen Tate.
Copyright 1931, 1932, 1937, 1948 Charles Scribner's Sons;
renewed copyright © 1959, 1960 Allen Tate.

For Lexa, Lizzy and Pat

CONTENTS

Praise for *An American Requiem* ᖾ

"A flawlessly executed memoir."
— **National Book Award citation**

"A work of the heart . . . perhaps the most moving drama of fathers and sons that I have ever read."
— **Christopher Tilghman,** *Washington Post Book World*

"Heart-breaking and heroic . . . autobiography at its best."
— *Publishers Weekly*

"James Carroll has written a profoundly honest and haunting memoir, which brilliantly evokes the love, loss, and heartbreak in his relationships with his father, his church, and his country."
— **Doris Kearns Goodwin**

"James Carroll, whose prose is always exceptional, has produced one of the most poignant and powerful American memoirs to emerge in many years." — **Tim O'Brien**

"A magnificent portrayal of two noble men who broke each other's hearts." — *Booklist*

"A personal and political memoir in a class by itself. Rich in ideas and historical detail, a personal story that makes you think — about politics, parents, children and God." — *USA Weekend*

"*An American Requiem* is one of those books that even as you are reading it, you know you will never forget. James Carroll is well recognized as a master storyteller. In this, his own story, he touches us as only a gifted writer can, and more so because it is true."
— **David McCullough**

"A healing and inspiring work."
— **Richard Hoffman,** *Boston Sunday Globe*

"Of all the memoirists who have set out to 'tell the truth' of a life and a crucial relationship, very few have ever succeeded so convincingly as James Carroll, in this poetic and achingly honest account of his lifelong struggle with his father to find a basis for mutual respect and love, an effort finally foundering on the Vietnam War. It is the story, never told better, of a generational faultline splitting households all across America. I couldn't put it down till its last, haunting sentence."
— **Daniel Ellsberg**

FRONTISPIECE

MY FATHER: not until years later did I appreciate how commanding was his presence. As a boy, I was aware of the admiring glances he drew as he walked into the Officers' Club, but I thought nothing of them. I used to see him in the corridors of the Pentagon, where I would go after school and then ride home with him. I sensed the regard people had for him, but I assumed that his warmth and goodness were common to everyone of his rank. I had no way of knowing how unlikely was the story of his success, nor had I any way to grasp the difference between him and the other Air Force generals. He was as tall as they, but looked more like a movie actor. I saw him stand at banquet tables as the speaker at Communion breakfasts, at sports team dinners, and, once, at a German-American Friendship Gala in Berlin. His voice was resonant and firm. He approved of laughter and could evoke it easily, though he never told jokes. His mode of public speaking had a touch of the preacher in it. He brought fervor to what he said, and an open display of one naked feeling: an unrestrained love of his country.

A fluent patriot, a man of power. Grace and authority were so much a part of his natural temperament that I did not mark them as such until they no longer characterized him. His relationship with his sons was formal — we addressed him as "sir" — but there was nothing stern in his nature. He never struck us. He never thumped the table until the pressures of the age made it impossible not to. We always knew he loved us. The problem was his absolute assumption that the existing social context, the frame within which he'd found his extraordinary success, was immutable. His belief in the world of hierarchy was total, and his sense of himself, as a father and as a general, depended on that world's survival. Defending it was his one real passion, his vocational commitment, and his religious duty.

And yet. One early Sunday morning in winter, when I was perhaps twelve years old, he got up before dawn to drive me on my paper route. This was an unusual occurrence. I normally wrestled the papers onto my red wagon, even the thick Sunday editions. I hauled my own way in several cycles around our suburban neighborhood, Hollin Hills, a new subdivision in Alexandria, Virginia. But a savage storm had moved in the night before, and now the wind was howling. Sheets of rain and sleet battered the windows. We bundled up and waited inside the front door until my distributor arrived, late, in his panel truck. Then Dad and I hurried out to load my *Washington Star*s into the back seat of the Studebaker.

The windshield wipers kept getting stuck in the buildup of grainy ice, which we would scoop away as we returned from running the bulky papers up to the houses of my subscribers, Dad on his side of the street, me on mine. It was raw, unpleasant work, but that morning I loved it. Indeed, in my mind it was a game, a version of "war," which we kids were always playing then. Those dashes from our car were sorties, I thought, bombing runs, commando raids. A stack of papers — artillery shells, mines, grenades — sat between us on the front seat. We would drive for fifty yards, jolt to a stop, snap into action. I would lean toward Dad, pointing through the fogged-up windows. I was the navigator, the bombardier. "That one, that one." Then we'd each bolt from the car, ducking into the freezing rain, splashing up driveways and across soggy lawns, propping the papers inside storm doors, then dashing away as if the things were going to explode. We achieved a brilliant synchrony, a teamwork that overstamped everything that might ever separate us. Drive. Stop. Fold. Open the door. Duck. Dash. Return. Way to go! Sir!

If my father had been the commander of a two-man suicide mission, I'd have followed him — not out of any readiness to die but out of the absolute trustworthiness of what bound us at that moment. I would have sworn that time itself could not undo it. "Neither principalities nor powers, nor things present, nor things to come . . ." I was an altar boy over whose head Saint Paul usually sailed, but these words had lodged themselves in me. ". . . nor height, nor depth, nor any other creature shall be able to separate us . . ." Paul, of course, was talking about the love of God, but my only real faith then was in the good order of the world over which Dad presided. Him. Nothing would separate me from him. That morning was delicious for being just the two of us.

When we'd almost finished, something hideous happened. My father had run up to a house and dropped the paper and was running back toward the car when the door of the house swung open.

"Hey, you!" a voice boomed. Even in that wind I heard the threat in it. This was on the far side of Hollin Hills, where the newer, smaller houses were. My distributor had signed these people up. I didn't know them. The voice was a man's, and it was laced with authority. "Get back here, goddammit!"

My father stopped and stood with his back to the man, still facing me. I searched his eyes to see what was in them, but the distance between us, and the rain, made it impossible to see.

"Get your ass back here, I said. Put my paper where it belongs."

I looked across and saw that Dad had dropped the paper under the overhang protruding from the lintel — dry enough, but not quite at the threshold. I thought of making the dash myself, to spare us all. But then I saw, on a low post beside my father, a sign with luminous letters on it. Dad was looking at it too. "M. Sgt. John Smith." *Master Sergeant,* I realized at once. The man was military. An NCO was barking orders at a general. A drill instructor bellowing at recruits.

Again I looked for Dad's eyes, and though it seemed I found them, I could read nothing of his reaction. Mine was stunned enough for both of us. Caught! was the feeling. Captured! Now they shoot us. I was frozen to a spot near the rear bumper of our car. Rain and sleet pelted my face, my soaked clothing, my slimy skin, my watery bones. A shudder coursed through me, a fever and a chill at once.

"Get back here, goddammit!"

My father's stare made me feel sure this was my fault. I started to sprint toward the house, to retrieve the paper and apologize. But as I was about to pass Dad, he put his hand up, stopping me. He turned and, with that low humping movement — ducking gunfire? — he retraced his path up the sergeant's driveway, dodging rivulets, scooting past a wheelbarrow and a mound of topsoil. Sergeant Smith's car was off to the side, and now I saw the bumper sticker identifying it with Fort Belvoir, an Army post a few miles away.

The sergeant had remained in the shadow of the doorway, out of the weather. He held the storm door half open. I could see only his arm and the dark bulk of his body. He was a big man. I had collected at the house once or twice, but from his wife. In the short time they'd been on my route, they'd never complained. I took a step forward as Dad bent to pick up the newspaper. He brought it the two or three steps to the door, held it out, and the man took it, saying something I could not hear. Then Dad was running toward me again, pumping like a halfback. "In the car," he called.

I scooted around to my side, and when he leapt onto the front seat so did I, as if we'd just pulled one off together. Our doors shut simultaneously. Dad dropped the car into gear, popped the clutch, and we lurched forward, away.

"What did he say, Dad?" I asked, but I was afraid of the answer.

"He said . . ." Dad looked at me, and I still could not read him. "He said, 'Don't let it happen again, bub.'"

"What'd you say?"

"No, sir!" His face cracked open with pleasure, sheer triumph. Sir! Even I knew how senior NCOs hated it when stupid punk recruits addressed them as if they were officers. "No, sir!" Dad repeated. Then we laughed and laughed, heads back. He slapped my leg. No, sir! I was swept up in a wave of gratitude, both that my father had not needed to pull rank on the bastard and that he'd found a way to prick him.

Our over-large reaction was about more than that, though, and now I know why. The order of the hierarchy, of the universe we shared, had just been upended. Years later, in literature class, I would learn that such reversal is the essence of comedy — and also of tragedy. But that morning, bound more tightly than before, my father and I found his near humiliation and his too sly but finally generous riposte only funny. Nothing would ever seem this funny to us again, certainly not the ordered world as eventually I upended it. But that morning, it was enough. We laughed until we got home, then found ourselves unable to explain to the others why. Which only made it better.

1

IN THE VALLEY
OF BONES

CATHOLICS CALLED IT Our Lady of Perpetual Help, but to the Jews and Protestants who also took turns worshiping there, it was just "the chapel." Mary's statue and the crucifix were mostly kept behind blue curtains — Air Force blue, the color of the carpeting, the needlepoint kneelers, and the pew cushions. The little white church with its steeple and clear glass Palladian windows could have been the pride of any New England town, but this was the base chapel at Bolling Air Force Base, on the east bank of the Potomac River in Washington, D.C. A block to one side, hangars loomed above it, and up the hill on the other side a Georgian mansion, the Officers' Club, dwarfed the small church — a reminder of what really mattered here.

On a Saturday in February 1969 more than two hundred people filed into the chapel. The statue of Mary and the wretched crucifix were on display. The paraphernalia of a Roman Catholic liturgy were laid out on the side table and altar — the cruets, the covered chalice, the beeswax candles, the oversize red missal, which the chaplain's assistant would spell "missile." The congregation included Air Force officers in uniform, since this event had the character of an official function. A number were generals who had come down from Generals' Row, the ridge road along the upper slope of the base, where the vice chief, the inspector general, and members of the Air Staff lived. These were the chairborne commanders of Operation Rolling Thunder, an air war that by then had dropped more bomb tonnage on a peninsula in Asia than the Army Air Corps ever dropped on Germany.

The generals and their wives, easing down the center aisle, looked for their host and hostess, and found them already seated in the front pew. They were Lieutenant General and Mrs. Joseph F. Carroll — Joe and Mary. He was the founding director of the Defense Intelligence Agency, the man in charge of counting the enemy and evaluating targets in Vietnam. Today he wore civvies, but with his steely hair, fixed gaze, and erect posture he looked like what he was. She, a staunch, chin-high Catholic woman, was nearly in possession of a lifelong Irish dream: she was the newly minted mother of a priest. But there was worry in her fingers as the beads she held fed through them. Her lips were moving.

A bell rang. The airman at the Hammond organ and a seminary choir began with a hymn, and the people stood, joining in with a set of coughs that moved through the chapel like a wind sent to rough up the chipper happiness of the seminarians. A line of altar boys entered from the sacristy in the rear, ambling into the center aisle, leading a procession of a dozen priests wearing stoles and albs, a pair of candle bearers, a thurifer, the surpliced master of ceremonies, and, last of all, the ordained priest come to celebrate his first Mass and preach his first anointed sermon. That new priest, with his primly folded hands and his close haircut and his polished black wingtips, was I.

A few minutes later, the Air Force chief of chaplains, Major General Edwin Chess, by church rank a monsignor, whom I had known since he accompanied Cardinal Spellman to our quarters for a Christmas visit at a base in Germany years before, stood at the microphone to introduce me. "In a day when our society is so disjointed," he said to his fellow generals, "it is a great joy to know that Father Carroll is on our side."

What? On *whose* side?

I was celebrating my first Mass here, as tradition required, because it was my parents' parish, not mine. True, I had served as an altar boy in this chapel nearly a decade before. My brother Brian had been married at the sister chapel, across the Maryland hills at Andrews Air Force Base. A rotation of Air Force chaplains had been welcomed into our family like bachelor uncles. When I had entered the seminary after a year at Georgetown University — where I was named Outstanding Air Force ROTC Cadet — it had been with the specific intention of becoming an Air Force chaplain myself. General Chess had been my spiritual director.

And no wonder I'd harbored that ambition. Air bases were like sanctuaries to me. I loved the places — the air policemen saluting us at the gates, the sprawling hangars, the regular roar of airplanes, the friendly sergeants in the Base Exchange, the Base Ops snack bar, the mounded ammo dumps amid stretches of grass on which I'd played ball. After Hollin Hills, Air Force bases were a realm of mine. I grew up a prince, a would-be flyboy, absolutely on the side of everyone in blue. But now?

On our side — when had that unambiguous phrase ceased to describe my position? Perhaps beginning in November 1965 when, below my father's third-floor window at the Pentagon, a thirty-one-year-old Quaker named Norman Morrison set himself on fire. It took a couple of years, but by October 21, 1967, I was standing on roughly the same spot below my father's window. No self-immolator, I merely chanted antiwar slogans — and I dared do even that only because tens of thousands of others stood chanting with me. I was sure it would never occur to my father that I was out there, and I was careful not to isolate myself from the throng. He never saw me.

As a seminarian I had embraced as an ideal Daniel Berrigan, the Jesuit priest and poet. Only months before my ordination, he and his brother led the infamous raid on the draft board offices in Catonsville, Maryland. On their side? Compared to the Berrigan witness, my anonymous participation in Washington's massive antiwar demonstrations was the height of timidity. In secret I had taken the stainless-steel model B-52 bomber that was my prize for that ROTC award out to a ravine behind the seminary and hurled it, the napalm machine, into a fetid swamp. I remember its gleaming arc as my version of the gods' dispelling in midair — their annihilation, not ours, as Wallace Stevens had it, "yet it left us feeling that in a measure, we, too, had been annihilated." Those photographs of little slant-eyed people with melted chins and no eyelids and charred blue skin and fused fingers had given new meaning to the old word "hit," as in "hit of napalm."

I had had dreams about the war, about flying airplanes in it, but my puerile fantasy had become a nightmare. Once I dreamed of crashing a jet plane into my parents' house on Generals' Row. But it was all a secret, and not just from them. When, only a few months before, General Curtis LeMay, a 1968 vice presidential candidate, had put the most savage warmongering on display, I could not square my shame with the near worship I had felt for him as our next-door neighbor at Bolling in the early sixties. That was a secret too. I dreaded the thought that my fellow protesters might learn who my neighbors were, much less my father. In public, standing alone, I had never declared myself on the war. But what did it mean to be alone? I was two people, and considered independently, each of my selves seemed to have a coherence and integrity that were belied by the fact that I could not bring them together. For the longest time I could not speak.

And now? What to my father surely seemed a proper obeisance had become to me the secret cowardice of a *magnum silentium*. He had reason to take for granted the reliable decorum of my first priestly performance. But my mother, with her worrying fingers, had reason to be anxious, for she had learned never to trust the arrival of a dream, even if she could not quite imagine how it might shatter.

Despite my clerical draft exemption, or because of it, mounting the tidy pulpit of that pristine war church felt exactly like conscription. *On our side?* The chief chaplain's words had hit me like a draft notice, and I felt naked as any inductee before my well-clothed brothers, friends, and neighbors; before a few of my fellow seminarians, hardly peaceniks; before beaming chaplains and generals; before my parents; before — here was the deepest feeling — the one-man congregation of my father. I could no more look at him than at God.

I remember looking at the other bright, uplifted faces. One was my brother Dennis, who before this year was out would be a draft fugitive. Another was my brother Brian, who before Dennis returned from exile abroad would be an FBI agent, catching fugitives like him. I remember the beveled edges of the wooden lectern inside my clutching fingers. The Scriptures in front of me were open to a text I had chosen myself, departing from the order of the liturgical cycle. And I remember:

"The hand of Yahweh was laid on me, and he carried me away and set me down in the middle of a valley, a valley full of bones. He made me walk up and down among them. There were vast quantities of these bones on the ground the whole length of the valley; and they were quite dried up."

A mystical vision? The prophet Ezekiel in an epileptic trance? Yet news accounts not long before had described just such a scene in the valley below a besieged hilltop called Khe Sanh. Curtis LeMay had proposed using nuclear weapons to break the siege. Casualties had mounted. Ten thousand men had been killed in a matter of weeks, and that carnage was in my mind when I presumptuously chose Ezekiel's text as the starting point of my first proclamation as a priest.

Dry bones: the metaphor rang in the air, a double-edged image of rebuke, cutting both ways, toward the literal Southeast Asian valleys of the dead and toward the realm of crushed hopes about which some of us had never dared to speak. "Can these bones live?" I now asked in my excursus, repeating Ezekiel's refrain. "Dried and burned by time," I said, "and by desert wind, by the sun and most of all" — I paused, knowing the offense it would be to use a word that tied the image to the real, the one word I must never use in this church, never use with them — "by napalm."

It was as specific as I dared get — or as I needed to. Others in that congregation may not have felt the dead weight of that word, but I knew my father would, and so would the other generals. No one but opponents of the war referred to the indiscriminately dropped gelatinous gasoline that adheres to flesh and smolders indefinitely, turning death into torture or leaving wounds impossible to treat. Napalm embodied the perversion of the Air Force, how "Off we go into the wild blue yonder" had become the screeches of children. There was a sick silence in the chapel that only deepened when I repeated, "Can these bones live?" Only now the meaning was, "Can they live after what you have done?"

That was not a real question, of course, about the million Vietnamese whose bones the men in front of me had already scorched, or the more than twenty thousand Americans who had fallen by then. They were dead. And even a timid, metaphoric evocation of their corpses seemed an act of impudence. "Can these bones live?" I realized that I had unconsciously clenched my fist and raised it. All power to the people! Hell no, we won't go! *My* fist upraised, as if *I* were Tommie Smith or John Carlos on the medal stand at the Mexico City Olympics, as if *I* were Bobby Seale. I recall my stupefaction, and now imagine my eyes going to that uplifted arm, draped in the ample folds of my first chasuble. "Can these bones live?"

I answered with Ezekiel's affirmation of the power of Yahweh, the great wind breathing life into the fallen multitude — an image of the resurrection hope central to the faith of Christians. I reached for the spirit of uplift with which I had been trained to end sermons, and perhaps I thought I'd found it. Yes, we can live and love each other and be on the same side, no matter what. "Peace," as LeMay's SAC motto had it, "is our profession." None of us is evil. God loves us all. Who am I to judge? Coming from one who'd just spit the word "napalm" at them, what crap this must have been to those generals.

Can these bones live? The answer to the question that day was no. We all knew it. In my mind now I look down at my parents, stiff in the front pew, my mother staring at the rosary beads in her lap, my father stupefied like me, meeting my eyes. He must have known that I had chosen this text. That violation of the liturgical order would have been enough to garner his disapproval. But a biblical battlefield? He must have known exactly what it meant. Bones? Vietnam? To ask the question was to answer it. My fist was clenched in my father's face. "Prophesy over these bones!" Yahweh commanded. And, coward that I was, I did.

In the Catholic Church to which I was born, the theology of the priesthood affirmed that the effect on a man — always a man — of the sacrament of Orders was an "ontological change," a transformation at the deepest level of one's essence and existence. It is an absurdly anachronistic notion, I would say now, but that morning I was living proof of it. My ordination in New

York the previous day by His Eminence Terence Cardinal Cooke — himself the military vicar, the warriors' godfather — had given me an authority I never felt before. In my first sermon as a priest, it prompted me to break the great rule of the separation of Church and State, claiming an expertise not only about an abstract moral theology but about its most specific application — an expertise that my father, for one, had never granted me. "I was not ordained for this," I would have said, sensing the wound that my timid reference had opened in him. "But I can't help it."

After Mass there was a reception at the Officers' Club, and I was not the only one who noticed when my father's fellow generals did not show up. They had no need to pretend, apparently, that my affirming peroration had undone the damage of my impudent reference to the war. My father stood rigidly beside me in the boycotted reception line. We were the same height, but his posture was better than mine and I thought of him as taller. Typical of me. Looking at it from his side, as I was conditioned to do, I saw that his presence next to me displayed a rather larger portion of parental loyalty than I deserved. I had already begun to see what I had done in referring to Vietnam not only as an act of smug self-indulgence but, conversely, as yet more proof of my cowardice. I had said enough to offend my father, and also enough to make me see what I should have said.

It wasn't cowardice, I see now. What an unforgiving perception the young man I was had of himself, but he had yet to move through the full cycle of this story, had yet to move away, that is, from seeing the world as populated by cowards and heroes. The point is, despite my act of resistance, my father and I, even at that cold moment, were not unlike each other. And yet we would be separated for good now. "These bones," I saw too late, were also the whole house of our relationship, and no, they would not live. There were two lasting effects of the sermon I gave on

February 23, 1969. The first, and most painful, was the breach it caused between me and my father. For more than two years I had feared that if I dared hint at my rejection of the war, if I hinted at my not being "on his side" in the home-front war against armies led by the Berrigans or even Bobby Seale, he would neither understand nor forgive me. In prospect, to a young man such a consequence is fearsome, but abstractly so. I anticipated my father's reaction accurately, yet I never imagined how debilitating to him would be, not my rejection, but all that it symbolized; nor how disheartening to me would be our lifelong alienation.

The second effect of that sermon was its manifestation of the kind of priest I had become. Alas, the wrong kind. Wrong for the country — both Berrigans would soon be in jail — and wrong for the Church. Pope John XXIII had famously opened the windows to let in fresh air, convening a council that was to end the era of Counter-Reformation rigidity. With the openhearted, beloved Angelo Roncalli on the throne of Peter, the day of a calcified, totalitarian Catholicism was supposed to be over. But Roncalli was gone. I didn't know it at ordination, but Church renewal had already failed a few months before, with Pope Paul VI's 1968 encyclical *Humanae Vitae* condemning birth control. Pope John's fresh air had moved across the valley of dry bones but had not entered them. I think now that my fate as one who, a short five years later, would violate his solemn vow and leave the priesthood was sealed in that inadvertently clenched fist of mine. The strident question "Can these bones live?" found an answer in Jesus' searing words: "Let the dead bury the dead."

During the Nixon administration, William Rogers defended the team ethic of the Vietnam War by saying, "There gets to be a point where the question is: whose side are you on? Now, I am the Secretary of State of the United States, and I'm on our side."

Because of accidents of my personal history, I associate the forcing of that question with an Air Force chaplain's remark and Ezekiel's vision of the dry bones. For me, the image of the death-littered valley has always overwhelmed the image of a promised restoration, those bones up and dancing. Even in the era when I could rhetorically evoke the magical breath of God, I did so dutifully. I was too innocent to know it, but my cherished version of the Good News was too thin, too devoid of irony, and too cheaply won to sustain me as a preacher, much less to carry the weight of what was coming. The death-littered valleys of Vietnam — within weeks of my first Mass, reports would surface of the one at My Lai — changed the way I thought of my family, my nation, my faith, and myself. Ultimately, of course, it was all a lesson in mortality: my parents died, although not before my infant daughter did. And now I know, as privileged twenty-six-year-old American men never do, that my bones too will be scorched, and the breath will leave my body forever. Far more devastatingly, I know already that I will die as my father did, as a man who fell far short of his first and most generous dream. I will die as the flawed compromiser I was already when I wounded him with a sermon that was not cruel enough. And why shouldn't this soul be sorrowful?

Yet from here, precisely in this am I seized, not by some falcon-Yahweh who lifts me up, but by the story. I am a writer, no priest. I believe that to be made in God's image is to do this: arrange memory and transform experience according to the structure of narrative. The story is what saves us, beginning in this case with Ezekiel, coming down through valleys and a blue curtain to Jesus, my only God, whose fate was and remains the same as my father's, mine, and everyone's. Telling His story, in my tradition, is what makes Him really present. And that is why this soul, also, can rejoice.

2

J. EDGAR, JOE,
AND ME

ROGER "TERRIBLE" TOUHY was a notorious bank robber, kidnapper, and killer in gangland Chicago, but he was also the key to my father's fate and then, of course, to mine.

By 1940, the year my Chicago-bred father joined the FBI, the G-man glory days were over. Al Capone had moved to Miami the year before, and would in time die of syphilis. Most of the other well-known Chicago hoodlums, like Touhy, were on ice in the Illinois state prison at Joliet. My father had only recently graduated from Loyola Law School, a blue-collar night school in the Loop. During the day, for the six years it took to complete the program, he had worked in the Chicago stockyards, first as a shit-kicking steamfitter's helper, then as a meat seller for Swift. He'd grown up in the rancid shadow of the packinghouses, in Irish Bridgeport, "Back of the Yards." Workers never got the stench of the place out of their skin, and it was his nightmare to end up there.

He was a tall, good-looking dark Irishman, bright enough to have ranked at the top of his law school class. He was a good-humored young man whom others liked, a ball player and a partygoer, even with his tight schedule. His classmates did not hold his *summa cum laude* law degree against him; they marveled at it. His fellow workers at the stockyards, on the other hand, did not know about it.

This was an era when fewer than one in twenty Americans attended college, and fewer still went to law school — and of those, most were the sons of the elite. Naively, my father had expected that his success in school would land him a job at a State Street law firm, but after a decade of the Depression, firms in the desolate Chicago Loop weren't hiring lawyers even from the Ivy League. By the time he graduated Loyola, my father felt lucky to land a job with the FBI. He assumed it would take him out of Chicago, and by 1940 that seemed lucky too.

Chicago was a hard-ass town, and young Joe Carroll had seen the roughest of it up close. As a boy he'd had to scramble for nickels and dimes to help feed his sisters. He'd collected discarded milk bottles on the lakefront beaches, competing with derelicts. He'd climbed to the roofs of buildings near Comiskey Park to retrieve the "Spaldeens" and softballs and White Sox hardballs that had been lost up there. Once a section of roof collapsed under his weight, which brought him crashing down into the owner's bedroom. His shirt was stuffed with balls: what to do but grin impishly and ask the man if he wanted to buy one?

The yards district was the home of Edward J. Kelly, the mayor and head of the Democratic Party machine, as years later it would be home to Mayor Richard J. Daley, and then, years later again, to Mayor Richard M. Daley. After the Capone syndicate was broken by the feds, Kelly's machine picked up the pieces. The mob's lucrative vice industry continued, only now run out of police stations, ward offices, and city hall. Beginning in the mid-1930s, the Kelly machine raked in $20 million a year from illegal gambling alone. At the same time Kelly, by delivering

Chicago to Franklin Roosevelt in 1936, made himself essential to the president, who repaid him with massive patronage through the WPA.

The newsstands and cigar stores where my father bought his *Tribs* and Camels were fronts for betting parlors, which had no need to hide the betting slips and numbers stubs the losers dropped on the floor. Nor was there shame in the machine's vote-getting technique, which Joe saw even closer up. His father's job as a janitor in a South Side ward house was contingent on the family's delivering ten certified votes in every election. When he came of age, my father was one of those votes, as, later, would be my mother. Once married, they would not be able to move out of the ward without having arranged for reliable replacements on my grandfather's voting list. Kelly's ruthless enforcement of machine discipline; his open collection of money from gamblers, pimps, and protection racketeers as well as from the coffers of the New Deal, which in a few short years funded Kelly's new airport, the State Street subway, and major expansions of Lincoln Park and Lake Shore Drive — it all left my father with what would be an abiding contempt for the hypocrisies of politics.

"Roosevelt is my religion," Kelly used to chant in a favorite speech, but so was Irish Catholicism. Whatever he did during the week, on weekends he was a good Bridgeport family man whose Saturday confession and Sunday Communion reinforced an Irish sense of God's mercy on a fallen world, which helped make him a complacent partner to criminals. My father was a different kind of Irish Catholic, the other kind. A fallen world? Its only hope was a firm attachment to the law, the letter of it. Despite his apparent good humor, my father, from an early age, had a ruthless conscience, and by the time he was a man — what else took him to school all those nights? — the idea of the law itself had replaced not only Roosevelt but, in some way, religion too. Didn't Edward J. Kelly represent the corruption of both? That was why my father hated Kelly and, taking Kelly as their archetype, all other politicians. The world is fallen, yes. But that is reason not for a winking laxity, but for rigidity.

Years later my father, with his partygoing days long behind, would describe himself to me as an Irish Jansenist. Cornelius Jansen was a seventeenth-century Dutchman who held that human nature is incapable of good. His sway was greatest just when Irish seminaries were being shut by the occupying English, and Irish clergy had to go to the Continent to learn Catholic theology. Condemned by Rome as heresy, Jansen's ideas had nevertheless found a niche in the besieged Irish Church. Eventually they spread like a virus to Irish-American seminaries, in one of which my father was infected. The trouble was that the harsh Jansenist judgment he applied to others he had first to apply to himself. Incapable of good? My father had reason to think as much of Kelly, the neighborhood boss, city tyrant, exploiter of his own father. But by the standard of immigrant Catholicism, at the deepest level of his existence, my father had reason to think as much of himself.

In 1934, Kelly's Bridgeport-based machine was reported by the *Chicago Daily News* to be taking in $1 million a month from illegal vice activities. That same year, my father returned to Bridgeport, a twenty-four-year-old disgrace to his parents, his five sisters, and to the parish that had sponsored him. After a dozen years in the archdiocesan seminary, preparing to be a priest since the age of twelve, he'd committed the sacrilege of quitting. He did so on the eve of his ordination to the diaconate, shortly before taking the lifelong vow of celibacy. The years of disciplined study in philosophy and theology — he'd been at the top of those classes too — had grounded him in a rigid moralism. There was a flinty ledge below the surface of an affability that was enough to make colleagues love him, but only to a point. And in his family he would always be at the mercy of an old self-rejection we would note but never understand. It would inflict itself on me, but not more than on himself. *Domine non sum dignus!* My earliest memory of my father, from when I knelt next to him in a pew I could not see out of, is the forceful thumping of his fist against his chest. When later I learned the words and gesture meant "I am not worthy!" I was not surprised.

As the son of a sporadically employed, heavy-drinking sad sack whose one season as a bullpen catcher for the Chicago White Sox — "Dike" Carroll, they'd called him — was a sole and, perhaps, ultimately inhibiting distinction, Joe Carroll would never have been educated except for his time on the track to the priesthood. But once well along that track — here was the catch, and I would feel the pinch of it myself years later — it was a virtual mortal sin to get off.

Young Joe had had a last meeting with the seminary rector, a bishop who told him that if he changed his mind, he could go to the North American College in Rome for his doctorate in theology, a slipstream Church career. But still he said no. No to the bishop. No to Holy Mother the Church. No to his own Irish mother, who'd already claimed parish primacy as the mother of a priest. And no to God.

Though my father's youthful choice would, without my knowing it, define my own, his refusal to become a priest remains a mystery to me. *Domine non sum dignus:* was he "unworthy" before he quit the Church or only after? His more secular motto might as well have been the running gag line of a 1930s radio show, "Don't open that door, McGee!" Unlike Fibber McGee, my father never opened his door. To my knowledge, he never discussed the meaning of his early status as a "spoiled priest," but that status and its consequences explain our two lifetimes. I still long to know how he mustered such an act of nonconformity, defying every expectation, every notion of virtue in which he'd been schooled, and, for that matter — what were his alternative prospects in the depths of the Depression? — every apparent note of economic self-interest.

There is a large hint in the fact that he began seeing my mother around the time of his fateful choice. She was a wise-cracking, lusciously redheaded working girl from the same South Side Irish enclave. Mary Morrissey was the second-oldest of eight children, a family split by "Irish divorce," meaning her father had simply disappeared. She had quit school at fourteen. She lied about her age, altering the date on her birth certificate, to get a job as a telephone operator. By 1934, aged twenty-three, she was a Ma Bell supervisor in the bright art deco Illinois Bell Building in the Loop, in charge of a whole floor of girls in headsets.

I have a boardwalk-concession photograph of a beach party, a dozen young people in surprisingly sexy bathing suits, taken at the Oak Street Beach off Lake Shore Drive. My father and mother are each leaning into someone else, but he is looking across at her, the one real beauty. It is easy to imagine his being smitten. He once told me that when they were dating, he could lift her up, his hands completely linked around her waist. When I asked her, she said that it was true, but that since then his fingers had shrunk.

Though I asked and asked again, my mother always refused to be pinned down on when exactly they'd become an item. She would discuss his decision not to be a priest no more than he would, but that refusal eventually made me see the truth embedded in it: if she had begun dating the dashing Joe Carroll after his break with the Church, she would have forever emphasized the fact — much as my own quite American wife, years later, firmly makes the point that she never knew me as a priest. In Irish Chicago, there was shame enough in having married a man who'd once been betrothed to God, but also to have been the occasion of his unfaithfulness — the very corespondent, as it were — evokes a pale green version of the scarlet letter. Unworthy? What does it do to a vibrant young couple when their passion for each other, however conventionally expressed, makes them feel sullied from the start? A song of the day went, "A fine romance! With no kisses! A fine romance, my friend, this is!" From that beachfront photograph, I imagine my parents coming together like Fred and Ginger, but there was no such sexual ease between them by the time I knew what to look for — and I think that "unworthiness" is why.

In any case, my father weathered, but also presumably withered in, the bishop's stare. How it must have accused him of stealing all that schooling, his erudition, and the self-assurance it took to walk out on God. Joe Carroll returned to Bridgeport, to the hedged life into which his boyhood chums had long since settled, as a stockyards shit-kicker. Fluency in Cicero, Aristotle, and Thomas Aquinas notwithstanding, he was a spoiled priest now, and in Chicago he always would be. His role in life would be to drink heavily and fail.

Yet he rejected that bleak outcome too. Hubris to others, to him a primitive will to survive, it took him downtown most nights for years, bone-weary and reeking of the slaughterhouses. What a relief, finally, to have a shot, if only at the FBI. That it would take him to Quantico, Virginia, Washington, D.C., and beyond could not have been bad news. He and my mother married in 1938. Less than two years later, having replaced themselves on the ward voting lists for the sake of his father's janitor's job, they kissed the world of Swift and Armour, of Edward J. Kelly, of St. Gabriel's parish, and of Cardinal Mundelein good-bye. They were the first of their large families to leave Chicago — a very few would follow — and it is impossible for me to imagine them doing so except with relief.

That should have been that, an arrow-straight midcentury American story, from the old to the new, from the parish to the world. But after training, and a brief assignment to Knoxville, Tennessee, the Bureau in its wisdom sent my father back to Chicago, a curve in the story. By 1942, Joe and Mary Carroll were living Back of the Yards again, not far from Mayor Kelly's. They were voting on the machine list in old Dike's name, as if they'd never left the parish. But the truth was that Mary, for one, felt a need to be near her mother, and an unexpected freedom to be. Mary and Joe had had their first son, Joe junior, on New Year's Eve of 1940. Only with the birth of my own first child thirty-nine years later could I imagine the transformation made possible by such an event. There is a signal of their transformation in my parents' self-affirming impulse to name the baby for its father. Unworthy? The saint for whom that baby was named was not Jesus' father but the baby's own. And why not? It became a joke with them: Joseph and Mary, and a baby whose initials would be J.C. A baby whose robust perfection and even beauty stunned everyone; a baby who could be taken only as a sign of God's approval, no matter what the parish biddies thought. Joe junior rebutted every notion of unworthiness.

The experience of parenthood, and perhaps even its consola-tions, were mysteries Mary contemplated more or less alone, not mainly because of the era's restrictive gender roles, but because the world emergency of the war proved to be as transforming for Joe senior as Joe junior's birth had been for her. He was working the fugitive squad out of the field office on the nineteenth floor of the Bankers Building in the Loop and, since Pearl Harbor, was rarely home. He wouldn't say it, but the irony of his position had to be like a carcass carrier's weight: enforcing the wartime Selective Service and Training Act meant making sure the South Side goof-offs he thought he'd left behind got out of Chicago while he stayed. FBI men, more essential than ever, were draft exempt and discouraged from enlisting. Joe Carroll assumed that he would never wear a uniform.

A million men had registered for the draft, and then the boards had begun issuing classifications and calling men up. My father could not have imagined how it foreshadowed the last large reversal of his own life — one son a draft dodger, another son an antidraft conspirator — but Joe Carroll's early work as an FBI agent was the knuckle-dragging humdrum of tracking down dopes who did not understand that events in Europe east of Wicklow had changed everything — that the draft law was for real. Those who knew that this Hitler meant more than Luke Appling saw big changes looming in the future, but the big change in my father's life came then from the past.

In September of 1942, Roger "Terrible" Touhy broke out of Joliet. His escape pushed the German installation of Pétain off the Chicago front pages. As an antidote to the gloomy news from Europe and the Pacific, the Bureau prepared to launch a glorydays gangster hunt again. But FBI jurisdiction was a prickly issue because, unlike the tax evader Al Capone or the border crosser Clyde Barrow, Touhy had never been convicted or even charged with a federal crime. Then my father had an idea. Touhy, in escaping from state prison, had failed to notify his draft board of his change of address, a violation punishable in wartime by federal imprisonment for up to five years. Thus Joe Carroll, a thirty-two-year-old junior gumshoe, but an expert at catching draft dodgers, was assigned to the Bureau's biggest case.

In the 1930s, FBI gangbuster exploits had been deliberately publicized as a way of acclimating citizens to the idea of an activist, interventionist federal government. Despite his legacy as an icon of the right wing, J. Edgar Hoover, master publicist, had been an enabler of the New Deal, implicitly preaching to traditionally wary Americans that Washington was a friend. By the early fall of 1942 other forces were at work. The Allied counterattack in Europe had yet to come — Torch Day, the Montgomery-led invasion of North Africa, was November 8 — and so the hunt for Touhy took on a subliminal meaning as a kind of substitute pursuit of the as yet unchallenged Hitler. Roger "Terrible" Touhy became familiar to newspaper readers across the country.

But then weeks went by and the Bureau had not caught him. Hoover sent more agents into Chicago. Torch Day came and went, but not even the Allied offensive got the Bureau off the hook. Agents were looking for Touhy all over the Midwest. My father, meanwhile, as head of a small squad that had honed its skills on draft fugitives, moved steadily through the old networks of the South Side Irish in Bridgeport and Canaryville, where the gangster had been based a decade before. One night, in an event that would become a family legend, Joe Carroll made the mistake of showing up at his own apartment still toting his submachine gun. Mary, with her new baby, would not let him in until he ditched the thing. We never knew what he did with it.

Finally, in a fleabag hotel they found a man named Stewart who'd been part of the Joliet jailbreak, and he told them where to find Touhy. "I was sleeping like dead," Touhy would write in his autobiography, *The Stolen Years*, "when a hoarse, bellowing voice awakened me. I thought at first that Banghart or Darlak had turned on the radio. It was that kind of voice . . . It was the voice of doom — the reveille bugle calling us back to Stateville.

"'Touhy! Banghart! Darlak!' the voice said, with an ungodly tone that must have been heard half a mile away. 'Touhy! Banghart! Darlak! This is the Federal Bureau of Investigation. You are surrounded. You cannot escape. Come out with your hands up — immediately. If you resist you will be killed.'"

Touhy and the others surrendered. He wrote that when he was cuffed, "The FBI kids looked at me blankly — a habit of theirs. That was it. The big escape was all done. The date was December 29th."

The FBI kid with the "hoarse, bellowing voice" threatening to kill and with the habitual blank look was my father. I have on the wall above my desk a photograph of him, taken during that period. He is standing tall and lean, in a trimly cut, dark three-piece suit. The steeple of a white handkerchief pokes out of his breast pocket. A gold chain, doubtless attached to a badge, not a watch, curves across his waist. His tie is knotted like a gemstone. A black curl falls on his forehead. He is standing in what could be a gravel pit. Behind him are a rotund black automobile, running boards and all; a low hill covered with scrub grass; and, on the ground, the long, thin shadow cast by his own figure, indicating that the time of day is early morning or late afternoon. His torso is presented to the camera, but his head is turned so that his face is in profile. His right arm is stiff, pointed away, and his hand holds a revolver off which the sun glances. The revolver hammer is cocked, and so is his eye. This is a photo taken at a firing range. His feet are slightly apart. His left hand is tucked casually in his trouser pocket. The ease of his marksman's stance contrasts with the rigidity of that gun hand and aiming eye. In this picture I sense the presence already of tensions I will much later label as between aggression and affection, between courage and compassion, between law and grace. Roger Touhy heard the bellowing voice and saw the blank stare, as I would, but even this photograph of a man at arms displays something else. I see it most clearly in the joyous relaxation of that left arm and hand, which have swept the jacket back to rest in that pocket. The tensions in this "kid," not conflicts, are the structuring principles of his identity — a Jansenist who chose love. If I sense anything here, it is what Touhy sensed, and what the bishop sensed before him — that this kid is more firmly anchored in who he is than he has any right to be. If he says no, even to God, it's what he means. If he tells you he will kill you, count on it. And if he uses the word "love" — but he almost never will. Suffice to say at this point that the organizing tension of this story is embodied in the movement over decades from, among other things, the pursuit of draft dodgers to the defense of one.

After my mother died two years ago, I went through her boxes, and in addition to the soiled linen bands in which my anointed hands had been wrapped by Cardinal Cooke at my ordination, I found a half-century-old letter addressed to my father from J. Edgar Hoover: "I want to express to you both officially and personally my commendation for the very excellent and efficient services which you rendered at Chicago on the Touhy case. Your assignments in this case were most important and were extremely dangerous . . . The courage and fearlessness displayed by you were far beyond the ordinary call of duty."

Touhy's arrest solved a big problem for Hoover. Still, his commendation might be taken as a manager's hyperbole, but within a year he ordered this FBI kid to Washington, out of Chicago once and for all. He named him chief of kidnapping and bank robbery investigations for the entire Bureau. Because of Touhy, Joe Carroll became one of the director's trusted intimates, and the trajectory of his rise to the top levels of government was set.

My father remained absolutely loyal to Hoover, even after the director had become a parody of himself, and no wonder. J. Edgar Hoover did for young Joe Carroll what the birth of Joe junior did for Mary, offering affirmation just when, having forfeited the affirmation of the Church and a felt sense of the affirmation of God, he needed it most. Hoover's letter concludes with the news that "as a result of the commendable manner in which you performed your duties in this particular case, I have recommended that your salary be increased from Grade Caf-11, $3800 per annum to Grade Caf-11 $4000 per annum, to be effective January 16, 1943."

The letter is dated January 18, 1943. Four days later, in a South Side hospital within range of the stench of the stockyards, and not far from the grubby apartment in which Roger "Tough" Touhy was arrested on the eve of my older brother's second birthday, I was born. Eventually Mary and Joe would have five sons, although she would have perhaps twice that many pregnancies. Not that my arrival was simple: I was a blue baby, deprived of oxygen in the birth canal, and they feared for my life. My father was present as the priest went into the operating room to baptize me. The commotion of the event is made palpable in the fact that the hastily summoned priest misunderstood what my name was to be and mistakenly christened me "Joseph." But Joe was already Joseph: what was this, Jacob and Esau? It speaks volumes about the choke hold of ecclesiastical legalism that the priest, having uttered that name over me while pouring water on my blue forehead, insisted that "Joseph" was it, no matter about my brother. The priest entered that name on my birth certificate. "James" was added later, after another priest, in the counterbalancing but only ceremonial church ritual, rechristened me. The confusion of names was an accidental but potent foreshadowing not only of my fate as the usurper of the eldest son's role, but of the soon-to-come disaster that would make such a fate inevitable.

I never imagined what my frightened parents thought while I struggled for breath, not until forty-three years later when a child of my own went through a version of the same thing, but unluckily. Her name was Jenny, and she spent almost her entire life in my arms, dying an hour and twenty minutes after she was born. In that brief period, I repented everything and promised everything, desperately bargaining with God. To no avail. So yes, now I can imagine my own parents reacting similarly, repenting and promising to beat the band, beat the devil. Promise Him anything, but give him your son. When I pulled through, a second healthy child at last, surely they took it as another confirmation, together with the almighty Hoover's, that the course they'd set for themselves, however fraught, was good.

3

STATE AND CHURCH

WHEN I WAS two years old, my mother held me in one arm at FDR's last inauguration. With the other she clutched my brother Joe's hand. He was four. She was determined that her two sons would glimpse the president once, and the odd arrangement of that inauguration gave her the chance. FDR had ruled that, because of the war, a large celebration would be inappropriate, although it was also likely that his unpublicized declining health — he died of a stroke a few months later — would not permit it. Roosevelt's health would, in fact, emerge as a contrasting thread in this story, but at that point my mother was like most Americans in feeling only admiration for the stoic reserve with which the president kept his affliction not hidden precisely, but in the shadows of public awareness. In 1921 he had been stricken with poliomyelitis. He'd been paralyzed from the waist down ever since. Very few knew of the severity of his condition. Of the 125,000 photographs of FDR on file at the Roosevelt Library in Hyde Park, only one shows him sitting in a wheelchair. We are expected to look back on the reticence of that era's press corps — those photographs not taken — as a better way, but would the disease of polio have been so consistently and universally taken as shameful if the president had stood openly in his braces, with his crutches, and declared, "I do not govern with my legs"?

In 1945 there was no inaugural ball and no parade. Roosevelt took the oath on the south portico of the White House. He spoke for five minutes to members of the public gathered on the lawn, the smallest audience ever to hear an inaugural address — a few hundred people, three of whom were Mary Carroll and her sons Joe and Jimmy. It is as if I can remember being there, so much have such events featured in my life. In 1949 our mother took us to the swearing-in of Harry Truman, a person, like her, of no schooling — the only president of this century not to have gone to college. Like her, he was of the unvarnished and unpuritanical Midwest — his Edward J. Kelly was named T. J. Pendergast Jr. Famously a man of plain talk, Truman was proof to a woman who needed it that, even in Washington, virtues of directness and common sense could triumph. For Truman, we stood in the throng at the Capitol, and images of my mother's beaming face and of the gleaming white dome play off each other in one of my first true memories.

Brian, Dennis, and toddler Kevin kept her home in 1953, so that year Joe and I, aged twelve and nine, went to Ike's inaugural on our own. That is the one from which I cherish images of the marching bands and soldiers, baton-swinging girls and cowboys on horseback — and Eisenhower's Homburg. I remember someone saying Ike was the first not to wear a top hat. Like good Democrats — Back of the Yards Democrats, Mayor Daley Democrats — Joe and I wore buttons that said, "I Like Everybody."

By 1961 I was a freshman at Georgetown. I had desperately hoped that my ROTC unit would be tapped to march in Kennedy's parade, but we were not chosen. It was deflating to be on the curbside again, but disappointment gave way to rampant joy when JFK drove by, no hat at all. More, almost, than anything else, his bareheadedness made him ours. It was so cold that button vendors had built fires in oil drums up the side streets from Pennsylvania Avenue. I recall that someone near me in the crowd was carrying a transistor radio, which seemed more a marvel even than Kennedy's speech.

I was present for Lyndon Johnson's parade, but my memory is blurred because a melancholy impulse had taken me back to the spot on Pennsylvania Avenue, near the National Gallery, where I'd stood for the funeral procession the year before. When I try now to picture a triumphant LBJ going by, I see instead the riderless black horse. Same bands, different music.

No longer living in Washington in 1973, I realized I had an unbroken string of inaugurations going, yet when I traveled there that year, it was to join what organizers dubbed "the counter-inauguration." The protest was an enraged reaction to the just past Christmas bombing of Hanoi, which, with a hundred thousand bombs dropped in eleven days, was the highest concentration of firepower in the war. When Richard Nixon's car approached — that year my spot was at Fourteenth Street, near the District Building — the crowd jeered the man who'd kept the war going despite his four-year-old promise to end it. My own readiness to join in was a measure of the distance I had come from my youthful worship of these men. I shook my fist and cursed the president of the United States.

All my life, inaugurations had been like a sacrament of the streets to me, rituals of rebirth, the one true American gala, a quadrennial instance of Jefferson's "peaceful revolution." At inaugurations, even including the glaring exception of 1973, because it *was* an exception, I had learned the basic lesson of this nation: how to put aside what divides us — *e pluribus* — in favor of a felt experience of what unites us — *unum*. At inaugurations, we could all wear buttons that said, "I Like Everybody."

I grew up, in other words, with a vivid and continuous sense of connection to what theorists called "the state," but which we thought of only as our country. From an early age, I understood that "we the people" gathered on the sidewalks of the avenue to cheer the president as a way of cheering ourselves. And our entire lives in Washington, with its child-pleasing monuments, museums, military displays, and becolumned white buildings, reinforced us in our attitude toward the political sphere — toward, we would learn to say later, the "secular" — as a realm of nothing less than (we didn't know yet to use this word either) the "sacred."

The Roman Catholic Church had set itself against the modern ideas of pluralism and democracy, and it was deeply suspicious of Protestant America. But Catholic Americans knew in their bones that democracy was good, and their influence, especially through figures like the Jesuit John Courtney Murray, was beginning to be felt in Rome. The American experience, filtered through theology, would end the era of Tridentine Catholicism. My mother and father would be constitutionally incapable of thinking of themselves as ecclesiastical liberals, but they unselfconsciously anticipated the coming breakthrough that would be so powerfully symbolized to American Catholics by the twin, nearly simultaneous arrivals of John Kennedy and Pope John XXIII. With a wartime jump-start, my parents embraced the life of Washington — of their nation — with a verve that I still remember as the electric pulse that brought me into my first awareness of myself not only as a citizen, but as a believer.

Our father would give us the motto *Pro Deo et Patria*, yet he was less the one who initiated Joe and me into the holy mysteries of Washington than our mother. Later our brothers were initiated too. They were born as Joe and I had been, in two- to three-year intervals, according to norms set by *Casti Connubii*, the Pius XI encyclical that "once and for all" defined "artificial" birth control as intrinsically evil. That doctrine was promulgated in 1930. It fixed my parents and their generation of Catholics — the meaning of *Pro Deo* — in the rigid sexual roulette to which so many of us, their children, owe our very existence.

Throughout our infancies and childhoods, our father was making his way from the outer circles into the starred chambers of real government power, first at Justice, then at Defense. But because we knew to associate him with the high and, even to us, evident purpose of the era's great crusade — he was catching Communist spies — his absence itself had the weight of presence. "Absence makes the heart grow fonder," he used to say to us, climbing into the car where we were waiting, half asleep. We often picked him up at night, and I still remember the odd thrill it was to have our mother at the wheel, him in the passenger seat, and her announcing that on the way home we would have a tour. As if she were his guide to Washington too, she would set off, hunched over the wheel of the Studebaker Champion. She loved the city's avenues and edifices, and displayed them as if they were hers to give us.

So much was hers to give. I know that she cherished me when I was little, and wanted to give me not just that city but the world. She is the first source of my pride and self-regard, the virtue of my worldliness. I knew from an early age what a rare woman she was, and I remember feeling the power of that knowledge when she would drive us through Washington at night: the stately flag-bedecked mansions of Embassy Row, the brooding Lincoln, Jefferson in solitary splendor at the Tidal Basin, the White House, the Willard, the ghostly white "tempos" along the Mall, the fairy-tale turrets of the Smithsonian, and the floodlit needle of the Washington Monument. The tours were especially vibrant if visitors from Chicago were along, and then our father would chime in with a rare recounting of tales of wartime Bureau work: the surveillance of diplomats at Dupont Circle, a stakeout at the old Carroll Arms Hotel on Capitol Hill, a rendezvous near the Soviet embassy on Sixteenth Street, and someone's suicide off a bridge into Rock Creek Park.

I cannot drive through the Doric canyons of Washington even now without seeing the flash of my parents' youth, my mother's enthusiasm for a world she would never have dared expect to claim as her own, my father's quiet assumption of an authority that would eventually be ripped away from him. The established classes of old Washington — Cave Dwellers, the Foxhall Road set, the high society of Ivy League men and women who set their clocks by Cissy Patterson's *Times-Herald* — would ruthlessly have kept in their place one-toilet Irish interlopers like my parents, but a social revolution had occurred during the war. The population of the city had doubled with the arrival of men and their women who'd come to save the nation, which they then did. The newcomers loved Truman, of course, because he seemed like one of them.

As for my brother Joe and me, the FBI was everywhere in our first remembered world, and we loved it more for that. My first experience of professional entertainment, one could say even of story itself, was listening on the radio in the late forties to *The FBI in Peace and War,* and I can still hum its theme. Joe and I, and then Brian too, huddled together by the old Philco, riveted because those tales of gangbusters, spy catchers, and G-men gave us glimpses of Dad, who couldn't be there to put us to bed. That radio program, and another called *This Is Your FBI,* filled that primordial need to draw close to him at night before daring to close our eyes — Joe in the bottom bunk, me in the top, Brian on the cot. Those episodes portrayed FBI agents as men of such competence and integrity, of such selflessness, that one could think of them as modern-day Knights Templars. In my mind, the image of the agent would blur into that of the priest, for some obvious and some quite obscure reasons. In recalling the power of that first ideal in which virtue was not the opposite of masculinity but the essence of it, I recognize that the man I still long to be is the one I first thought my father was.

Joe and I had a wealth of uncles and aunts. Between them our parents had a dozen or more siblings — we never knew for sure how many. The totality of their break with Chicago is evident in the sad fact that even now I have no remote notion of how many first or second cousins I have. But in those early years in Washington, our Back of the Yards relatives arrived at our garden apartment in Arlington in a regular parade. Someone from Chicago was always sleeping on the couch, under the replica painting of Lady Davenport that Joe and I thought was of Mom. The visitors came as if to verify the regular, and to them incredible, reports of Joe and Mary's ascension. And every visitor, whether Morrissey or Carroll, or member of the old gang at the phone company or Loyola, got the nighttime tour on the way to pick up Dad.

Two buildings loomed in importance. Careening down from Capitol Hill, crowded into the Studebaker, we would fall silent at a certain point on Pennsylvania Avenue, passing the wedding-cake Archives Building where my mother would slow down. At Tenth Street she would point to the innocuous desk-sized marble block that was Franklin Roosevelt's self-appointed and only monument — hidden in death as he was in life — and then, craning at the windshield, she would point at a set of grand corner windows three stories above. "J. Edgar's office," she would say with a familiarity that always impressed the South Siders, and had me convinced for years that Hoover was more her personal friend than Dad's mentor.

After the Touhy case, Hoover had brought Dad into his inner

circle and begun to depend on him as a Bureau troubleshooter. My father went from kidnapping and bank robbery investigations to the more urgent wartime tasks of counterespionage. The Germans and Japanese proved to have been ineffectual penetrators of Washington security, but, as the nation would learn soon enough, they weren't the only ones trying. Joe Carroll came into his own as the war ended and a renewed Red scare began, a true reversal of the short-lived American assumption of invincibility.

In a few months in the summer and fall of 1949, the postwar euphoria evaporated suddenly, as illustrated by the contrasting findings of two Alger Hiss juries. The first jurors, in July of 1949, were unable to reach a verdict in the perjury trial of the patrician State Department official. The second, in January of 1950, found him guilty in a matter of minutes, not because the evidence was any more conclusive, but because the atmosphere in which charges had been brought was entirely different. In the period between the two trials the meanings of America's past and future were both upended. In August the Soviets exploded their first atomic bomb, which Truman announced to the world in September. In October Mao Tse-tung took control of Peking, prefiguring his imminent takeover of all China. In December, after being cornered by an energized FBI, the eminent Los Alamos physicist Klaus Fuchs admitted to being a Soviet spy, source of the information that had enabled the Reds to build the Bomb a full decade ahead of expectations. The intermediaries between Fuchs and Moscow, it would be revealed, included low-level Los Alamos functionaries, one of whom had a sister named Ethel Rosenberg, wife of Julius. Although the authentic villain, Fuchs, would serve only nine years in prison before returning, upon release, to a hero's welcome in East Germany, the Rosenbergs would be sentenced to die a week after the North Koreans invaded the South. For more than a generation, Americans would argue over these events and claim their fundamental identities in terms of them. Notwithstanding all the controversy, the one undeniable fact, obvious from the start, was that the most closely held secret in the history of the United States had been penetrated by agents of the Soviet Union, which was how Joseph Stalin, the moral twin of Adolf Hitler, obtained the Bomb. Why shouldn't Americans have been anxious?

And why shouldn't my mother's voice have been full with pride as she pointed up at J. Edgar Hoover's windows? But the FBI wing of the Justice Department Building would not remain the high point of our family tour. By a stroke of fate that must have seemed of a piece with other momentous changes, the Pentagon became the destination of all our tours, the place where Dad worked now, and from which he would emerge at the end of another Free World–saving day, cheerfully greeting us and whoever that night's visitor was.

The life-changing Touhy letter from Hoover was dated, as I said, four days before I was born: three days before that, on January 15, 1943, the new Department of War Building was completed. Not one building actually, it is five distinct pentagonal structures arranged concentrically around a five-acre open court. These "rings" are joined by ten spokelike corridors, and its five stories (seven, counting the two below ground) are connected by broad ramps. Why ramps? "Because," as my mother always said, heading across the Fourteenth Street Bridge to the pharaoh's temple on the west bank of the Potomac, below Arlington Cemetery, largest tombstone in the world, "the building was designed to be converted into a hospital after the war was over." Ramps, she insisted, were for the movable beds and vets in wheelchairs, proof that we were an unwarlike people. I believed it for years, but my mother's explanation was a sweet piece of Washington apocrypha: Pentagon planners assumed the building's ongoing function as headquarters and records center of a massive military. The ramps ensured the smooth movement of wheeled file cabinets in the world's largest bureaucracy. Beginning in 1947, my father was one of the multitude working there.

Approaching the river entrance along the tidy George Washington Parkway, my mother loved to enumerate the wonders of the place: the Pentagon covered thirty acres and had three times the floor space of the Empire State Building, more even — here was something to impress Chicagoans — than the Merchandise Mart. It was a mile in circumference, had eighteen dining rooms that served sixty thousand meals a day. But the wonder of wonders was that her Joe worked there. A mere eight years after finishing night school, quitting the stockyards, and marrying her — he who, in growing up, had never crossed paths with a soldier or sailor much less an officer, never served a day in uniform, never saw a moment's service overseas, and had hardly ever been in an airplane — he had become an instant brigadier general in the United States Air Force. At age thirty-seven, he was the youngest general in America.

My brother Joe and I, and our Uncle Tommy, say, would laugh and laugh as Mom described how on his first day in uniform Dad went to work wearing one brown sock and one black. We'd howl as she described him at the bathroom mirror, practicing his salute. We wouldn't dare laugh about such things in front of him, but there was no mockery in us. We took our cue from Mom, and her pride in his accomplishment was bottomless, like her delight.

We had no language with which to express this, of course, no way to know it even, but looking back on my mother's giddy satisfaction at his rocketlike success, I sense its meaning as an apparently final reversal of the shame they'd felt in Chicago, a vindication of the risk he'd taken in rejecting the priesthood, and she'd taken in marrying a man who'd once promised himself to God. Wasn't the miracle of his success in Washington a sign of heaven's favor? How could their embrace during that period not have been edged with a feeling of release? Compared to the brothers, sisters, and friends they'd left behind in their indifferent hometown, and certainly compared to what, in their heart of hearts, they'd expected, they were surely the luckiest two people in the world, free or not.

Here is how it happened. In 1947 the Air Force was established as an independent service. The first air secretary was Truman's Missouri protégé Stuart Symington. He approached J. Edgar Hoover for the loan of an FBI expert in investigations and counterintelligence to devise a structure for an Air Force security agency. Symington wanted an operation more like the efficiently organized FBI than the Byzantine OSS or the Army's fief-ridden CIC. Hoover was duly flattered, which always helped. He assigned to Symington a man he described quite simply — this is my mother speaking — as his very best. "Your dad," she'd say; or, to Chicago visitors from his side of the family, "Your Joe"; or, to her own, and here was the phrase into which she put her every curl of feeling, pride, and love, "My Joe."

Symington quickly replaced Hoover as a mentor. My father might have been loyal to the FBI director, but he was no masochist. The initial assumption was that he would remain a civilian and return to the Bureau after six months. But the organizational structure he recommended for the Air Force posed a problem. It violated military taboos, and the brass hated it. For one thing, the new agency would be accountable not to local superiors, or even to theater commanders, but to a director in Washington. In order to avoid being intimidated by senior officers who could be subjects of investigations, its agents would dress as civilians, not disclose their ranks, and stand outside the chain of command. The authority of OSI agents could supersede that even of generals.

The generals did not like the idea, and said so. They said it would not work, and implied they would not carry out such a proposal. But the operation my father outlined was exactly what Symington wanted. He went to Hoover, Congress, and President Truman. In short order, extraordinary legislation was passed, the Air Force Office of Special Investigations was established, and the ex-seminarian and former stockyards worker was released from the FBI, commissioned to the rank of brigadier general, and appointed director, a job he would hold for a decade. Instead of six months, my father would be in the Air Force for a quarter of a century.

A few years ago, I encountered a retired colonel who had been an assistant to my father in the early days of OSI. The mystery to me had always been how my father won over the hostile Air Force brass. The hard-boiled Curtis LeMay, for example, became his strongest early booster. I asked the colonel if he knew how it happened. He told me this story. In the late 1940s the great Pentagon contest was over who would be given main custody of the nuclear arsenal — the Navy with its proposed fleet of aircraft carriers and submarines or the Air Force with its new generation of strategic bombers. Politicians on the House and Senate Armed Services Committees would decide, and they seemed to be favoring the flyboys, largely because of the popular appeal of the Air Force chief of staff, hero of the air war against Germany, General Hoyt Vandenberg.

At a crucial point, however, a congressman sympathetic to the Navy produced an anonymous letter that labeled Vandenberg an adulterer and a liar. Negative publicity undercut the Air Force case just as the vote was to be taken. Symington asked the newly appointed General Carroll to find out what he could about the

letter. And what Carroll did that very night, operating on a gumshoe's hunch, was burglarize the Pentagon offices of the secretary of the Navy and the chief of naval operations. Acting alone,
he took type samples from all the Navy typewriters and, still in
the middle of the night, brought them over to the FBI laboratory
on Pennsylvania Avenue. By morning Joe Carroll had established that the anonymous letter slandering Vandenberg was
written on a typewriter in the office of an undersecretary of the
Navy. Using FBI-prepared photographic blowups comparing
the "fingerprints" of the typescript, he briefed first Symington
and Vandenberg, then the congressional committee members.
Apparently no one asked whether this warrantless intrusion of
the Navy offices was a violation of the law. Hearing about it
from that elderly colonel, I thought immediately of my father's
denunciations — "The ends don't justify the means!" — of Catholic peaceniks who burglarized draft board offices during Vietnam.

Later, I would read an account of the same incident, although
without explicit reference to my father's role, in *Iron Eagle*, the
biography of General LeMay by Thomas M. Coffey. The anonymous letter levied charges of corruption among the highest officers in the Air Force, including LeMay. Coffey writes, "The
author of the document was not so anonymous after all. He was
identified as a man named Cedric K. Worth, one-time Holly-
wood script writer who was now a special assistant to Undersecretary of the Navy [Daniel] Kimball." The colonel to whom I
spoke told me that after my father's congressional briefing exposing the Navy ploy, the pro-Navy congressman who'd produced the letter apologized, and the committees took their votes.
The first nukes went to the Air Force, which led to its ascendancy
and, not incidentally, to LeMay's, with the formal establishment
of the Strategic Air Command. After that, the colonel said,

young General Joe Carroll could do no wrong with the Air Force brass. He could wear any color socks he wanted.

I have a photograph in front of me that shows my father in his new uniform, shiny brass buttons, flap pockets and all. He is standing on the lawn outside our Arlington apartment. I am standing next to him. He is holding my hand. I am four years old. My father in his peaked cap is looking off to the left with a benign smile that has always made me hope he is looking at my mother. I am wearing a uniform too, a fringed cowboy vest, gun belt, and boots. My eyes are in shadow, but otherwise the expression on my face is slightly stunned, as if I appreciate all that has happened to us in a few short years. Perhaps I know something else already, the other large event, the countervailing catastrophe that instantly and permanently undid every feeling my mother and father had of being lucky. The precise timing has always been unclear to me, but one day in this same period, my brother Joe fell down, and he could not get up again. Our mother took him to the doctor, who knew at once what to look for. Our father was summoned from his office, and this time he came. Their first-born son, the seal of a love that wasn't to have been, the issue of flesh that was weak, a child conceived in the Irish Church's idea of sin, my older brother, my lively partner in the world of radio, in the cult of bunk beds, my teacher and first friend, the one with whom I secretly shared a name — Joe had infantile paralysis, poliomyelitis, Roosevelt's disease, polio.

I remember the living room of our apartment on South Sixteenth Street, the Lady Davenport on the wall, the red couch, the figurine-laden glass shelves in the window. Four or five years old, I am sitting on the couch when they bring Joe home from the hospital for the first time. My father is carrying him. Joe smiles at me, as if privileged. I refuse at first to get off the couch, where he must lie now. My mother screams at me, the first remembered time. I run from the room, fighting off the consoling pleasure of my knowledge that Joe cannot run after me.

Behind and above my father and me, in this photograph, stands a telephone pole. This same picture sat on my table when I was a seminarian, and I recall the day I first saw that telephone pole as a crucifix. "The end of learning," Samuel Johnson wrote, "is piety." And the end, also, of a hard-won self-acceptance. There was a time in my life when I saw crucifixes everywhere — in soaring airplanes, in the joints of windowpanes, in radiator grilles, in the fall of toothpicks on a table. Polio brought the cross back into our family, where it belonged. Our religion meant one thing only, that God came onto the earth to show us, so vividly, so unforgettably, that every human being has, as Mom would never tire of saying, "a cross to bear." The phrase deflects from its own meaning, that each of us — "Drink ye all of this" — is crucified. Joe's fate — he would have a severe case of the disease, undergoing a dozen operations over the next fifteen years, forfeiting his childhood and walking with a savage limp for life — seized my parents like claws reaching up from the stockyards bog to haul them back into the fetid world from which they came, a crone chorus — Irish hags, the nuns — screeching, "Who did you think you were? How dare you think you can escape!"

After Joe got polio, our roles reversed. I did not openly claim the name in which I too had been baptized, but I usurped his place in other ways, a pseudo–older brother, sibling born to lead, to try things first, to help with chores, to mind the baby, and, later, to be the outgoing one, the Carroll boys' little representative. I did everything asked of me, and more than was expected. Yet my every success, since it came at Joe's expense, would feel like failure — a sad pattern grooved into my psyche to this day.

Mom did mute penance, nailing herself to the cross of her first son's suffering. The rest of us would compete for the dregs of her attention. His having caught one of the three viruses that caused polio — Joe and I agreed that he'd gotten it drinking from the creek that ran near our apartment house — was her fault, wasn't it? What else had she to do in life than protect her children? Or was it somehow my fault? Had I been first to slurp the forbidden water, giving him the idea? It was as if I were already older, guilty for giving bad example. I remember Joe telling me that if one of us had to get polio, he was glad it was he, a sentiment that seemed in no way noble to me. I envied him his suffering.

Mom became our own Pietà. The spontaneous, wisecracking, affectionate young woman I first knew, as it were, simply packed up and moved out, to be replaced by the Mother of Sorrows herself, a woman privileged to be in pain. Our father, meanwhile, fleeing the sure Jansenist knowledge that his own hubris, not polluted water or "germs," was the true cause of his son's polio — a perfect punishment if ever there was one, just at the time of his great achievement — he fled from us too, Joe junior for sure, a rebuke embodied; and long-suffering Mary; and also me. One might have expected that with our mother entirely taken up with Joe, I would have had more of our father to myself, his attention, talk, play; but not so. I remember sitting in the car with him, outside one hospital or another, waiting for Mom to come out from visiting Joe. He would sit at the wheel ignoring me, compulsively whistling a tune I would much later recognize as "Beautiful Dreamer." I hear it now, and it makes me sad.

Our parents would be sexually intimate again, but lovers? Properly unprotected prophylactically, they would be protected from each other in every other way from now on. I can claim only intuitive knowledge here, but my conviction is that the

shock of my brother's illness broke the spell of the golden escape
— the beautiful dream — they'd woven for themselves. They
would be alienated from each other hereafter. She would be giving her all to her children. He would be saving the Free World
from Communism. I would be the secretly beloved child of
a quietly scorned woman, which would lead years later to a
boundless embarrassment around sexual assertion. Now I understand my mother's forever unstated difficulty with male sex-
uality, mine in particular. The lesson of polio to all of us was that
our bodies were plainly not to be trusted. Devastating as my
brother's illness was in itself — year after year of his real agony
— its resonance as a kind of Irish curse against a spoiled priest,
his woman, and their children is what made it the radioactive
mushroom cloud of our family. Certainly it hung over me.

Friends and relatives from Chicago stopped visiting. Mom
stopped packing us into the Studebaker to go pick up Dad at
night. Instead of wonder tours of Doric Washington, she did her
driving now to doctors' offices and hospitals in Alexandria and
Washington. Instead of past the White House and down Pennsylvania Avenue, she now drove the Studebaker every chance
she got to the far northeast of D.C., an area around Catholic University called Little Rome because of its concentration of seminaries, convents, monasteries, and oratories. When Joe was in
the hospital, she took me and a succession of my infant brothers
to the Franciscan Monastery, where visits to the papier-mâché
catacombs and concrete-over-mesh grottoes of Lourdes and Fatima earned something called "indulgences," which Mom flam-
boyantly "offered up," as she said, for Joe. I once asked a Friar
Tuck monk why he had hair on his chin and not on his head, and
the relieved pleasure I took in my mother's laughter makes me
realize now that it had become unusual. Sometimes, in a wheelchair or on crutches, Joe would come with us. He could be impe-

rious, ordering me to fetch, to wait, or to carry, but I had developed the habit of responding instantly. To do so solved the ache of my not being crippled myself.

If it wasn't the Franciscan Monastery or the Poor Clares Convent we visited, it was the National Shrine of the Immaculate Conception, in those days a crypt church still under construction. Completed, it is the largest Catholic church in North America. Even incomplete, the Shrine had a well-stocked religious goods store, where my mother bought scapulas and miraculous medals for Joe to wear, sacred oil and relics to rub on his scarred and withered legs. I went along mutely, increasingly agnostic as I saw no improvement in Joe's condition. Mainly I was learning the great lesson that religious faith has everything to do with suffering and unhappiness. I was four years old, five, six . . . eleven, twelve, going to and from these places with my mother and brothers. The Shrine especially was the North Star of my childhood. When Joe was in the hospital, it seemed we went there after every visit. I knelt below the crucifixes, all that writhing, legs as bruised as Joe's; I said my rosaries and learned carefully to deduct my time from purgatory. With the cultivated appearance of a fervor I never felt, I imitated my mother in lighting candles at the snake-ridden (virus-ridden?) feet of the Blessed Virgin Mary. After a while, and without ever believing any of it was helping Joe, I realized that these rituals had become for me what they were for my mother, a bond with her after all, and a rare — perhaps the only — source of consolation.

Latin Masses and communally recited rosaries were unintelligible rituals to me, but the act of kneeling next to her was emotionally comprehensible. I learned to bury my face in my hands, a dark focus that offered a release I had no way of understanding — and which is still available to me when, in certain circumstances and blank-minded, I assume that posture all these years later. Faith in a crucified God, son of a heartbroken mother, consoles without providing any particular hope of salvation, solution, fix, or escape — that was the first principle of my credo, and it remains the last.

Two blocks down Fourth Street from the National Shrine of the Immaculate Conception, behind a pair of looming stone pillars past which we drove every time, was a pseudo-Gothic, crenelated mausoleum that had already branded itself on my unconscious. It was St. Paul's College, a seminary. Seminary: when I first heard the word, I took it to be "cemetery," another Arlington, like the one sprawling up the hill behind my father's office at the Pentagon. Seminary: at the word I always looked for grave markers. St. Paul's College on Fourth Street was the institution where, years later, in my pathetic effort to resuscitate the mortal happiness of that fugitive young couple and their first son, their first Joseph, I would, a willing mystic Houdini, entomb myself.

4

THE POPE SPEAKS

THE MAN WHO embodied everything triumphant, timeless, and secure about the Catholic Church also embodied everything rigid, morose, and moralistic. He was Eugenio Pacelli, Pope Pius XII, and he figured in my life as the avatar of a piety to which I felt both drawn and condemned. His photograph — a severe face in profile, eyes cast downward, lost in the glint of rimless spectacles — was everywhere in my world: the classrooms of St. Mary's School in Alexandria, the altar boys' robing room behind the sacristy, the cover of *The Pope Speaks*, a monthly magazine that came home with us from Mass, and framed cheaply on the wall above the plastic holy water font in the front hallway of our house in Hollin Hills.

Eventually, I went for high school to the Priory School at a Benedictine monastery, one of the rarefied religious communities near the National Shrine of the Immaculate Conception. Joe preceded me at Priory. It was a small, demanding school for a would-be intellectual elite, run by English monks on a British model. I was always sure I had been admitted because of Joe, who had compensated for the impairment of his polio by becoming a good student. I had compensated by doing what I was told. I hated Priory but never said so. Even here, a place of cultural sophistication, His Holiness was revered. On the wall inside the front door hung his gilded portrait. To me, by then, the pope had become a figure of such familiarity that I felt I knew him.

Pius XII was a decidedly foreign figure to other Americans — brooding, austere, authoritarian. He could have been the stereo-typed figment of priest-baiting nativists for whom the papacy had long been the devil's den. Pacelli had been the apostolic delegate to Berlin and an admirer of the Germans. His scrupu-lous neutrality during World War II — to him the Nazi death camps were a moral horror, but so was the Allied bombing of urban populations — should have made him even more hated in America. But long-standing anti-papal prejudice and leftover resentment from the war gave way in the raw climate of the 1950s to broad American recognition that Pius XII was a crucial ally in the greatest struggle of all, the one against what we knew as "atheistic Communism." It was a telling phrase, a key to un-derstanding the odd difference in Catholic responses to Fascism and Nazism, on the one hand, and Marxism on the other.

The premise of twentieth-century papal politics, from the Vatican concords with Mussolini in 1929 and Hitler in 1933 to Vatican condemnations of class-struggle liberation theology in the 1980s and 1990s, is that Bolshevism is a greater threat than Fascism. That is so precisely because, in its ideology, the former explicitly targets religion. Demonstrating what he could have done against the Fascists and Nazis but never did, Pius XII in 1949 solemnly excommunicated, with one pronouncement, every Communist in the world.

Coming within months of the Soviets' first atomic-bomb test, Stalin's final takeover of Czechoslovakia, and Mao's capture of Peking, the pope's decisive act endeared him to most Americans. Neutral no longer, the pope was a powerful ally, and as news broke of priests and nuns being murdered and bishops being imprisoned in China, Poland, Czechoslovakia, and Hungary, Americans realized that Catholics were on the front lines *for them.* A Catholic doctor, Tom Dooley, sounded alarms about Communists in a place called Vietnam; a Catholic senator, Joseph McCarthy, exposed them in the State Department; a Catholic bishop, Fulton Sheen, preached on television the old dogma of martyrdom in its new form: "Better dead than Red." And a Catholic cardinal, Francis Spellman, would profess the new American faith — "Our country, right or wrong" — by citing half of Stephen Decatur's toast.

Pro Deo et Patria — first my father's motto, then mine. The old threat of conflict embedded in that *"et"* evaporated in the warmth of American appreciation for Pius XII. His merciless rigidity and stern moralizing were not derided now, but admired as the very virtues the Cold War called for. Alliance with the Vatican had the practical consequence of undergirding the American sense of moral purity, even as blocks of the American strategy of nuclear deterrence were put in place. In the 1950s, Pius XII set aside his earlier abhorrence of the deliberate mass targeting of civilians. He powerfully reiterated the Catholic Just War theory for the Cold War context, emphasizing its notion of the acceptability of "unintended but predictable consequences." The deaths of millions in a nuclear exchange were predictable but, according to this casuistry, unintended, and therefore acceptable. Thus a morality with roots in Saint Augustine and Saint Thomas Aquinas was used to justify — and my father could articulate it better than anyone — what became known as Mutual Assured Destruction, or MAD.

Silencing what little dissent there was, as for example from Dorothy Day's ragtag band of Catholic Workers, Pius XII declared in 1956 that "a Catholic citizen cannot invoke his own conscience in order to refuse to serve" in a legitimately declared war. That absolute repudiation of conscientious objection reinforced the U.S. government's, and depriving them of the appeal to religion that Quakers and Mennonites had, sealed the fate of many Catholic boys. Like his colleagues in the Bureau and the Pentagon, my father welcomed the pope's statement, I'm sure. As an American he believed in the right of conscientious objection, but as a Catholic he accepted the subjugation of conscience. Doubtless he took the pope's edict as an affirmation of one of his own core principles — Roger Touhy arrested for draft violations! — and as yet another reinforcing of ranks against godless Communism. Who could have known — unintended and unpredictable — that eventually it would make of two of his sons an outlaw and a half?

As I approached adolescence, however, I shared my father's view entirely. That is why the grim and ascetic pope — Cornelius Jansen in a white skullcap, fierce symbol of a judging God who, for your eating meat on Friday, would send you to hell forever, to the unconsuming and inextinguishable fire, to infinite pain and an infinite ability to feel it — why this calculatedly inhuman figure made me proud.

But then the unthinkable happened. In October 1958 His Holiness died. It was as if the natural law had been not fulfilled but violated. In the minds of American Catholics, Pius XII was identified with their own clear self-definition, the clean authority that made their Church a standard against which all other organizations, and especially other Churches, fell short. The leadership of Pius XII had been perfectly matched to an institution that unapologetically proclaimed itself "a perfect society," unchangeable and "out of time."

His Holiness dead? But Pius XII had bridged — a "pontifex" precisely — the centuries-old gulf between America and Catholics. Indeed, under his reign, while the Catholic Church was quietly collapsing in Europe, it was coming into its own in the United States. Since 1950, this nation's Catholic population grew by 44 percent; the number of students in Catholic schools grew by 66 percent. In 1950 there were 43,000 priests in the

United States. A decade later there would be 54,000. Seminaries grew in number from 388 to 525, and seminarians from 26,000 to 40,000.

Pius XII dead? His "apocalyptic pessimism" had, despite all these triumphs, been proved accurate after all. Yes, His Holiness was dead, and the American Catholic reaction, an instinctive sense (which I recall very well) that something ominous had happened, would be proved accurate too.

Smoke rose black from the Sistine Chapel repeatedly, indicating that the Consistory of Cardinals was having trouble choosing the next pope. Some said, outrageously, that the cardinals were deadlocked between liberal and progressive factions, but such secular political analogies defiled the workings of the Holy Ghost. We knew that the cardinals were seeing to nothing less than the apostolic succession, the central fact of Catholic supremacy, the spine of the faith, and the Holy Ghost's way of staying with the Church through time. Critics would call that dogma of the literal chain of hands-on-heads going back to Peter an absurdly mechanistic notion, but not until later.

One afternoon in late October the bells in seminaries and convents and parish churches around the world began to toll. The smoke in Big Rome had come up white at last; the cardinals had burned their ballots without wet straw. *"Habemus Papam!"* An old man whom no one had described as *papabile* had been elected pope. Indeed the cardinals had been deadlocked, and if the Holy Ghost tapped the aged, ineffectual Angelo Giuseppe Roncalli, it was because the crimson-hatted power brokers knew they could control him for the few years he would last. Then they would put a real pope, one of themselves, in the shoes of the fisherman.

Mom would surely have taken us all out to Washington's Little Rome to hear its bells pealing, the American Catholic subculture's resounding celebration. But that fall we were living in

Germany, in a baroque mansion in the lovely spa town of Wiesbaden, nestled between the Taunus Mountains and the Rhine. Dad was a two-star general now, and although I could not know it, his promotion from the still marginal OSI to the position of chief of staff of the Air Force in Europe did not signal full acceptance into anything. He was in charge of pilots, of warplanes and nuclear weapons. As always, the officers and staffers who worked for him were enthralled by the unusual warmth that was still a mark of his public mode, and some colleagues valued his forthright lack of curves. But others, and certain of his superiors, feared him. He was "that cop" to them, forever a threat with his broad authority to investigate everything from carelessness to informal graft — bringing an extra duty-free Mercedes home to sell, billing Uncle Sam for family trips to the Alps — to real breaches of security. It's likely that his assignment to an overseas line position was made in the hope that he would learn what a general's life in the off-the-books Air Force was really like — and lay off. If so, the hope was disappointed.

The day Pius died, less than two months after my start at the Air Force–sponsored high school in Wiesbaden, the assistant principal announced that Roman Catholic students were excused from study hall to attend a special service, to be conducted by Colonel Chess — Monsignor Chess to us — in the chapel across the street. What I remember most about the service is that the girl I sat next to in English class did not attend. Delivered as I'd been from an all-boys school, such stirrings in class were new to me, and I was at their mercy. The curve of that girl's calf had kept me from my prepositions, nouns, and verbs. Once she'd caught me looking at her, then had looked away before I could. I had learned in the corridor to watch her at her locker, how her skirt hiked when she stooped for books — a thigh, the press of her ass. And not only that. I had never seen such a neck before, how long it was, and her perfect throat at the center of which was a cameo medallion, the profile of a queen. I'd begun to dream of futures built around this girl, but then . . . I knew enough to be sad about His Holiness, but what crushed me in the chapel was her absence, proof that the secret object of my true devotion was not one of us.

Us: the word still meant, primarily, Catholics.

I remember kneeling in that chipper new church, which would have been the pride of any suburb, as that bright American enclave in a still ravaged Germany would itself have been the suburb. I remember burying my face in my hands, the one sure spiritual act I knew how to perform. And I remember the surprise it was, the unexpected satisfaction — despite having just realized that my dream classmate was not a Catholic, or because I had — that here in the dark warm cave of my hands where before I'd always found God, the omnipresence of a consoling spirituality, I found instead the face of a girl. The body of a girl. Was this a first, fully admitted sexual desire, or "lust" as I was conditioned to call it? Certainly it was a wish for a fate other than the one I'd seen coming since the nuns had seconded my family's assumption about my "vocation."

In the seventh grade, at St. Mary's School, I won a nun-sponsored speech contest, a first achievement of my own — but not really of my own. The theme, forced on all contestants, was "Many Are Called, but Few Are Chosen." My particular oration was written with a large assist from Dad. I do not know whether I asked for his help or whether he volunteered it. "Indubitably" is one of the words he imposed on the text, and I can only imagine what the nuns thought of an eleven-year-old using such rhetoric. I remember what a nightmare that word was to pronounce, and I remember wondering why I didn't just say "undoubtedly." That I won the contest seemed proof that Dad's word was right. That I won seemed proof, as well, that I was "called" and "chosen" both.

Vocation: it was a word I'd carried into high school like a hidden birthmark. If I'd found it on an antonym quiz, I'd have paired it with "sex." The nuns. The priests. My father. My mother. Especially her. I learned early that to follow my own sexual desire would be to abandon her to a world of power — male power? — that would abuse her. An unspeakable dread surrounded these feelings, so naturally I did not speak of them. Nevertheless, the feelings efficiently packed themselves into that one word, vocation. Unlike all these other happy kids, I had one. Vocation was a word without windows, a word with bars on the door, a word I associated above all with the dour, rimless-eyed profile of the pope who, as he wanted to, embodied the very Church to me and my place in it. The pope is dead — here was the outlaw feeling I was having suddenly — but I'm not.

The years in Germany were our family's best. The nation, defeated and disgraced, nevertheless worked a spell on us, and so did the shock of aristocratic living for which we were in no way prepared, but which senior generals took for granted in those gravy days early in the Cold War. When our ship docked in the harbor city of Bremen, we were met by blue-uniformed baggage carriers, drivers, and limousines that took us to a waiting U.S. Army train. We were shown into a posh lounge car staffed with orderlies and stewards. In our prior life in the cheery Virginia suburb, fifteen miles down the Potomac from D.C. and the Pentagon, our only contact with the military had been the uniform in which Dad left the house each morning — and that sergeant whose paper I delivered. When the mood between our parents was right, we checked his socks to be sure they matched. Otherwise, for the way Mom, Joe, I, and my little brothers lived, centered on the parish school and church activities, Dad could have been an insurance broker or a meat salesman.

But now — at first we were impressed that Dad's rank entitled us to our own railway car, until we realized that the entire train, locomotive, sleeper, and caboose too, was his. We'd been told he had his own airplane (a converted B-29 bomber), but a private train? Beginning with the exotic sights we saw from the windows of that railway car, beginning with the canapés served that day on silver trays by Air Force sergeants who from then on would be our family servants, my brothers and I were astounded by the world we found ourselves in. Germany's sad mysteries alone would have kept us amazed, but the Air Force culture too was a kind of Oz. Once ensconced, we roamed Wiesbaden as if we were heirs of the man who owned it. In relation to the Germans in that occupation era, we were. "We come as conquerors" were the opening words of noble Eisenhower's first proclamation to the German people, and though he went on to add, "We stay as friends," it was the first assertion that was true. The Allied triumph still showed, not in ruins because Wiesbaden had not been bombed, but in a subservience of the populace. The ingratiating deference of Karl, our gardener, of a *gemütlich putzfrau*, of neighbors on Biebricher Allee, embarrassed us and put us on guard, which of course that sort of passive aggression was intended to do. The sprawling, lavish house we lived in had been built for a kaiser's marshal, and it dominated one of the city's two hills. On the other hill sat Hainerberg, the American enclave with its housing blocks for servicemen, its tidy subdivision for officers, its shopping center and theater — the AFEX — and its cluster of schools, including mine.

I remember climbing out onto the roof of our house to look across the city and up at Hainerberg. I would sit there watching the light of day fade and the windows of houses in the valley turn bright, and then stars overhead would fill the sky. I remember hearing what I knew then only as "classical music" drift up from a neighbor's terrace, and realizing how full of beauty the world was, and that it was put there for me.

We were like heirs of the owner in relation, also, to Americans — because of rank. Our mother, the eighth-grade dropout and former telephone operator, was thrust into the role of grande dame of the Officers' Wives' Club, presiding at teas in white gloves, arranging Christmas parties in the wards of the vast headquarters hospital, and hosting receptions for German, French, and British dignitaries. My brothers and I learned in the Air Force–sponsored schools that our father's rank was a fact that took precedence over every other.

I attended H. H. Arnold, the high school named for the famous bomber-general of World War II. My brother Joe, a valiant survivor of a dozen operations, still had a pronounced limp, and the state of his health was always a question. But he was away at college now, and for the first time in my life — Hap Arnold High to myself! — I was out of his shadow. Sprung as I was from the all-male pinched milieu of Priory, the large all-American public school with its hilltop view of the magic city, its bright cafeteria, sports field, locker-lined hallways, girls in swirling skirts, and talentless football team, the Warriors, on which I could shine — it was heaven. Suddenly, instead of being known as the crippled kid's brother, I was the general's son. The feeling was, Wiesbaden gave my father back to me.

I remember especially the early *bierstube* sessions with a first group of chums, sons of lower-ranking officers and NCOs, when it hit me that my father's primacy in this pecking order was my own primacy; that the essence of his status was power, mine as well as his; that it was more determinative than our being Catholic. It hit me that, in relation to my friends, this was all grossly unfair — like my not having polio was unfair to Joe — and that I loved it.

To be on an American-sponsored school's sports team in postwar Europe was a special glory, because most weeks we traveled to the capital cities where the great Army, Navy, and Air Force posts and bases were. Our big rivals were the high schools in nearby Frankfurt and Ramstein, but the games we really looked forward to were against Munich and Paris. One trip took us to Berlin. In those pre-Wall days we careened down East Berlin's Stalin Allee in a rented Opel, a drunken classmate at the wheel while the other four or five of us waved red bandannas out the windows, singing in honor of the heroes of the airlift, "Off we go into the wild blue yonder." We sang our own praises for making it back into the American sector without being challenged by the Commie "Vopos," or Volkspolizei, but then we were pulled over by a pair of stalwart Negroes, American MPs who seemed to know what we'd been up to. They were not amused. Looking at my dependent's ID, noting my father's rank, one of them said to me, "You should know better."

The high school travels gave me a feel for that peculiar American empire: we came as conquerors indeed! But my golden memory is of a home game late in the season. I remember it as the biggest game of my senior year. I was the starting right end, which perhaps explains why our team had yet to win a game. I had stopped hoping that my father would attend one, and also stopped minding, since we were so bad, that he never did. He was busy keeping Khrushchev at bay. Those were the years of "flashpoint Berlin," and why should such a father have had any idea that his son was becoming another kid entirely?

It was enough for me that my girlfriend was a cheerleader, and that after the dance that night, win or lose, she would let me push the palm of my hand against the wired cushion of her breast.

By the fourth quarter, the game was still scoreless. The quarterback was John Blaha, a lean hero who, like me, was planning to go to the Air Force Academy in Colorado Springs. He would actually do so, eventually becoming an astronaut and space shuttle pilot. In the huddle he called yet another play that sent me downfield, a decoy. I shot from the line of scrimmage, fooling no one. Then, when I crossed into the end zone, I looked back expecting to see the play action far away. Instead I saw the soaring football in descent toward me. I was horrified. My girl-friend and the grandstand full of kids would see me drop it. My father's rank would do me no good now.

The ball hit me in the throat, and by some miracle I managed to get my arms around it. Tacklers jolted me, and I remember picturing my fumble, but I held the ball. I hit the ground hard. A few yards away, at the sideline, the band struck up the fight song. I heard the word "Touchdown!" The crowd made a new sound, and I wanted to see their faces, but mine, in dirt, was pointing the other way, toward the opposite sideline where the pole-vault track was. I remember lying there for a long time, not moving, looking across the field, my eyes unable to focus, quite, on the odd blue shape that did not belong.

Blades of grass in the foreground gave way slowly to a sleek, long limousine, the most familiar car there was. I knew without seeing them that two stars would be on its bumper plates. How long had that car been there? A man in uniform and peaked hat, stars on his shoulders, was leaning on the front fender, hands in his trousers, a cigarette at his mouth. Daddy. Or rather, Dad.

My first touchdown. Our first victory. And he had seen it. Not only that: the whole school, including my girl, had seen him doing so.

In the huddle, the others knew. I sensed the rush of their excitement, as if the general had pressed an instant's imprima-tur — General Patton at the front — on them too. For the extra point, Blaha called the same play, slot two, down and out, Carroll fly. As we lined up, I did not dare look over again. I shut the layers of my concentration down to the numbers. Hut! Hut! The snap. The running. The head fake. The flight. The ball coming at me again. And once again — first Lourdes, then Fatima — I caught the thing. By that one point we would win the game.

When I looked toward the limo now, ready to wave, it was gone. I thought I'd looked the wrong way, and so I turned. The car was not there. How had it disappeared? I took my helmet off and looked again. He was gone. For a second I wondered if I'd dreamed him, leaning against the fender, smoking that Camel, watching. But I knew I had not. He had been there. He saw the touchdown. And he left. And in a flash — flashpoint Wiesbaden — I understood.

The others would think he'd had to leave because of Nikita Khrushchev, the tension in Berlin, the things a general has to do. The others would feel the affirming afterglow of the general's presence, however brief. But not me.

I knew why my father had left abruptly. Because he saw me in my moment of success. Success here, in this culture, with these kids, with a girl watching, was the enemy of my father's ancient and implicit plan for me. Silly as it seems to say so, crossing into the end zone with that football was crossing out of the zone of my selection. Daddy had been right in the first place to stay away from me in this new world. He could not see me exhibit what he had repressed. His coming to my game was his mistake. Doing well in front of him, basking in the applause of my new friends, putting my happiness on display — these were mine.

The Eagle Club was a requisitioned mansion in downtown Wiesbaden, near the casino and the park. Even grander than the house we lived in, it had reputedly served as Queen Victoria's residence when she'd come here for the spa. On better authority, it was said to have served as General Eisenhower's headquarters for a time in 1945. But by 1958, its distinction to us teenagers was even more pronounced, for the Eagle Club, now a servicemen's bar and music joint, was rumored to be an occasional hangout of Elvis Presley.

Elvis, famously a GI by now, was stationed at an Army post thirty miles away, near Frankfurt. Word was that he drove trucks, and at a certain point a hot rumor had it that he was dating an eighth grader in the junior high across the street from H. H. Arnold. No one believed it. When even hotter rumors identified her as the daughter of an Air Force colonel, a prim girl on whom my eighth-grade brother, Brian, had a crush of his own, I *really* did not believe it. But I would remember her chiseled prettiness years later — 1967, Priscilla Beaulieu — when Elvis married her.

The main reason I could not believe that Elvis would seek out a girl that young was that it did not square with the libidinous image we had of him, or with the license he gave us to imitate it, albeit with a decidedly fifties-era inhibition. Even we straight-arrow military dependents mimicked Elvis with our pomaded hair, curled lips, slouches, suede shoes, piping on our trouser seams, and cultivated air of obsession with sex. Pregenital, making-out, feeling-up, French-kissing, going-halfway sex, but sex all the same. A little song, a little dance, a little seltzer in the pants. That's entertainment.

Those who did their double-clutching in the next decade, to the rhythm of the Rolling Stones, could hardly sustain such heights of tension — the point of "satisfaction," we believed, was to yearn for it — as the ones we approached to the strains of (what else?) "I want you, I need you, I love you." Of course today the truth of what drew that secretly lost young man to cute but as yet sexless Priscilla is obvious, though we swore then that the rock 'n' roll star was up to his olive underwear and their garters in *fräuleins, mädchens* and *schatzies*. Well beyond the eighth grade ourselves, we teenage boys knew, nevertheless, that we weren't ready for the German prostitutes whose Marlene Dietrich gams decked every corner for blocks around the night-time *buhnhof*. Still, those girls were barely older than we were. We tested them, testing the language and ourselves, with sly, pidgin exchanges. (*"Was costen?" "Mit goumi? Fünf mark." "Zu muchen!"*) Then we'd hustle back to Hainerberg, great balls of fire, hoping for a slow drag at the sock hop. The music of Elvis, like our idea of sex, was all about dry humping.

Even so, lewd Elvis embodied the opposite of all that I'd been raised to be. The showy sexlessness of my parents' relationship and the aggressive puritanism of my parish and monastery schools had established a standard of repression that we called morality. I was dying to fall short of it. I had been conditioned, like every parochial Catholic, to an exquisite vigilance against "impure thoughts" and "illicit pleasures." Vigilance means paying acute attention, which I did. The nuns and priests had told me that temptation was the great enemy. I recognized temptation as my steady companion, and eventually as a friend. Having been so breathlessly warned against upheavals of carnal desire, I found that when they came — whether through photos in a magazine, the sight of a classmate's bra strap, dancing on a dime with my girlfriend, or, marvelously, when the pearly gates of her teeth opened to my tongue — those upheavals were volcanic. Recalling them later always left me feeling alone, afraid, doomed.

Until Elvis, "Hound Dog," "Love Me Tender." I was a boy with four brothers and no sisters. Elvis, like a fifth, did nothing to dispel the haze that mystified my every notion of what a girl was, but he taught me how to dance with one, how to touch her hip, and how to take the wild disapproval of parents and church, teachers and chaperons, as a signal that these feelings, as much erotic as rhythmic, were rightly ours. Because of Elvis, I found myself belonging to a new group — not Catholics, the parish, school, or even family, not the military either, but "youth."

The American Youth Association, the AYA, was the teen club beside the high school, and every day we adjourned there for Cokes, which never tasted sweeter, and for the jukebox, the jitterbug, the stroll, and bop — for slow dancing with our knees inside each other's thighs, the unacknowledged teenagers' braille that told me girls were as much on board this express as boys. For the first time in my life I had something that belonged to no one else in my tight family, not my parents, of course, not Joe, who would never dance, and not my other brothers, who were — Priscilla notwithstanding — still too young. Elvis himself, sadly, was already a musical has-been, though who could have imagined that in 1959? Eventually he would be called The King, but he was already king to me, my truest lord, the one in whom, at the AYA, I found my first identity, not as my father's kind of Catholic or my mother's kind of son or my siblings' kind of brother, but simply as me.

The AYA was for weekday afternoons. Saturday nights were for the Eagle Club and the permanent dream of seeing him, the one who'd made us who we were. The GIs and airmen who frequented the club were not much older than I was, and no more able to appreciate the glories of the physical setting. The mansion's ornate fence, curving driveway, and baroque entrance evoked the elegance of a bygone era, but the smoky interior and the dim lighting of a would-be nightclub blotted out the carved marble and crystal sconces to which the farm boys, rednecks, and buffalo soldiers would have been indifferent anyway. Jazz groups and rock 'n' roll bands performed on the stage at one end of a former ballroom. In the center of a circle of stein-cluttered tables was a dance floor, always crowded with servicemen clinging to or jumping with blank-eyed German girls, some of whom were secretaries or clerks at headquarters, some the daughters of sycophantic locals seeking contacts, and some the leggy *schatzies* from the shadows near the *bahnhof*. It was a regular shock to see the hookers here, how much less alluring they looked than the girls who might say no.

High school kids were forbidden admission to the Eagle Club, and except for some of the tougher girls who dated GIs, few bothered to try to get in. That was less a problem for me than a further condition of my joy in the place. I learned early in Wiesbaden that such rules did not apply to the general's son, especially since my father's driver, a forever ingratiating staff sergeant, moonlighted as a club maitre d'. Once I arrived with my girl on my arm, her twin sweater set a demure contrast to the hookers' cleavage. The sergeant greeted us with a mock salute and took us to a table with a placard that said "Reserved." More typically he would wink, admitting us, and we would lose ourselves in the crowd. We would drink the German beer, and dance, and lean into each other's bodies, but always with one eye peeled for Elvis. Often we would hear he'd arrived on a night the week before, just after we'd left, and that, responding to the hoots of his buddies, he'd climbed to the stage and sung a song. Calculating our arrival to be later, we would hear another time that he'd just left. We never doubted these reports, and the sexy frenzy of the Eagle Club always seemed to justify them.

When I saw Elvis at last, not long before he rotated back to the States, the single most striking thing about him was his hair — how short it was, and how unglistening. He looked as much the straight arrow as I did. I savor the memory of Elvis leaping onto the stage in his khakis, his field hat through the epaulet on his left shoulder; Elvis swooping the microphone and diddling his leg, that pelvis thrust, and making the crystal chandeliers jitter to the mournful squeal of "Heartbreak Hotel." I savor the memory, but instead of being what happened, it's what I'd always imagined happening. In fact, Elvis walked into the smoky nightclub and, instead of his Army buddies hooting a welcome, the room fell silent, which cued everyone to look his way. I caught the briefest of glimpses before his head disappeared as he took a chair at a corner table. A buzz of amazed exchanges swept the room, but it was instantly clear to me that this crowd was no more able to think of Elvis as belonging to it than we would have been at the AYA. All the stories about his easy camaraderie were false, and judging from the stupefied air, I realized that so were the reports of his regular Eagle Club appearances. Elvis was Elvis, here and everywhere. By the time I had maneuvered my way around the room for another glimpse of the greatest man alive, he was gone.

Elvis's quick disappearance was a potent revelation that the man who'd set me free was himself anything but. It was a lesson not only in the imprisonment of celebrity but in the untrustworthiness of even our most absolute assumptions. If Elvis was not free, how in the world had I begun to think that I was? Not long afterward, Francis Gary Powers, in a flight originating in Turkey and plotted to bring him to Wiesbaden air base, was shot down over the Soviet Union. President Eisenhower said the U-2 was an off-course weather plane. I recall how, at H. H. Arnold High School, the sons and daughters of the air base maintenance crews and traffic controllers raised eyebrows at each other: weather plane? After a week, Khrushchev ambushed Ike, exposing his dishonesty to the world with Powers's own testimony. Dwight D. Eisenhower, a liar like Charles Van Doren? And that was not all. "The CIA promised us that the Russians would never get a U-2 pilot alive," John Eisenhower said, expressing his father's sentiment. "And then they gave the SOB a parachute!"

I had seen noble Ike inaugurated twice. If he was not virtuous — here was the next weighty question — how had I thought my father was?

*

My life in Wiesbaden ran along a pair of tracks that seemed parallel but weren't. On one, I sought to recreate myself as the beau ideal of the American high school boy, a chipper, clean-cut version not of Elvis but of an Elvis fan. Of all the many surprises in Germany, the biggest was the ease of my own self-transformation, which was more instinctive than calculated. The feeling was that I'd been given license at last to be who I really was. No longer the student who wasn't quite smart enough, or the phony who felt obliged to make a show of piety, I became instead a tintype football hero, a cheerleader's lover boy, a dance contestant, a class officer, a card — a phony of another kind entirely. Successes came in a cascade — Stage Manager in *Our Town*, yearbook editor, Lettermen's Club — yet even I knew it was less because of my many charms — this freckled face? these Alfred E. Neuman ears? — than because that particular track was well greased by my father's rank. No dope, instead of hating my privilege, I embraced a new ambition for myself. I would make that privilege permanent by cruising that glistening track right into adulthood. Off we go into the wild blue yonder, fucking-A. By senior year I was a self-declared candidate for the U.S. Air Force Academy. At H. H. Arnold a culture of academic mediocrity prevailed, and I was content to be a C student. The college counselor assured me, however, that the Air Academy's competitive admission process would hold no obstacle for a boy of my special qualification. General Junior. Mr. Shoo-in. This track was inside.

But the other track was there as well, incrementally diverging. "All hail rock 'n' roll," yes. But also, always, "Hail Mary, full of grace." At home, in the kaiser's marshal's mansion on Biebricher Allee, just up from the Henkell champagne factory, the Church was more palpably present than ever, but in a confusing new way. Instead of the Jansenist gloom of the old monsignor at St. Mary's — once, when he dropped the sacred host on the sanctuary floor, and when I, his altar boy, instinctively reached to pick it up, he stomped my hand with his stout Irish boot — our house was full of the raucous laughter of manly Air Force chaplains. Monsignor — Colonel, and later General — Ed Chess was a cigar-chomping Chicagoan who'd nearly overlapped at seminary with Dad. Learning the game on the same clerical course at Mundelein College, each had become a scratch golfer. Now, in Germany, they became weekly partners, playing on the requisitioned course of an elegant old German hunt club near Frankfurt.

Sometimes I caddied for them just for the rare thrill of sharing their fellowship. They bet on greenies and "pushed" each other, a gambling trick I never understood. Monsignor Chess offered Dad cigars, which to my surprise he took. I loved listening to their exchange of stories from seminary days and gossip about priests they knew. When they slapped each other's shoulders, laughing, I glimpsed more fully than ever the rare warmth that marked my father's relationships outside the family. No wonder his colleagues were dedicated to him. No wonder disparate groups, from the seminary to the Bureau and even to some quarters of the military, wanted him at their centers. With Monsignor Chess, my dad's irresistible affability was on full display, and so was his manliness. I was awed by the power of their booming drives, rifle shots down fairway after fairway. On the golf course, and only there, they called each other by their first names, and at times during those leisurely Saturday afternoons, I pretended that my father had become a priest after all. Sometimes I forgot about the Air Force Academy, even about my girlfriend, and pretended that I had become a priest too.

Those golf games were a dream of intimacy that, it seemed to me, was made possible by the transforming presence of a priest — a priest my father and I both came, without ever saying so, to love. For the first conscious time, and because of that priest, I linked a bond of feeling for my father to a like bond of feeling for God. That it was happiness pure and simple I know every time, even now, that I taste lentil soup, because lentil soup was a feature of the hunt club's kitchen. The three of us finished every round of golf by eating that porridge, with rough black bread, in the grand room of a timber-framed lodge that reeked of the ghosts of barons and Prussian generals we had defeated. What chance had the Nazis had against men of such virtue and such prowess off the tee? Monsignor Chess would eventually become the chief chaplain of the Air Force, in part, I suspect, because of his friendship with Dad, formed here. General Chess's concelebration at my first Mass a decade later would redouble both its meaning for my father and, then, the shame of my betrayal.

The younger captains and majors among the Wiesbaden chaplains, given to bright crew cuts and stainless-steel ID bracelets, spit-shined shoes and aviator sunglasses, forced a new idea of the priesthood on me. The same was true of my mother. With these men, she was extroverted and flirtatious, delighted by the power her status gave her. In Germany she was the baron's wife, the baroness. The chaplains were champions of her court. She seemed as amazed as I that our religion, given to us in sorrow, for the vale of tears, could suddenly seem so glamorous. One chaplain drove a Thunderbird convertible, another a Mercedes gullwing. Instead of clucking nuns, grimacing monks, old ladies of the sodality, and a stern Irish pastor, we had brush cuts, loafers, ID bracelets, fast cars, and the good-humored informality of a clerical masculinity calculated to appeal to American GIs. It appealed to me.

At the high school I kept it as secret as I could, but all the time I was angling for position at the yearbook and in class elections, and all the time I was chipping away at my girlfriend's sexual inhibition and my own, I was showing up also for early morning

Mass at the chapel across the street. It thrilled me to see as servers sergeants or lieutenants in uniform instead of robed altar boys. Sometimes I took their place. As I stood by with cruets and finger towels, féeling naked in my uncassocked chinos and sweater, I imagined the young chaplain spreading the sacred cloth over the hood of a jeep on a cratered hillside in Korea, say. I saw myself as his assistant, holding the golden plate under the chins of GIs who, shortly after this last Communion, would die like heroes.

In relation to Mom, my question, like every high school boy's, had become, How to be a son and a man both? A developing relationship with a girl — by senior year my cheerleader and I were going steady, talking lifelong love — could have opened the way to one kind of answer, but in the frenzied push-pull of my sexual confusion, my girl herself had come to seem like, in another loaded phrase of the era, an occasion of sin. She was, in fact, an occasion of my own true selfhood, but that, given my long-set fate, was what could seem the sin itself. Thus the power of the alternative represented by these military priests, new objects of my mother's affection and unexpected images to me of a holiness that was not quite sexless. They began to seem, much as I did not want it anymore, the answer I was born to give.

The most dramatic consequence of our ascension to the upper ranks, not so much of the military but of military Catholicism, was the friendship it made possible between my parents and, as he was called, the military vicar, a no less exalted figure than Francis Cardinal Spellman of New York.

Spellman was a short, round-faced eunuch — although his biographer many years later would report that "rumors abounded" about his homosexual activity. Many of his priests assumed it. His own first bishop, William Cardinal O'Connell of Boston, had called him many years before "the fat little liar."

Some would describe Spellman as a pederast. The thought that at the very time I was trying to repress my own sexual urges, key Church figures at whose behest I was doing so may themselves have been promiscuous is enough, even today, to wrench my stomach with anger and disgust. The issue is not homosexuality, but dishonesty and abuse. By the 1990s the pathetic exploitation of the young and the weak by priests had become an old story, but in the 1950s this pathology was deeply hidden. As the secret became exposed, Church officials would work hard to make the misbehavior of priests seem marginal, yet it was central. The pathology was and is endemic to the repressive, deceit-ridden culture of celibate clericalism. Cardinal O'Connell's biographer would expose him, an active homosexual, as a liar too.

I was at war with myself, habitually committing, then confessing, the mortal sin of illicit sexual pleasure, "alone and with another." But without knowing it, I was at war also with the sexual lie at the heart of Church practice. My father, years before, had said no to clerical celibacy and all that went with it, not imagining that many of the vicious slanders American anti-Catholics had hurled at priests and bishops were literally true. Now celibacy was an issue for me too, but the renunciation of sexual intimacy implied the "virtuous" embrace of a spiritual power that was actually profoundly temporal, and no one embodied this more fully than Spellman. "The Powerhouse" was how his residence on Madison Avenue was referred to in rectories, in boardrooms, in government offices, and in foxholes. The key to Spellman's power was the well-known fact — he made sure it was well known — of his closeness with Pius XII. From his being the pope's valued friend and counselor flowed his wide-ranging influence over Church and State alike.

To Catholics like us, he was the avatar of Irish-American ambition. The son of a storekeeper, a graduate of the North American College on Rome's Humility Street, the Vatican factotum at home with the high and mighty, he was also as well proven a friend to GI Joe as Bob Hope would ever be. Presidents Roosevelt and Truman had used Spellman as a back-channel diplomat. Eisenhower depended on him as a fellow Republican. Thomas Dewey, Joseph Kennedy, and Clare Boothe Luce regarded him as a confidant, if not as a confessor.

It was J. Edgar Hoover whom Spellman had in common with Dad, but that would not have been enough to soothe my father's impatience with Spellman's vociferous support of Senator Joseph McCarthy and McCarthy's pit bull, Roy Cohn. My father hated them both for making a proper anxiety about Communist infiltration seem only paranoid. Still, the memory of Spellman in military fatigues, saying Mass on Heartbreak Ridge and Pork Chop Hill, had made His Eminence a permanent hero on Army posts and Air Force bases, and therefore to the likes of us.

When Cardinal Spellman visited the troops in Europe at Christmas in 1958, protocol put my father at his side. That was the first of several occasions when he was a guest in our home. As he stepped from his limousine on Biebricher Allee, he was even shorter than I'd imagined, and with his cherub face and frock coat, the word that popped unforgettably to mind was leprechaun. I glanced inside his car behind him and saw the seat strewn with cartons of cigarettes, a mystery until later when I saw that the packages of Luckies had been specially manufactured to include the cardinal's own picture inside the cellophane, along with a printed promise of a papal benediction. Holy Smokes.

Arriving at the door of our house, Spellman was greeted, as per rehearsal, by Kevin, the youngest at six years old. Kevin was a curly-haired redhead with a winning smile, the one at the center, then and always, of everybody's affection. But when he said, "Welcome to our house," he addressed His Eminence as "Your Enema," causing his stunned brothers to choke on laughter while red-faced Spellman blushed even redder. Mom endeared herself to the cardinal by hugging flummoxed Kevin and smiling broadly at the prelate. She said, "Now we have to become friends." And they did.

At one point, after an intimate and, by me, wholly unauthorized conversation with my parents, Cardinal Spellman put his hand on my shoulder and said, "When you're ordained, Jimmy, it will be, God willing, by me." Not since the move to Germany had my long-determined fate been so openly referred to. I recall the pride in my parents' faces. I also recall feeling, despite myself, a momentary thrill of selection: Many are called, but few are chosen. The moment passed: Many are cold, but few are frozen. As a love-smitten teenager who was working hard to re-imagine himself a junior air cadet, a married man, a fighter pilot, I was thrown off balance. My simple, half-formed, run-of-the-mill ambition for myself seemed shoddy, even shameful — a secret. "Yes, Your Eminence," I said, blushing furiously, a true coward who was thinking, as I always would then, Enema.

"He's no pope," Cardinal Spellman had said to his aides about the newly elected Roncalli. "He should be selling bananas." Upon Roncalli's election, Spellman commissioned a life-size wax dummy of Pius XII and displayed it in a glass case at the rear of St. Patrick's Cathedral — the image of the real pope. As John XXIII, Roncalli immediately, and mainly by his behavior, undercut what had been taken to be Catholic absolutes — that Protestants and Jews are doomed, that priests are ontologically superior beings, that error has no rights, that the pontiff himself, no mere "bridge," is a kind of God. In his great encyclical *Pacem in Terris*, John would call into question not only his predecessor's rejection of conscientious objection, but also the basic assumptions of American military strategy, and therefore of my father's life. The pope would do so by declaring, "It is hardly possible to imagine that in the atomic era war could be used as an instrument of justice."

Pope John stunned the world by receiving and embracing Nikita Khrushchev's son-in-law. After their meeting, His Holiness advocated a Catholic dialogue with Marxists. Dialogue? With atheistic Communists? To discuss what? Even more momentously, he announced in January 1959, only two months after his election — and a month after Cardinal Spellman's first visit to our house — that because the Roman Catholic Church was out of step with the times, he was convening an Ecumenical Council. It would be the first in nearly a century, and its purpose would be, he said, to usher in *aggiornamento*. He was going to open the Church's windows, he said, to let in fresh air.

John XXIII's arrival, in other words, was a disaster for the likes of Cardinal Spellman, curial officials and Church moguls whose power under the rigid Pacelli depended on the triumphalist ecclesiology of the Counter-Reformation. If the Church was a perfect society in no need of reform, then its princes held power unassailably, and of course unaccountably. But for Pope John himself, and for an entire generation of European Catholic thinkers, the myth of the sinless Church had been exploded by the near-total capitulation of the Roman Catholic hierarchy before Adolf Hitler. As for the Vatican itself, when Pope John was asked what to do about Rolf Hochhuth's play *The Deputy*, which savaged Pius XII's complicitous silence, His Holiness replied, "Do? What can one do about the truth?"

As wartime apostolic delegate in Istanbul, Roncalli had personally signed thousands of forged baptismal certificates to give Jews the one credential enabling escape, but he knew that his effort fell far short of redressing Catholic responsibility. Sinful? Papal silence early — say, when Mussolini decreed an end to the rights of Jews in 1939; and Papal silence late — say, when Nazis rounded up Jews in Rome in 1943 for transport to Auschwitz — silence is one thing, but what about active cooperation with the tyrants? What else was it when, in Italy in 1929, Pope Pius XI agreed to Mussolini's demand to suppress University Catholic Action, the last organized resistance to Fascism? Or when, in Germany in 1933, the Vatican acceded to Hitler's demand to suppress the Catholic Center Party, the last opposition to Nazism? In each case — the Lateran Pact and the German Concordat — the Vatican put its institutional rights ahead of resistance to the dictators. The record of the moral failure of the Church in relation to the Final Solution is well known; even a number of formal Church statements have acknowledged the culpabilities of national hierarchies and individual prelates. The Vatican as such, however, has never openly faced its own role in the Holocaust, much less repented of it. But the pervasive malaise of European Catholicism that prompted Pope John XXIII to call the Ecumenical Council was surely a consequence of the popes' and bishops' having failed the moral test of the century. Even though his successors would fall short of his vision and impede the implementation of what it implied, Pope John, if only by refusing to exempt himself from the confession of sin, was a prophet of the Church's historic corruption. Which is why, to Spellman's ilk, he was anathema.

But for my family, as for ordinary Catholics everywhere, Pope John was something else. Not only a big-eared bear hug of a man whose warmth kindled the world's affection and ours, he was also attuned to the morbidity of Church structures, theology, and governance, which stood in marked contrast to the instinctive moral vitality of the Catholic people. For example, in the United States my parents' generation, with little or no guidance — although at times with opposition — from pastors or bishops, had enthusiastically and unembarrassedly embraced the national consensus, its respect for freedom of conscience, its assumption of the virtue of pluralism, and its determination to leave behind the old religious intolerance of Europe. My father's arrival as an American general was a small version of the imminent arrival of John Kennedy. Both represented a change in America and a change in what immigrant Catholicism expected of itself. Such change urgently required some equivalent shift in the Church's understanding of itself and some revision of the face it showed the world. Even Catholics who, like my parents, thought of themselves as traditionalists could only welcome it when Pope John opened the windows of the Church by opening his Council. This pope's religious hope meshed with our American optimism. People like my parents were never more themselves than at that time.

"Holy Father, General and Mrs. Joseph Carroll and their sons Joseph Jr., James, Brian, Dennis and Kevin . . ."

These words are written in Gothic calligraphy in a gold-framed certificate below a photograph of the smiling, large-nosed pope. In the four corners of the certificate are sketched scenes of Vatican City: St. Peter's, the Apostolic Palace, Bernini's square, the walled gardens. The framed object sits on the edge of my desk before me, leaning against the wall. I found it in one of my mother's boxes when she died two years ago, one of a matched pair of gilded frames. The other holds a color photograph of our family flanking Pope John XXIII in front of the red damask wall of his throne room in which we had our audience. In the photo, my blue father with his gleaming buttons and stars is on one side of the pope, together with Joe and Dennis. My mother, in a Lady-of-Spain mantilla, is on the other, with Brian, little Kevin, and me. I am beside her. My hair, in front, is a cresting wave, a small hint of Elvis, but my sideburns are not so long that my ears do not protrude.

The Gothic calligraphy, evoking the ghosts of Tetzel and Luther, continues, ". . . do humbly beg your fatherly and Apostolic Blessing, and a Plenary Indulgence at the hour of death on condition that being sorry for their sins but unable to confess them, or to receive Holy Viaticum, they shall at least with their lips or heart devoutly invoke the Holy Name of Jesus."

The petition is presumably answered with the scrawled signature of some monsignor and the pressed seal of the Keys of the Kingdom. This event was the absolute highlight of my parents' life, and it was something for me too. It took place in my senior year, toward the end of our time in Europe, within weeks of the chill midnight when my girlfriend and I, on the edge of the Hainerberg football field overlooking the twinkling spa city of Wiesbaden, fumbled our clothes open. The Puritan verdict "Found in Unlawful Carnal Knowledge," someone told me, gives us "fuck." My girl and I were not "found," and we did not quite consummate our "knowledge," but fucked was what, arriving in Rome, I felt. Sex was going to be my secret way out of the religion.

I have little or no memory of the papal apartments, the tapestries or great paintings. I am told that somewhere there hangs a fifteenth-century map that marks the American continent as "Terra Incognita," but I did not see it. Years later, in the statue-lined corridors of the Vatican Museums, I would notice that the male genitalia of all the Greek and Roman nudes had been chiseled off. I would learn of the artist Daniele da Volterra, ordered by Pius V — always Pius? — to cover the loins of Michelangelo's naked figures, earning for himself the sobriquet "Il Brachettone," the trouser maker. But at the time of this, my first visit to the Vatican, I was blind to such signals of the Church's genital obsessiveness, no doubt because I was so conflicted about my own. Sex evil? All I knew by then was that God was right to regard the sexual feelings of creatures as supreme competition. At times my longings obliterated the existence of everything else, including Him.

By now, the effort to recall this phase of my personal history has succeeded at least in evoking my sad pity for the affected, frightened lad in this photograph with the freckles, big ears, and mini-pompadour; his carefully constructed surface — that Windsor knot just so — layering over a seething insecurity; his dread of a future that seemed a trap or a dead end; the tumult of his hidden unbelief, sex, and filial subservience. This lad whose brothers knew nothing about him, and whose parents could see only in the unsteady light of choices they themselves had made twenty-five years before. This lad whose ability to be consoled by a sweet, pretty girl who claimed to love him, who'd trusted him with her near nakedness, was blown to smithereens by the certain knowledge that, despite himself, in every gesture of affection and word of promise he had lied to her about an open future. This lad — how, in seeing him in this photo now, I would love to embrace him, pressing in all that I have seen and learned of acceptance and forgiveness and affirmation. He is my younger self, of course, and there is nothing I can do for him.

Yet just such a thing, by a miracle of the same fresh grace that has swept the Church itself, is done then to the very same lad. It happens when Pope John turns from my brother Joe to me. He is most of a foot shorter than I, his face as red as his shoes, his cassock pure white, a gold cross, a jewel on his finger. I bend toward him, and he surprises me by reaching up and taking my shoulders firmly in his hands. His head is close to mine. I smell the scent of incense, also of soap. He holds me for a long time, pressing in all that he has seen and knows. His accent is thick, and so I do not understand what he is saying. The interpreter stays apart, as if this is private. Confession. He seems so much more affectionate with me than with my brothers that I can only assume, as with Spellman, that someone has told him of my ancient designation, my "vocation." But now instead of the claustrophobia of my hypocrisy, I feel elation. He is seeing through to the core of me, he knows my secret, and he shares it.

This is the moment of my conscription. After this encounter I will abandon the false dream of following my father into the Air Force. The romance with my girlfriend will not survive the separation following high school graduation. I will enroll at Georgetown University. In summer I will work as a clerk at the FBI, a job my father gets me. There will be other girls, and more of the panic of sex, but no more lies. I will cut short my time at college to enter the seminary — the one past which Mom drove so often when we went to lay our sorrow down at the feet of Mary. I will spend the next dozen years in a religious order, ultimately — pre-ordained? — to be ordained a priest.

Why? For a hundred reasons and for one. Here in Rome, the city itself inside a gold frame, for the first time in my life the Call feels entirely addressed to me, and not from Mom or Dad. In the person of a pope, a counter-Elvis, I glimpse the transcendence of the Church, which Michelangelo saw in flashes. The Church is a way that God has touched the earth. I know that its rituals and symbols satisfy the deepest urges of human beings because here, for a moment, this man, its chief symbol, satisfies the very thing in me. My turbulent self-consciousness is replaced for a moment — the first one — with peace. For a moment I do not think of any of this in relation to my parents.

What can we know? Why is there anything instead of nothing? What is the reason and meaning of reality? What ought we to do? Why are we here? Kant's questions, and every adolescent's. Pope John's face is close to mine, his sweet breath blows across mine. I stop asking these questions because, for a moment — the first one — I believe in God.

Now another question: how could anything ever seem more important than this faith? To ask it is to answer it. I genuflect, and His Holiness blesses me with something not his own, not my father's, and not mine. The Hound of Heaven has me. God. And how can I not make a life of Him?

5

JOY TO MY YOUTH

"Introibo ad altare Dei," the priest says at the beginning of Mass. "I will go unto the altar of God." *"Ad Deum qui laetificat juventutem meam,"* the altar boy replies. "To God who gives joy to my youth."

One night we are cruising along on the ridge of South Capitol Street, above the river-plain city of Washington, D.C. It is the summer of 1960. "Kennedy Nominated on First Ballot," the headline blared this morning. Below it, another read, "Moscow Bids U.N. Convene at Once on RB-47 Incidents."

Dad has worked late at the Pentagon and, earlier, has let his driver go. I have driven across the Potomac to pick him up. I am a hotshot college kid now, and for the summer a cryptanalyst's aide at the FBI, but I am not so worldly as to pass up the chance to take the Lincoln out at night — or to be alone with him.

The headlines have steadily charted the ratcheting up of tension between our country and the Soviet Union. "Khrushchev Warns of Rocket Attack on Bases Used by U.S. Spying Planes," one read earlier this week, and I knew enough to think of the U-2 hangar at Wiesbaden. The U-2 crisis in May had turned the heat up on Berlin again: "Khrushchev Establishes New Deadline." This time, if the Allies fail to withdraw from the beleaguered city, the Soviet leader says, he will close its access route through East Germany. GIs will have to go in behind tanks. A war will start. We will quickly drop our atom bomb on Moscow, and they will drop theirs on this city, here — the one outside our window. What a view we have, the twinkling lights, of Ground Zero.

The road takes us along the edge of a plateau. To our left and above are the looming turrets of St. Elizabeths Hospital, where the traitor-poet Ezra Pound has been locked up, nuts, for more than a decade. To our right, across the blue runway lights of Anacostia Naval Air Station, is the Potomac River, and in the distance the similar lights of National Airport. I know that Khrushchev's threats are what has kept Dad so late at the Pentagon.

When he finally came out, he surprised me by letting me stay at the wheel, which he had never done before. Instead of taking my place he got in next to me, a passenger. I was glad to have a chance to show him how well I'd learned to drive — both hands on the wheel now, of course, no finger-steering, no arm across the backrest.

Up ahead are the gleaming runway lights of yet another airport, Bolling Air Force Base, where we have lived since returning from Germany, and where my mother and father and brothers will live for the next decade. Westmoreland Avenue, Generals' Row, a gracious house next door to Vice Chief Curtis LeMay. There is a buzzer under the dining room rug for summoning the orderly to clear the dishes. There is a Red Telephone, which will ring when the war begins. There is a pool table in the rec room. When we pull through the main gate, an air policeman will salute us because of the stars on the front bumper. He salutes even when it is just me, and I salute back as if I am the general.

Behind us the Washington Monument and the Capitol dome are still illuminated, so I know that it is not yet midnight. Washington and I have become well acquainted. It is a recovered paradise to me. There are fabulous girls at work — the typing pool, the file clerks — although I have been too shy to approach them. A clique of the sons and daughters of the high and mighty hang out at the Officers' Club swimming pool, and seem ready to invite me to join. Soon I will be haunting mixers at Visitation, Cathedral, and Goucher. I will meet Lynda Bird Johnson, and take her dancing at the Shoreham Terrace. I will squire girls to hear Charlie Byrd at the Showboat Lounge and Count Basie at the Carter Barron Amphitheatre. At Georgetown I will join the Young Democrats, staking a claim on the New Frontier. Washington — impossible thought — shows promise of the very joys I thought I'd lost. "It's like Wiesbaden," I'd crack to my new chums, a stab at true worldliness, "but it's better because here the hookers speak English."

My Life as a Hooker was the title of a book I would give Dad one Father's Day — the story of Bob Hope's golf game. Otherwise the word would never be mentioned, the profession never referred to. Not just hookers, but girls in saddle shoes, nursing students at Georgetown, pickups at the library, flirts in the mailroom — I would mention none of them at home, as if sex did not exist, as if I were not aching with desire and loneliness.

Tonight Dad is in a somber mood. He is not whistling, as he often still does, "Beautiful Dreamer." He is smoking, flicking ashes out the window. He has said nothing. Finally he crushes the cigarette in the dashboard ashtray and turns to me. "Son, I want to say something to you. I'm only going to say it once, and I don't want you asking me any questions. Okay?

"You read the papers. You know what's going on. Berlin. The bomber they shot down last week. I may not come home one of these nights. I might have to go somewhere else. The whole Air

Staff would go. If that happens, I'm going to depend on you to take my place with Mom and the boys."

"What do you mean?"

"Mom will know. But you should know too. I'll want you to get everybody in the car. I'll want you to drive south. Get on Route One. Head to Richmond. Go past it. Go as far as you can before you stop."

He didn't say anything else. As I remember it, neither did I. We must have driven the rest of the way home in silence. I do remember very distinctly, though, the two halves of what I felt. The first was fear. Until that moment, even in Berlin itself the year before, tearing down Stalin Allee, red bandannas out the window, I had not felt afraid. Despite all the talk of war, I had believed that my father and the others like him — Curtis LeMay, Tommy White, Pearre Cabell, Butch Blanchard, our neighbors on Generals' Row — would protect us from it. Now I saw that Dad himself no longer thought they could. I felt my father's fear, which until then I'd thought impossible. I began to be afraid that night and I stayed afraid for many years, first of what our enemy would do, later of what we would.

The second thing I felt was an unprecedented intimacy with him; the trust he placed in me had less to do with the prospect of that drive down Route One than with his readiness to let me see his fear. You are ready "to put away childish things," he might have said, with Saint Paul. Like what? I might have asked. Like your wish for self-realization, for carnality, for pleasure, for the world; the way you want a girl, companionship, relief from the loneliness that properly belongs to men like us.

I felt a rare happiness in the car with him that night, the wish only to be what I already was, a father-pleasing son. I remained silent, but I could have said, Of course, Dad, that other stuff is for 'the boys,' for women, for those not chosen — I am chosen, and I admit it. The doom of my privilege, that's what I felt. A lifetime of exactly this servility. The loneliness I recognized in him was so familiar, and yet because he let me sense it, my version of the same feeling seemed not just tolerable, but like a badge, a sign of our belonging to each other. Loneliness? If I could have him, my dad forever, I would never be alone again. The silence was the seal of what bound us now.

Another time, we did put some of this into words. It was that same summer. The international crisis had passed. In late August, Dad took me and Joe with him for a short vacation at Ramey Air Force Base in Puerto Rico, a SAC base on a remote bluff overlooking the azure Caribbean. Its golf course made the base a favorite R & R destination for the brass, and though Joe could not play because of his legs, golf was what took us there. On the course, I felt the old tug of guilt knowing Joe was back at the VIP bungalow, but also I prized the time alone with Dad. It felt like a reward for the inexorable, gradual surrender I was making, what later I would learn to call my abandonment to the will of God. By which I meant, in every way but consciously, my father's.

The golf course lapped like a winding emerald lagoon at the edges of the huge concrete air strip. This was one of the bases from which a third of the nation's strategic bomber fleet was kept airborne at all times, to avoid being surprised on the ground. Ramey was a mammoth reservation, bordered by blue water on one side and rain forest on the other. The golf course was lush, dotted with palm trees, swept by a constant breeze, broiling in a tropical sun. On one particular hole, the green abutted the front edge of the longest runway, and Dad and I were about to putt when a fleet of silver motes appeared on the horizon. We watched them approach and heard the faint roar grow louder. It was a wing of H-bomb-laden B-52s returning from its global patrol. Once Dad had pointed out the B-52's wingspan, how it exceeded the distance of the Wright brothers' entire Kitty Hawk flight. At an air show at Andrews Air Force Base, I had sat in a B-52 cockpit. It was the first and only machine I ever fell in love with. And now this was the first and only time I saw it in naked flight from just below. The screaming eight-engine plane, first one, then a succession of them, swooped down to within dozens of yards above us. The earth shook with the noise. My father held his putter and waited five minutes, ten. Ten warplanes, twenty. When the last B-52 had landed, he exchanged a glance with me, addressed his ball, and stroked it into the cup.

He was not so cool later that night. With an ample glass of bourbon in his hand, after Joe had gone to bed, and after another mute period spent listening to the bombers taking off one after another above our bungalow, he told me in so many words that World War III was inevitable. "The world is going to end in a ball of fire — of our own making," he said. I knew he was a little drunk, but in those days I thought that guaranteed that what he said was true. Within a few years as head of the Defense Intelligence Agency, he would be the one to discover hard evidence of the Soviet missile sites in Cuba. "General Carroll Saw Something," said a missile-crisis headline on the front page of the *Washington Star*. I would keep that page in my boxes, and would have it copied and framed years later for each of my brothers. During the crisis, I would glimpse Dad on television behind President Kennedy, but that would be all my family saw of him. For those ten days he disappeared. I was gone by then, and no help to Mom. Later, when I asked why she'd never gotten into the car and driven south, she explained that she and the other generals' wives at Bolling took turns driving down to the remote corner of the flight line where evacuation helicopters waited that would ferry the brass to Thunder Mountain. As long as the choppers were still there, she knew the generals were still in Washington and war was not imminent. During those ten days the helicopters never left the ground, so my mother never bundled her remaining sons into the car.

At Ramey that night, swirling his whiskey, Dad said, "Man has never created a weapon and not used it." An irrefutable fact; on this subject my father's authority was absolute. "The nuclear war is inevitable."

"I know," I said, feeling the pull of his fatalism, a sickness that even now curdles the juices in my throat. "That is why," I continued, aware of my words as a declaration, "I want to be a priest. I want to be a priest, Dad."

He looked at me, not speaking.

Now that I was saying them at last, the words poured out of me: "Because what's important now are the spiritual things, the eternal things, the things that last. The political and social and philosophical things have all already failed, the worldly things." I could have added, "The flesh." I could have said, "The devil." I could have said, "Indubitably."

He nodded, a quiet gesture of agreement and approval. The cold stone floor, the bamboo furniture, the stucco walls, the silence. I remember the unbroken silence, a stunning aftermath not only to my declaration but to the end-of-the-world shrieking of the B-52s. The silence was a warning that, having said those words, I would have to live them now. The silence was a warning also that the warplanes might never return.

Is my memory of this moment only melodramatic? In what way exactly were such fears founded? In fact, my father's fatalism was appropriate to what he knew, and so was my readiness to take a large cue from it. As the secret files of the Cold War are declassified and made public, in Moscow and in Washington, we discover that the world teetered closer to the nuclear precipice than has been thought. The risks of the Cuban missile crisis are assumed to be well known, yet recent revelations, summarized for example in Robert McNamara's memoir, *In Retrospect: The Tragedy and Lessons of Vietnam*, tell us that had the United States invaded Cuba, as the Joint Chiefs of Staff and civilian leaders alike recommended, the Soviet commander in Cuba was under orders to unleash the 162 nuclear warheads, mostly tactical, already in place. McNamara concludes, "No one should believe that, had American troops been attacked with nuclear weapons, the United States would have refrained from a nuclear response. And where would it have ended? In utter disaster."

This scenario, dreadful as it is, presumes that the United States would use its nuclear arsenal only in retaliation — and that has been taken as a tenet of our nuclear posture from the start of the Cold War. But in April and May of 1954, according to Mark Perry's *Four Stars*, a history of the Pentagon, Admiral Arthur Radford, chairman of the Joint Chiefs, proposed using nuclear weapons to defeat Vietnamese Communist forces at Dien Bien Phu. President Eisenhower refused. In February 1955 the Chiefs, with only General Matthew B. Ridgway dissenting, proposed the use of nuclear weapons to preempt China's anticipated attack on Formosa. Again Eisenhower refused. And we know, as of 1993 declassifications, that in 1961 around the time my father was confiding his dread to me, the National Security Council, with President Kennedy's participation, was seriously debating whether to launch an unprovoked surprise attack against all targets in the Soviet Union while it was still possible to preempt their retaliation. "The Burris Memorandum," summarizing one such meeting and dated July 20, 1961, includes this sentence: "The President asked if there had ever been made an assessment of damage results to the USSR, which would be incurred by a preemptive attack." That same summer Kennedy confirmed McNamara's appointment of my father as founding director of the Defense Intelligence Agency, and I am sure the shadows of such assessments fell on him.

At that time, American citizens were being urged by their government to build bomb shelters, always with the assumption that it would be Soviet fallout that threatened. But in the Burris Memorandum about a U.S. first strike, "The president posed the question as to the period of time necessary for citizens to remain in shelter following an attack." The answer was two weeks, but what citizens would be sheltered from was the earth-encircling fallout from our own weapons. At the end of his meeting, Kennedy remarked in an aside, "And we call ourselves the human race."

History records that after such experiences with the Pentagon leadership, Kennedy went on to turn the tide against the nuclear mindset. His American University speech in 1963 and the Test Ban Treaty, which led to the Nuclear Nonproliferation Treaty, were signals of that effort. But the heart of it was Robert McNamara's struggle to reimpose civilian controls on the World War II generation of generals and admirals — a struggle in which, since his abrupt commissioning to the rank of general by Stuart Symington, my father had played a part, and would continue to under McNamara, ultimately with disastrous personal results.

In his 1995 memoir, McNamara specifies occasions in 1964, 1966, and 1967 when the Joint Chiefs put forward Vietnam proposals that advocated "utilizing the nation's full military capability, including the possible use of nuclear weapons." This is a first public admission of what our government long denied — that the use of nukes in Vietnam was seriously considered. The common perception is that Curtis LeMay, who proposed bombing Hanoi "into the Stone Age," was a loose cannon, but his was far from the only Pentagon finger on the nuclear hair trigger. McNamara's record of conflict with the military leadership, well known as a key factor in the debacle of Vietnam, cannot be understood apart from the unacknowledged civilian-military struggle over use of nuclear weapons. And any assessment of McNamara's role that fails to credit him for finally thwarting the open-ended escalation toward nuclear use in Vietnam is inadequate.

But in 1960 this conflict was just being joined. LeMay, our neighbor at Bolling, was riding high. He had more than 200 first-generation ICBMs in place, and he wanted 2,400 of the new Minuteman ICBM missiles; LeMay's successor as head of SAC, Thomas Powers, wanted 10,000. Eventually McNamara would impose a limit of 1,000, infuriating the Joint Chiefs, who had begun that year's public panic about a "missile gap" with the Soviet Union. There was a gap, but it was heavily in our favor. The Soviets had, even into 1962 when the Cuban missile crisis occurred, only a few unreliable ICBMs. Their long-range bomber fleet consisted of 100 vulnerable Tupolev Bears and 35 May Bisons. By comparison, the United States had 1,500 B-47s and more than 600 B-52s.

The subtitle of the film *Dr. Strangelove* was *How I Learned to Stop Worrying and Love the Bomb*. Perverse as it seems, I loved the B-52. A screaming wing of them had adorned the cover of my high school yearbook, called "Vapor Trails," a copy of which is still in my boxes. Within a year of this moment at Ramey Air Force Base, as a freshman at Georgetown, I would be presented with the stainless-steel model B-52 I spoke of earlier, my prize for being named ROTC Cadet of the Year. Even I knew, by the way, that that award was attributable more to the cadet commanders' awe at my father's rank than to any distinction of mine. I did, however, have the most magnificently spit-shined black shoes in the corps. At inspections, the officer would put his shoe next to the cadet's, aiming to outshine, but he never did in my case. Nor did my ROTC superiors ever learn that I was wearing my father's shoes, which had been brought to that mirror finish by the countless hours' work of Dad's orderlies.

I would take my model bomber to the seminary with me. The "heavy hammer" of the nuclear triad would sit on my modest bureau — a perfect symbol of my unbreakable bond with my father, and of the motivating impulse that turned me, in fear and also despair, to God.

Vietnam would change the meaning of the B-52, of course. By 1969, the year of my ordination, it would be flying 1,800 sorties a month from Thailand and Guam, a strategy of "carpet bombing" and napalm runs. By then I would have unceremoniously thrown my stainless-steel model into the ravine behind the seminary — that "annihilation of the gods." The B-52 would embody all that divided my father and me.

But not now. The noise of the bombers had prompted his confession, which prompted mine. Now each of us was stuck. Within a year or two, the urge I felt could have taken me into the Peace Corps, or an inner-city tutoring program, or into a "helping profession" like counseling or social work. But in that pre-Kennedy summer, for a Catholic boy like me, what Robert Coles would dub "the call of service" could only mean the Church. And in my case, in addition to the call of service there was the call, though I did not know it yet, to fill a void. His. My mother's. Joe's. Anyone's but mine.

My father's quiet approval was, in fact, satisfaction that mitigated the despair he'd let me glimpse. Peace Corps? Tutoring? Social work? My inchoate sense of having filled a transcendent need of his would make such other ways of filling my own the moral equivalent of picking up an English-speaking prostitute on Ninth Street. Me? My call to service, my own personal strategy of deterrence — Myself Assured Destruction — was to stave off the war with an act of sacrifice. Given those terms, I did so willingly.

Thirty-five years later, the B-52 is still flying — seventy-four of them remain in service as I write. A third of the bomb tonnage in the Persian Gulf War in 1991 was dropped by B-52s. But in an odd turn of fate, the survival of the old workhorse has made it possible to reject successor bombers — the B-70, the B-1, and the B-2, which would have been even more destructive and would have forced yet another arms race escalation. The Air Force intends to keep the B-52 flying for another decade, as the mission of the heavy bomber melts away in the thaw of the Cold War. So ironically, the B-52, by its very longevity, may last long enough to be our final cover while bomber production shuts down once and for all. The B-52 as a kind of ploughshare: I could not have imagined it at Ramey in 1960. Or wanted it.

After 1993, when Russia and the United States stopped targeting each other's cities, and only then, I would stop being afraid of the nuclear war with Moscow. The American first-strike warmongers of the early 1960s had been held off, and their equivalents in the Soviet Union had been disarmed. In that contest, I know now, my father was on the right side, and I will return to the story of what it cost him. Suffice to say that he ended his career as an opponent of a Nixon-sponsored effort to escalate the nuclear arms race. I would feel a belated gratitude to him, and I would remember how the peculiar knot of love, in our case, was tied up with fear. Fear, no doubt, of the unconscious terrors of sex and success, true freedom and change; but fear, first and foremost, and quite consciously experienced — that Doomsday Clock — of an imminent nuclear war. It was a fear that did not come true, in some small part, I believe, because of him.

What matters now is not the fact of what he did but of what

he let me see, what I infer from it, and how it shapes my soul. The evidence of his role in secret Pentagon debates will always be ambiguous, and while they were going on, I was ignorant of them. But now I believe that even as I was giving up a world I loved for peace, so was he. He could not forgive himself, and so he could not forgive me. That inability was tied up in that other knot that bound us — of our priesthood. As a young man, I did not do what my father asked but never required — heading down to Richmond with Mom and the boys. But I did what he required without ever asking.

Introibo ad altare Dei. I went to the altar of God, and it was true. He did give joy to my youth. An odd joy. An unexpected one. A relief. A release. An escape. A discovery. A renouncing of the self, but a reinventing of it too. Joy, defined in words I still remember: "To live in the midst of the world with no desire for its pleasure . . ." This nosegay was on holy cards and graven plaques everywhere in the seminary, above the name of its author, to us an otherwise unknown Frenchman named Lacordaire. For a long time, such a card, bordered with a chain of thorns and roses, was displayed on my bureau along with my B-52. ". . . to be a member of every family, yet belonging to none; to share all suffering; to penetrate all secrets; to heal all wounds; to teach and instruct; to pardon and console; to bless and be blessed forever. O God! What a life! And it is yours, O priest of Jesus Christ!"

6

A RELIGIOUS
EDUCATION

ST. PAUL'S COLLEGE, the Paulist Fathers' seminary, was a crenelated faux-Gothic castle dominating the hill around which the colleges, seminaries, monasteries, and convents of Little Rome had sprouted like tiger lilies in the rich humus of midcentury Catholicism. Nearby were the National Shrine of the Immaculate Conception, completed now as a towering Byzantine beach ball, and the kitschy Franciscan Monastery with its cement-over-mesh grottoes and catacombs — both of which had been such consolations to my mother and me during the early rounds of Joe's bouts with polio. St. Paul's would be my home from 1963 to the beginning of 1969, an island of relative calm in that typhoon of decades, but also, so unexpectedly, an incubator of my own personal and unwanted revolution.

The Paulist Fathers were a small, relatively new American order numbering fewer than three hundred priests. Yet they were widely known for efforts to bridge the gulf between a huddled, defensive Church and an often hostile American culture. The order was founded a hundred years before by the convert Isaac Hecker, a friend of Emerson and Thoreau. Hecker's own life gave the Paulists their mission, a dual task of opening the eyes of immigrant Catholics to the virtues of their new country and mitigating nativist suspicions of a foreign religion.

An undivided love both of the Catholic Church and of America fueled the Paulist project from the start, and this love served to undercut the rigid triumphalism casting the Church as a divinely established perfect society that had nothing to learn from the broader culture. The Paulists promoted an interplay between Church and society by publishing books and magazines, sponsoring radio and television programs, roving from parish to parish preaching "missions," and serving as chaplains at what were referred to as non-Catholic colleges and universities. The Paulists began the Newman Club movement at the University of California, Berkeley, in the first decade of this century, and after seminary I would serve as Newman chaplain at Boston University. Outpost Newman Clubs were a potent symbol of the difference between the small order and, for example, the massive Society of Jesus, which in the same period reinforced the spirit of immigrant rejection by creating an alternative system of higher education just for Catholics.

At Georgetown, where in all things save ROTC I was an underachiever, I chose the Paulists over my Jesuit professors for none of these reasons. I'd never heard of Hecker, and except for the Air Force Academy, it had not occurred to me to go to a non-Catholic college. Though my parents, like their hero John Kennedy, were participating fully in the new American consensus, no one openly questioned yet the Church's rigid self-definition as an ideal structure set apart. Certainly not me. I cast my fate with an unknown and implicitly dissenting religious community for the goofy reason that the one Paulist priest I met wore penny loafers.

He was a "vocation director" interviewing candidates at Healy Hall, below an austere portrait of Georgetown founder

John Carroll, a Maryland aristocrat to whom I was decidedly not related. John Carroll was famous to Catholics as the nation's first bishop. His cousin Charles Carroll signed the Declaration of Independence, the only Catholic to do so. I know now that John Carroll was a remarkable figure who challenged Roman Catholic triumphalism as much as nativist prejudice, but at the time he was just another prelate to me, an ancestral Spellman. His glum visage above us seemed an emblem of all I feared about entering the Church.

My fears were contradicted by the young and informal Paulist priest who shook my hand warmly and pulled a chair out for me. He was handsome and jocular, like the Air Force chaplains I had known. Something in his breezy, hip manner made it seem that I could be a priest after all without torching the fragile structure of an independent self I had worked so hard to erect. Years later, I would recognize that instinctive, wholly uninformed choice of the Paulists as a life-shaping treasure, and I still feel a debt to that priest, a man I never got to know and whom I remember now only as Father Kelly. It does not dampen my gratitude to realize, as I did not long after entering the seminary, that the open-hearted camaraderie I found so irresistible was part of his pitch, and that, even with those loafers, I'd been had.

Instead of requiring a sacrifice of the self, the Paulists would help me — as a Christian if not as a "good Catholic," as a true American if not as a military chaplain, as a man if not as an obedient son — to lay full claim on my self for the first time. I entered the seminary in largest part to please my parents, but I left it — that first sermon in the pulpit at Bolling Air Force Base — the kind of priest Catholics like my parents held in contempt.

Before I took up residence at St. Paul's College, three months after the death of Pope John XXIII and three months before the death of John Kennedy, I lived like a monk in rural isolation for a year and a day, the canonically prescribed period of novitiate, a kind of spiritual basic training for life in a religious order. The Paulist novitiate, Mount Paul, was a former hunting lodge — a rugged retreat with its own manmade lake, the bull's-eye of ten thousand surrounding acres of deer-studded woods in the Picatinny Mountains of New Jersey, two hours west of New York City. Like many Catholic institutions of the kind — seminaries, colleges, and retreat houses from the North Shore of Chicago to the Hudson Valley to the Cliff Walk of Newport — it had once been the playland of robber barons, who sold off such places when income taxes, property taxes, and the wages of servants made them too costly.

My classmates were mainly working-class Irish, the sons of cops and electricians, getting their first taste of life in really beautiful surroundings. My first had come courtesy of the U.S. Air Force, in that Prussian general's mansion atop a hill in Wiesbaden. And then Rome, in all its Renaissance glory, had taught me that Catholicism was far more than the pinched, kitsch-ridden immigrant atmosphere of parish life in America. Still, the stone gates and the mile-long private driveway and the meticulously landscaped grounds around the tidy buildings — one a timber lodge dating to the hunters' era, the other a modern brick residence with a soaring glass-walled chapel; the blue diamond of a lake with its white cuticle of a beach, Adirondack chairs arranged on a terrace, flowers everywhere — the sight stunned me and made me feel out of place.

I was bound to feel that way, of course, embarking as I was on a journey I had so long hoped to avoid. Only the week before, winding up my glamorous FBI job, I had met President Kennedy at a White House reception for summer interns. I was still warm with the glow of a last date with Lynda Bird, a dreamy twilight trip with her parents down the Potomac River aboard the vice president's yacht, *Sequoia*. I remember the chief petty officer in whites piping us aboard, the gleaming brass and mahogany rails, the firing of the small foredeck cannon in salute to George Washington as we passed Mount Vernon. Then and always, I remember Lynda Bird as shy and kind, and her mother as generous and welcoming, and it was on that trip that heretofore aloof LBJ had brought me into what seemed the inner circle of his affection by saying, "You don't have to call me Mr. Vice President anymore, son. You can call me Mr. Johnson."

But I wouldn't be calling him anything now. I was Thomas Merton giving up Columbia. I was Isaac Hecker giving up Brook Farm. I was Augustine giving up a life with *Deodatus*. I'd had the inside track, and I'd dropped out of the race. Inhibiting me most of all, upon my arrival at Mount Paul, was a clinging emotional hangover from a recent misadventure in New York City where, aching with loneliness and desire, I'd gone by Trailways bus determined to complete a transaction with a prostitute. This last-inning wish to get laid also amounted, no doubt, if far more subliminally, to a wish to avoid the doom of celibacy. What would prove my unworthiness for the life of poverty, chastity, and obedience more irrefutably than a flagrant mortal sin committed with money?

Alas, all I succeeded in doing was replaying a reel of ineffectual flirtation — those teasing *liebchen* in the shadows of the *bahnhof*. Only here I drew the dead-eyed stares of pimps hovering in the alleys and alcoves, terrifying me. The girls on Forty-second Street and on Seventh Avenue in their skin-tight, liquescent pedal pushers and short-shorts lacked entirely the waiflike, wounded air that the postwar Germans knew how to flaunt. These girls were gum-snapping hip swayers, tongue flashers, redheads whose wigs were too obvious, or — this suspicion finished me — not even girls. I wandered New York, ending up on the Staten Island ferry in the middle of the night. From a windswept railing, I stared forlornly back at the glittering city, seeing it as the world I would never have. I felt grief-struck for the loss of girlfriends past and future, wallowing in guilt for wanting to have sex, in self-hatred for being unable to. I could not get out from under that primordial, binding, implicit but still potent challenge from my father: carnality, pleasure, personal ambition, those things are for "them," not for us. Afterward, I would dutifully regard my sad plunge into depressed, repressed puritanism as a sign of temptation overcome. That my "virtue" would always secretly feel false would be a sign of my essential mental health. But what did I know then? I arrived at beautiful Mount Paul in the rolling hills of Rockaway Township, feeling that my life was over, and that it deserved to be.

One day about a month and a half later, some of us were standing on the edge of the lake. We were all garbed in the black cassocks that were to be our uniforms from now on. In a few years, the requirement to wear such things would evaporate, as would Latin and the rules of fasting and abstinence, but as novices, we had already acclimated ourselves to a discipline that dated back to Saint Benedict, more than a thousand years before. "Keep the rule," we'd been taught, "and the rule will keep you." It was also making us a little odd.

The leaves had already turned and begun to fall into the lake. The changing season prompted an argument about when the lake would freeze over. It was the size, say, of a suburban shopping center's parking lot, perhaps three hundred yards across. None of us had been there the previous winter, but ignorance did not prevent us from taking firm positions on the subject: January at the soonest! Late November! Christmas! Lent! We argued about such things at Mount Paul.

Finally one of my classmates, a short, stocky Boston kid named Patrick Hughes who had said nothing until then, declared, "On December eighth, I'll skate across this lake. Who wants to bet on it?" Just like that, the discussion turned from a bunch of experts pronouncing to a handful of guys who had to put up their bets or shut up.

The novitiate was like ravaged Europe after the war in that we didn't use money for currency. In Europe they used cigarettes and silk stockings. At Mount Paul we used desserts, our rice puddings and Jell-Os, our kadota figs and Sunday apple pies. If I lost a dessert in a bet, the winner could wait until something he liked was served, and then send the waiter, another novice, over to collect. Desserts were not only our currency but our one source of power, totems of our subliminal defiance of two of the three vows. That Patrick Hughes had offered to bet all takers made his gamble a monument of daring and foolhardiness. We all took him up on it, and soon Patrick had desserts for the next four months riding on his ability to skate across that lake on December 8.

By Thanksgiving the lake showed no sign of freezing. Patrick would get up early every morning, don his cassock, slip down to the water to check, and then walk up to the chapel for morning prayer. We all knew what he was praying for. On December 3, when we woke up, there it was, the first thin glaze in the corner of the lake. That afternoon there was a delicate necklace of ice around the shore. Having bet against him, we gathered on the shore and groaned. By December 5, a thin sheet had spread all across the lake, but it would hardly hold a leaf. On the nights of the sixth and seventh, the temperature dropped, and in the daytime the sun hid, because on the morning of December 8, the ice looked good — or bad, depending on your bet. Desserts as the sublimation of poverty and obedience, if not chastity; all those coins, all that power. We knew nothing of these meanings, but neither could we have explained why the condition of the lake that morning had come to matter so much.

Right after chapel, hiking our cassocks, we clambered down to the water's edge. Not water. Ice. Someone picked up a rock the size of a softball and dropped it on the surface, and the ice held. We all groaned except for Patrick, who sat down to put on his ice skates. Then someone else picked up a bigger rock, the size of a football, and threw it out. The rock broke the ice easily and disappeared. We all cheered. But Patrick kept lacing up his skates. An undeclared expertise was on display. Later we would learn he'd been captain of the Boston College hockey team. I, for one, had never seen shoelaces handled so deftly.

I stepped out onto the ice with one foot. I bounced it a couple of times, then my foot went through. "Pat," I said, "you can't do this. It's impossible."

My words registered not at all with him. He stood and went up the hill a little, to get a running start. I felt a real fear for him. To the sound of a gun inside his head, he took off, launching himself out onto that shimmering surface. He hit it in stride, his legs pumping away. But he hit it with a great crack, and sure enough the ice broke. It *was* too thin. It was too soon. Oh, Patrick!

Then we saw that the ice was breaking and opening not under him but behind him. He was ahead of the break, skating so fast and so lightly that even the thin ice was support enough for the instant he needed it. All of us on that shore, watching him barreling across that lake, were transformed. We forgot our desserts and all they meant to us. We began to cry after him, "Go Patrick! Go Patrick!" As he shot across that ice, leaving behind a great crack, a wedge of black water, we knew we had never seen such courage before, not to mention such savvy knowledge of the ice, a Quincy kid's knowledge. We had never seen such a capacity for trust — a man's trust in himself. Even before he made it all the way across, and of course he did make it, I thought, This is a man I want to be with.

My friendship with Patrick Hughes became one of the pillars of my life. We helped each other get through the seminary. He taught me how to sail a boat, and I taught him how to use the Library of Congress. He introduced me to the Red Sox, and I helped him write sermons. He was a great athlete, a skilled carpenter, a singer and banjo player, an entertainer, a rare man whom others instantly trusted, yet he used to act as if our friendship were his privilege, not mine. Patrick was the first person who did not respond to either my cultivated self-importance or my deep-seated, mostly hidden conviction of worthlessness. He made me feel that, as he used to say to me, I could do no wrong. In that uptight, homophobic era, I never used the word "love" for what Patrick and I felt for each other — later I would — but the simple, pure pleasure I took in his presence remains one meaning by which I measure love today. I learned to measure happiness by the knowledge, which eventually became rock certain, that he rejoiced in my company as much as I did in his.

Friendship with Patrick opened me to friendship generally. It was the precondition of the first of three distinct but related revolutions — interpersonal, religious, political — that I underwent as a Paulist. I had grown up with four brothers, each of whom I now cherish, but for whatever reason — Joe's polio, our parents' emotional inhibition, my own narcissism, or, for that matter, the Irish Famine's melancholy legacy of bitterness and self-doubt — I knew little of the consolation of fraternal intimacy. Gradually I began to feel, first with Patrick, then with other Paulists, even including priests on the seminary faculty, a warm comradeship, intellectual and emotional both.

The Paulists were bright and energetic men. They regarded

the community life as, in Hecker's terms, one of the "two poles of the Paulist character." The common room was a raucous place, and its rituals of game playing, conversation, and libation were sacred. But at times it could seem like a minefield too, strewn with bursts of sarcasm, which were always styled as ironic wit. "Still cranking 'em out, Jim?" a Paulist priest asked me decades later, at the door of his church as I was leaving Mass one Sunday. He was referring to my sixth novel, which I'd come to his city to promote. The remark brought back the efficiency with which we had used barbed repartee to cut each other down to size, and a sick feeling that reminded me I'd never been much good at it.

"You ought to try it, Joe," I answered lamely. "It beats cranking out apologies for this pope."

"Still have your authority problem, eh, Jim?"

"Not my problem, Joe. My solution."

Indeed so. The dark underside of the repressed, authoritarian milieu could manifest itself, to take another example, in the veiled cruelty of endemic nicknaming, which ingeniously exploited points of vulnerability. "Fuzz," for one whose chronic facial acne inhibited shaving; "Spade," for another whose nose, from a certain angle, was said to resemble a shovel. I made the mistake in my first year of wearing my old high school letterman's sweater — that touchdown — and the gold *W* for Wiesbaden earned me the sobriquet (from the French for "chuck under the chin") "Mr. Wonderful." For a long time, whenever I entered a room, I braced myself, waiting to hear some bastard humming the first few bars of the show tune. Patrick Hughes seemed to get off light, called "Hugger," but I hear now a sly implication of homosexuality in the moniker, a putdown after all.

The rule anathematized "particular friendships," as if intimacy were ever general. In fact, friendships flourished. Despite a climate of forever unstated insecurity about the love of men for men — we had our own rooms, were forbidden to cross the threshold of another's, and never did — life among the Paulists was an antidote to the deep loneliness I had long before concluded was a constituent part of my personality. This was more than a matter of camaraderie, lively conversation, the common work, and the thrill — part New Frontier, part *aggiornamento* — of building the new American Church together. Patrick, Paul Lannan, Bob Baer, Al Moser, David Killian, Jack Kirvan, Floyd MacManus, Jim Young, Michael Hunt, Stan MacNevin, Jim Donovan, George Fitzgerald, John Collins, David Pilliod, Ed Guinan — these men were my companions, and more. After many years together, sharing every aspect of our lives, we knew each other well, very well. Eventually, it seemed they knew my secrets, without my ever having revealed them. That "Mr. Wonderful" punctured — and rescued me from — the phony, Erector Set, general's son persona I'd begun to construct in high school, not in favor of the obsequious and pious ideal I had already rejected for myself, but of something new. A multi-year counseling relationship — spiritual direction — with a benign and holy priest, Al Moser, was at the heart of an unsentimental directness that slowly but surely eroded even my self-isolating sense of being different.

In large and small ways they let me know they thought that I too had what it took to hurl myself out onto thin ice and skate ahead of a great crack. Over time, getting wet, I began to think so too. The entire project of moving through the seminary in the 1960s — thin ice *and* a minefield — began to feel exactly like such an act of abandon. The priesthood itself would seem an ultimate leap like that. We thought of it, with Kierkegaard, as a leap of faith.

The most fateful and unexpected affirmation I received from the Paulists was as a writer. Nothing obvious in my family history had made such an ambition likely, although my love of and knack for storytelling were gifts from my mother — those twilight tours of Washington, when she repeated and elaborated wartime tales about every monument and office building she pointed out. But the story I had to tell was different.

"I carried inside me a cut and bleeding soul . . ." In Saint Augustine's *Confessions*, no less, I came upon a familiar story. ". . . and how to get rid of it I just didn't know. I sought every pleasure — the countryside, sports, fooling around, the peace of a garden, friends and good company, sex, reading. My soul floundered in the void — and came back upon me. For where could my heart flee from my heart? Where could I escape from myself?" The answer that suggested itself to me, as to Augustine: instead of escape, try expression. I wrote my first poems and stories in seminary English classes. Paulist professors, especially Al Moser and John Kirvan, who would later edit my first book, considered my efforts good enough to tell me what was wrong with them. (One story's resolution depended on the main character's being run down by a Fiat automobile, as in *Fiat voluntas tua*.) When, in the "Cellar Theater," a seminary version of a sixties coffeehouse, I read aloud not from Eliot or Stevens but from compositions of my own, I heard no humming of "Mr. Wonderful." Some of the fellows made me feel my poems were good. The poems themselves, meanwhile, made me feel whole.

How had I come to poetry? I see now what it meant to be reading the work of writers who were themselves wrestling with demonic angels. I was responding not only, say, to the complaints of a celibate cleric — Gerard Manley Hopkins's "Thou art indeed just, Lord, but so is my plea!" — but, equally piquant, to the agonized howls of those we think of now as antiwar poets. I never recovered from Galway Kinnell's meditation on a B-52: "I hear its drone, drifting, high up / in immaculate ozone. And I hear, / coming over the hills, America singing . . ." I think still of X. J. Kennedy's poem "Vietnamese": "Upon our village / The fire fell, making sure. / I would have fled. / I was old, though, and poor." In that poem, Kennedy has the B-52 pilot say, "Each thatched shack where old men had sat in thought / I tore out of the village like a page. / The air keeps quiet. Nothing will engage." Wordsworth defined poetry as "the spontaneous overflow of powerful feelings," taking "its origin from emotion recollected in tranquillity." Through the 1960s, I had more than I wanted of powerful feelings and just enough of tranquillity to begin my own naming of the nameless powers of the dark.

My teachers recommended me, and the Paulist superiors approved me, for a special program to study writing in the summers. That led, in 1966, to a life-changing encounter at the University of Minnesota with the poet and critic Allen Tate. A member of "the Fugitives," a Southern agrarian group of writers, Tate was associated with John Crowe Ransom, Robert Penn Warren, Hart Crane, and T. S. Eliot, all of whom I was now discovering. As editor of *The Sewanee Review,* he had helped shape mid-century American literature, and only recently I'd begun seeking out back numbers of the magazine. In Tate's poems, in his novel *The Fathers,* and in his book of essays *The Man of Letters in the Modern World,* I began to see the shadowy form of a new idea of myself.

Tate was known as a Southerner, but he had spent summers as a boy in Washington and nearby Virginia, where I, a would-be Johnny Reb, had experienced such confusion. To discover in his masterpiece "Ode to the Confederate Dead" Tate's own confusion, a final inability to glorify those dead even while grieving them, was a lesson in the way poems reveal us to ourselves. At the end of *The Fathers*, a son sees his father as "arrogant," but also, more compellingly, as "beautiful." The mystery of holding two such perceptions in one act of love drew me irresistibly in. The thought of actually traveling to the Midwest to study with this writer came to me like an epiphany that year, and the permission that made it possible seemed miraculous. I allowed myself to dream that Allen Tate, the famous friend to writers, would be a friend to me.

There was no impertinence in my approach to him. I arrived in his classroom feeling like an interloper, but feeling also that a door was opening. In effect, he stood at that door inviting me to enter an entirely new room. He was a slight man with a head that seemed overlarge for his body. Wispy hair half covered his pate, but his white mustache and linen suits and British shoes gave him a dandyish air. One always expected to see him sporting a cane as an item of apparel. He was glamorous, a literary Fred Astaire, the beau ideal of the Man of Letters in the Modern World.

He was also a teacher. During his office hours I imposed on Tate, and he let me. I showed up early in the term with a sheaf of poems, hoping to leave them with him. He took my folder, flipped through it quickly, and handed it back. My heart sank. He said nothing while, slowly and deliberately, he opened a new pack of cigarettes, took one out, and lit it. He waved the match out. Then he said, "Come every Thursday. Bring two poems each time. We'll see what you can do."

Those sessions taught me more about reading and writing than anything I had experienced. Tate was a severe critic, but he was also the most courteous teacher I'd ever had. I left every session determined to be worthy of the next one, but eventually I realized that, to him, I already was. At the end of the summer he told me that, yes, I was a poet. Allen Tate's approval allowed me to think of myself as a writer, and the difference that has made in my life drives my own energetic commitment to teaching young writers today. When, in 1974, the Paulist Press, under Jack Kirvan, published my collection of poems, it carried this comment from Tate: "James Carroll's first book of verse, *Forbidden Disappointments*, is impressive. The general theme is the conflict between belief and existential disorder. 'Resurrection Poem' and half a dozen others announce a new, original talent." It is shameless, perhaps, to include here what was after all a blurb, but those words were as much a laying on of hands as anything the cardinal archbishop of New York could ever do for me.

At one point in that Minneapolis summer, I asked Tate to sign my copy of his *Collected Poems*. He wrote, "Inscribed to James Carroll with all good wishes for his two vocations." He watched me read what he'd written. When I looked up at him, he said sadly, "You can't have both, you know."

I think now that my Paulist superiors sensed that in time my vocation as a writer would take me away from the community, yet their support and encouragement never flagged. Paulists produced my first play, in the seminary. Years later, a group of them showed up at the Berkshire Theater Festival in Stockbridge, Massachusetts, for my first professional production, though it literally marked my break with the order.

Against their own institutional interests, Paulists affirmed me in other ways than as a writer. When, during the Vietnam era, I spent a night in jail, the president of the Paulists, instead of rebuking me, named me chairman of the order's Social Justice Committee. When the cardinal archbishop of Boston complained to headquarters that I was counseling Boston University students to use birth control, the Paulist president refused to transfer me. Eventually, it was through him that I made a formal request of the Vatican for dispensation from my vows. Having steadfastly supported me in each of the steps that took me out of the priesthood, he wept with me as I explained my decision to leave it. And then he gave me his blessing, another laying on of hands that touched the very core of me.

The Paulists as a group, in other words, finally gave me a version of the affirmation that had begun with Patrick — that I could do no wrong. It was not literally true, of course, as we all knew. But what a relief to find in their tested support a way to let go of the much older, deeper feeling — one derived not, perhaps, from parents or brothers but from the pulse of my own heart, the true effect in me, I'd long since concluded, of the doctrine of original sin. This feeling — that if it was *my* act or *my* desire, it *had* to be wrong.

Three personal revolutions, I said. The second revolution, the primordial one, was, to use a loaded word, religious. This aspect of my fits-and-starts transformation is hard to describe without falling into the mushy pit, but "religious," after all, is the technical word for what I'd become in joining the Paulists in the first place. I had the great advantage, despite my years as an altar boy, or because of them, of arriving on that scene with no authentic religious training. I was biblically and theologically illiterate. The catechism, even the highbrow version laid out in mandatory religion classes at Georgetown, had not come within a mile of touching anything but my good manners and guilty conscience. Thus I had less need of conversion, *pace* Hecker, than of initiation.

In the seminary, facts that now seem mundane hit me like the boulders of an avalanche. An example: the divinely inspired Bible is nevertheless a human composition subject to the laws of history and literary form. The great twentieth-century developments in biblical studies of the historical-critical method had impinged not at all on the Catholic Church as I had experienced it. It jolted me to hear professors and classmates discussing what I had taken to be God's great interventions in time and space as myth and story, constructions that may or may not have "really happened," heroes of the faith who may not have existed. Adam and Eve. Noah. The Tower of Babel. The Parting of the Red Sea. The Fiery Chariot. David and Goliath. Stories all. I struggled to get my mind around the new idea that fictions could surpass "facts" as a revelation of the truth. Once I grasped that, my own real journey of faith — what would become a fiction writer's faith — began.

Form criticism undid my notion not only of Noah but of Jesus. It staggered me to learn that Gospel accounts were anything but historical records of Jesus' life and ministry. Theologians said these "faith accounts" reflected the beliefs of Christians living a generation or longer after the death of Jesus. I learned that none of the Gospels was written by an eyewitness; that the exalted Roman Catholic Church began as scattered groups of Jews who sensed the presence of their Lord in their own decidedly unreligious acts of eating and drinking together; that the oral telling of His stories — sources of the Gospels — was a way of making Him present; that those stories said almost nothing about the historical Jesus; that the portrait they offered was of, in Rudolf Bultmann's phrase, "the existential Christ of faith."

Bultmann was a Protestant, as were most of the leading figures in biblical studies. Hard as it is to credit now, it seemed exotic, almost dangerous, to be taking cues from "heretics" like Søren Kierkegaard and Karl Barth. Early in this century, the Vatican erected walls against the challenges coming from new biblical studies. Indeed, certain Paulists were excommunicated as part of the Vatican crackdown on modernism. Hecker himself had been considered suspect, the inspiration of a heresy called, of all things, Americanism. But by midcentury, Catholic scholars like Pierre Benoit and Roland de Vaux had clawed through Vatican resistance, and breakthroughs like the discovery of the Dead Sea Scrolls in 1947 destroyed what remained of it. It was the otherwise reactionary Pius XII who declared, in *Divino Afflante Spiritu*, "The interpreter [of the Bible] must go back wholly in spirit to those remote centuries of the East and with the aid of history, archeology, ethnology, and other sciences, accurately determine what modes of writing the authors of that period would be likely to use, and, in fact, did use." This principle, once applied to the underpinnings of a calcified Counter-Reformation faith, caused its superstructure to crumble. The foundation-shaking work of these thinkers, Protestant and Catholic, laid bare the anachronistic absurdity of the denominational divisions that at the start of this process had seemed so absolute.

All of this required a new way of thinking of the Church; it too was subject to the laws of history. Much of what I'd been told was timeless had been put in place only at the Council of Trent (1545–1563). The monarchical papacy, the law of celibacy, the idea of infallibility, the form of the sacraments, the cultic priesthood toward which my whole life was aiming, none of it had been instituted or even imagined by Jesus Christ. I wasn't the only one having to come to terms with such radical notions: the bishops meeting at the Vatican Council had to do so. Indeed — and here was the real rarity of Pope John's initiative — it was because the bishops of the Church dared consider such questions that the rest of us could.

At remote Mount Paul in New Jersey, we were forbidden to watch television, but an exception was made within a few weeks of our arrival that fall of 1962. An oval-framed Motorola was hauled into the common room. We gathered around it one night and the bespectacled face of my own Pope John appeared on the screen. He was sitting on the great throne behind and above Bernini's altar in St. Peter's Basilica — which itself, because of indulgences sold for its construction, had been a cause of Luther's break and all the subsequent malaise it was this pope's intention now to undo. I had to resist the urge to punch the novice next to me and say, "I've been there. I've met the pope. He kissed me." I didn't tell him or anyone else. As was true of so much of what I'd been given, I kept it a guilty secret for reasons I never understood.

The papers in Pope John's hands shook slightly as he addressed the robed throng. And even at Mount Paul, knowing nothing of what prompted the words, and hearing them rendered in the halting voice of an unseen interpreter, we felt the heat of the pope's blast at "prophets of gloom, who are always forecasting disaster, as though the end of the world were at hand. In these modern times, they can see nothing but prevarication and ruin. They say that our era, in comparison with past eras, is getting worse, and they behave as though they had learned nothing from history, which is, nonetheless, the teacher of life."

The Council would run in a series of sessions from 1962 until 1965. In the "Pastoral Constitution on the Church and the World," the bishops would declare, "The Church has always had the duty of scrutinizing the signs of the times . . . The human race has passed from a rather static concept of reality to a dynamic, evolutionary one." And not only "of reality" but of the Church itself, was the point to us. During those years our once fixed attitudes toward the Church and priesthood, toward the meaning of sin and salvation were turned upside down. When I arrived in Washington in 1963 to begin the six-year course in philosophy and theology at St. Paul's College, the Council's impact was just beginning to be felt. In our classrooms we read the works of heretofore suspect theologians — John Courtney Murray, Pierre Teilhard de Chardin, Henri de Lubac, Karl Rahner — whose liberalizing program was finally being vindicated. Our Paulist professors and superiors were as enthralled as we, although the rigid Tridentine seminary discipline continued to inhibit us.

In the beginning, magazines like *The New Yorker* were forbidden to us, but when the classic series "Letter from Vatican City," by the pseudonymous Xavier Rynne, began detailing the behind-the-scenes maneuvering and competition between Church liberals and conservatives, we passed contraband copies among ourselves, as if *The New Yorker* had a centerfold.

Rynne was rumored, and later revealed, to be a Redemptorist priest, Francis X. Murphy, a theologian who, when not in Rome, was at Catholic University in Washington. His residence was only a crisp seven-iron shot from the lawn outside my room. No wonder he knew so much about the Church. The thought of a priest not being cowed by a tradition that claimed there were no such things in Catholicism as power grabs, turf fights, and self-protective secrecy took our breath away. Where was his piety about the Holy Ghost? Murphy's work in *The New Yorker* transformed the way the Council was reported elsewhere in the secular and, ultimately, religious press. But its more immediate impact on us, aside from the magazine's suddenly showing up in the seminary library, was the new view of the Church it offered. By shining a light on its hidden corners, Murphy made the institution seem more limited, fallible, and flawed. All at once the magnificent, intimidating, timeless Church was made to seem hospitable to the limited, fallible, and flawed members we knew ourselves to be.

The book that had broken open our minds, preparing us for Xavier Rynne and helping us to grasp what was really at stake in the Vatican Council, was *The Council, Reform and Reunion* by the young Swiss theologian Hans Küng. That book contained this shocking statement: "Renewal and reform of the Church are permanently necessary because the Church consists, first, of human beings, and, secondly, of sinful human beings."

It was no news that *I* was a sinful human being. A pointed sense of my own fallenness had been attached to my heels like a shadow ever since my brother, through some fault of mine, had contracted polio. I was the son of an Irish Jansenist, and why else did we have the sacrament of penance? But Küng was talking about the Church as such. The communion of saints, he was saying, is a group of sinners. No one is exempt from this judgment, not Cardinal Spellman, not the pope, not all the bishops in the Council. The revolutionary meaning of this all too obvious truth? First, that no human being has the right to sit in absolute judgment of another. Second, the essential note of our relationship to God, and to each other, must be forgiveness. Beginning with this idea, articulated by Hans Küng, I would learn to criticize the Church and to love the Church as the only true home a "wretch like me" can hope to find.

Wretch indeed. I committed my first serious breach of my solemn promises of poverty and obedience when, sneaking off to a downtown bookstore, I "bought" my own copy of *The Council, Reform and Reunion.* I accomplished this in that pre–credit card era by convincing a clerk to send the bill to my parents. He agreed to do so not because of my status as a seminarian but because of my father's rank, the best credit reference in Cold War Washington. I was still the general's son. Within days, racked with guilt, I went to the seminary rector and confessed what I had done. This incident — first defy the rule, then bend to it, miserably — was typical of the pinball course on which I'd been launched. Often I would be in my spiritual director's room, weeping inconsolably with confusion and fear as the pillars and posts of my flimsy faith fell apart. The only language I had for the experience prompted me to insist that I was not worthy to be a priest. My father confessor kept telling me that was why I'd be a good one.

Hans Küng told me that too, which was why I'd so wanted my own copy of that book. I know now that the seminary rector was as moved by Küng's vision as I was, but he did not let on. He could have expelled me, but instead he confiscated the book and sent me away. I choked with humiliation and shame. The rector's response was rooted in his own conflict between the liberal moment and the long-standing authoritarian system imposed even on the Paulists, his version of our being caught in two worlds at once. And we seminarians sympathized with him no more than student protesters would with the anguished college administrators whose offices they later occupied.

Our resistance to authority was less direct, more passive-aggressive, and probably more personal. We grew to hate the rector. In the summer we would stand on the edge of our little camping island in Lake George, New York. We would face south toward the main Paulist retreat, a pair of rambling Adirondack arks where the rector and faculty were housed twenty miles away. We would holler his name — let's call him Joe Blow — and the sound would curl across the water and lose itself in the hills on either side: "Come and get me, Joe Blow!" Or, in later years, the era of free speech, "Fuck you, Joe Blow!" Once a small motor boat pulled up to our island and a camper from a site down the lake asked, "Who is this Joe Blow? I've been hearing his name in the air for years."

Another time, I helped to organize a seminary conference on LBJ's Great Society legislation. We'd landed the pioneering community organizer Saul Alinsky as a speaker, something I recognize now as a signal of a new spaciousness of political imagination, a sign of my growing capacity to transcend the narrowness of my upbringing. I was proud of snagging Alinsky, and I asked the rector if I could invite an old friend of mine, namely the president's daughter.

"The president of what?" he asked with a condescending sneer. I took mortally sinful pleasure in replying, "Of these United States."

Perhaps the real beginning of the transformation of my authority "problem" into a "solution" was not Hans Küng's book but the impact of his personal presence when he came to lecture in Washington. Although I have a distinct memory of Küng's appearance, the incident I have in mind could have involved Bernard Haring, Edward Schillebeeckx, Karl Rahner, or another of the touring European theologians who came through Catholic University during the Council. But as I recall it, Hans Küng's lecture was explosive. I was one of the first people to arrive at the hall. We Paulists took pride in our distinctive habit, a sashed black soutane with a high Marine Corps–like collar, a linen-covered "leather neck," in fact. In gatherings at CU and Georgetown, with the multitude of Old World monks, friars, and Jesuits with their cowls and sandals and body odor, we always felt like an American elite, not Marines but liberals. That evening seminarians, scholastics, and student nuns came from all over Little Rome, and soon the auditorium was packed. The Beatles would not have been more eagerly awaited, nor Elvis.

But instead of the ovation I expected we would give the curly-haired, bright-faced Hans Küng when he appeared, the room fell into a hole of amazed silence. He was barely older than we were. It was him. But no one applauded. We remained mute as he was introduced by a white-robed Dominican, one of the sponsoring theologians. Then we listened fearfully, hardly believing our ears as Küng let loose a withering attack on the cruelly restrictive structures of Catholicism. He could have been quoting John Stuart Mill: "My love for an institution is in direct proportion to my desire to reform it." Faced with such forthright criticism of the Church, I finally recognized the ways Catholics, especially us would-be priests, had been kept dependent, puerile, and timid. The young Swiss firebrand made me see how the system I had only recently embraced depended on a scheme of sanctions, excommunications, and anathemas that were authoritarian, even un-Christian. The divisions among denominations, which the smug Catholic assumption of superiority guaranteed, struck me as a scandal too. Luther was right, I imagined Küng declaring. To me he sounded like Luther himself.

But Küng, like Haring, Schillebeeckx, and Rahner, was no mere revolutionary. These theologians were widely regarded as giving voice to the dreams and visions of Pope John XXIII, who had died only months before. When we heard them defend the Council's promise, Küng and company spoke with an authority unprecedented for institutional critics — Luthers with a mandate from Rome! We could thrill at their iconoclastic vision without feeling disloyal.

A few years later, this audience of young clerics would form the core of a protest that shut down Catholic University — a "pontifical institute" — after another theologian, Father Charles Curran, was fired for dissenting from *Humanae Vitae*. That defiance, like the anti-papal defiance of which I am guilty to this day — here is the heart of what Küng and the others gave us — was and is only an act of faithfulness to Pope John XXIII. Hans Küng, embodying John's vision, awakened in me a passionate hope for the future of the Catholic Church which has yet to be quashed, in part because Küng himself, long condemned and marginalized in the era of Pope John Paul II, has nevertheless steadfastly continued all these decades to defend and articulate that vision. The same is true of Schillebeeckx, Curran, and Haring, and probably would be of Rahner, had he lived. The greatest Catholic theologians of our time are regarded with suspicion by today's Vatican. Despite the thunderbolt sanctions and threats of anathema regularly hurled at them, they have never yelled "Come and get me!" much less "Fuck you!" Nor have they refused to speak the truth to power.

That night in the lecture hall, what struck us even more powerfully than Küng's words, what had struck us dumb, undercutting our ability to applaud him when he'd first appeared before our black- and brown- and white-robed pieties, was the disorienting fact that Father Küng was not wearing a cassock or a black suit and Roman collar or any kind of "clericals." He was dressed in a trim gray suit and a blue necktie. His getup itself was a thesis nailed to the door. A priest in mufti! A priest looking like everyone else! A priest with a phallic symbol hanging down his chest! A priest a man.

"Oh, the slow shall be fast . . ." Küng got his ovation and more at the end. We cheered him wildly. He was our Elvis, our John Lennon, our Bob Dylan. ". . . and the first shall be last." A rafter raiser. A shindy kicker. "Oh, the times they are a-changin'."

All of the transformations, even sartorial ones, ushered in by the Vatican Council were rooted in the momentous changes brought about by the prior and esoteric revolution in biblical studies. After the advent of form criticism, the historical-critical method, and a fuller understanding of what a Bedouin shepherd had found in the caves of Qumran, it was as if, all at once, the magnifying, scorching lights of Copernicus, Galileo, Newton, Darwin, Einstein, and Freud were focused on the heretofore immutable Word of God.

I read the Bible, actually read it, for the first time in my life. In the classroom, the Book became a living thing. I found myself turning to it even when I wasn't required to. Except for that old impulse to bury my face in the abyss of my folded hands, the only overt show of piety to which I am still given, prayer had meant nothing to me, though I had never admitted that to myself. By prayer I mean purposeful attention to the presence of God. Gradually I realized that prayer had become the content of my encounters with the Book. When, say, I recited psalms in unison with my brothers at lauds, matins, and compline, or when I turned over in my mind the stories of Exodus or of the Galilean peasant, the Scriptures themselves could seem shockingly addressed to me.

"In my inmost self I dearly love God's law" — this passage from my new patron, Saint Paul — "but I can see that my body follows a different law that battles against the law which my reason dictates. This is what makes me a prisoner of that law of sin which lives inside my body . . . Who will rescue me from the body doomed to death?"

In other words, sex.

But perhaps not. I was urged to read Paul's lament not as a description of the struggle with the flesh but as a description of the struggle against the ancient human impulse to flee from the burden of history — these bodies doomed to death — into absolutes.

Here was proof that all those popes had been right, that reading the Bible could be dangerous. For a Catholic boy of my generation, this was a nuclear question: what if the sin to watch out for is not sex but what the Bible calls the worship of false gods, the making of idols? In the Bible, I learned, that is in fact the first definition of sin. Golden calves? We create a golden calf, I learned, every time we take something of the earth and declare it exempt from the laws of history. In effect, I entered the seminary to learn that the tendency to claim eternity for what is only temporal corrupts both patriotism and piety. It is the oldest story there is, although lately we have worshiped not golden calves but our nation, and our Church.

My Paulist professors, one of whom was the first Roman Catholic scholar ever to receive a Protestant doctoral degree in the theology of Martin Luther, challenged my inbred assumptions about the Reformation, helping me to see it as the beginning of a great modern refinement of the faith. The reformers rejected the self-absolutism of the Catholic Church. Rome, they said, is not forever. Not even the Eternal City is eternal.

But Luther and his followers absolutized something else, the Scriptures. "Scripture alone!" they said. Nowhere is the idolatry of the Bible more obvious than in the desperate insistence that its affirmations are exempt from the laws of history, of time. The literal reading of miracle stories, the use of Biblical data to justify anti-Semitism or the second-class status of women or hostility toward other religious traditions or prescientific ideas of the origin of the cosmos — are all common forms of the idolatry of the Bible. Alas, it followed upon Luther's isolating the Word of God from the principle of authority that interprets it.

That is why the historical-critical deabsolutizing of Scripture in this century has been so invigorating. The lifeless oracle of fundamentalism, in its Catholic as well as Protestant forms, was replaced by a vibrant understanding of the living community out of which the Scriptures grew, and out of which new insights into faith continue to grow. When the Bible was deabsolutized, the modern renewal of the entire Church was launched — and I was there!

That was not all. Soon it became clear even to Christians that, like the Church and like the Scriptures, Jesus had been made into a kind of idol. He too needed to be deabsolutized. What Jesus never did Himself, His followers had been doing ever since —

exempting Him from the laws of time according to one of which Jesus is gone, simply gone, which is what it means to say that He died. His body too was doomed. A Jesus who meant it when He claimed to have been abandoned by God at the end — what else is death? — reveals far more about God than the triumphal Christ on a gilded cross.

But Jesus *was* God, wasn't He? The Church's true answer, I learned, is yes and no. The notion of Jesus-as-God that had been pounded into me by nuns, monks, and monsignors, and that had been taken as gospel by my mother and father and every Catholic I knew, was in fact heretical. We had been taught to believe that the divinity of Jesus was such that He had only, as it were, pretended to be human. Which meant that as an infant He gurgled when He could have given speeches to rival Pericles. As a boy, for His own amusement and when no one was looking, He could turn birds into little stone statues, snap. And as a man He went through the motions of anxiety, suffering, and death, but He never really experienced such things. The Resurrection, a magic trick that He Himself worked from the grave, was proof that He was God.

All wrong. The heresy of Docetism. Most of the divine wonders attributed to Jesus in the Gospels — beginning most obviously with the virgin birth and nativity narratives, extending more problematically to the Resurrection appearances themselves, including perhaps the phenomenon of the empty tomb — were mythic constructs intended to make a point of faith, not fact. I learned that the starting point of any train of thought about Jesus must be His humanity. The Nazarene was a fully human person, fallible and mortal. He never considered Himself to be divine. He came to be conscious of His own prophetic character through a spiritual awakening in relation to John the Baptist. Jesus repented and was baptized and saw something new about Himself, about what He called the Kingdom of God. He embraced a life mission to preach it.

What kind of kingdom was this? Jesus told us everything we needed to know when instead of as a king riding in a chariot, He came to us as the parody of a king. On Palm Sunday we still remember his "triumphal entry," but this is the king who arrives on a donkey. Even the story of the crucifixion — the purple robe, the crown of thorns, centurions hailing the king of the Jews — has the form of purest irony. It is a revelation of the folly and tragedy of wanting to be exempt from the laws of history.

For the first time in my life, Jesus was not a remote and almighty savior but a man whom I came utterly to identify with. Not identify as with a Christ figure from some messiah complex (my mother's name is Mary, my father's name is Joseph, my initials are J.C.), but only as somebody who ached to do what was right, and for the longest time didn't know how. I recognized Jesus' spiritual awakening, His feeling ambushed by a "vocation," conscripted into a mission, compelled by an urge to tell the story, but unlike the Baptist, never immune to the sirens of eating and drinking and the company of women. I turned Jesus' openness to prostitutes into a particular point of connection, seeing it as a version of my own youthful, nervous curiosity.

But the connection that really solidified my, yes, love of Jesus was the transcendent and ongoing crisis we shared. His central struggle for identity was tied up with what that word "God" meant to him. The key lies in the fact that Jesus called God "Abba."

I still recall the musty basement classroom in which I sat — the rows of unvarnished one-armed desks, the green blackboard, the window at shoulder height opening onto corrugated iron half-pipe sleeves of light shafts, and clanging heat pipes — the day I understood that "Abba" means "Daddy."

"'Abba,'" the professor said, "is *ipsum dixit*" — one of the few words recorded in the Gospels that the historical Jesus can be said to have actually used. "Abba," not Yahweh, Mighty One, Wholly Other, or Being Itself — but Daddy. Jesus came to understand Himself by understanding His father. And why shouldn't the same thing have been happening to me? The Bay of Pigs, the assassination of JFK, the Cuban missile crisis, the Vatican Council, the words of Hans Küng, the challenge of Martin Luther and of Martin Luther King, and the first stirrings of the sixties revolution — remote as I was from Bolling Air Force Base, the Pentagon, and the life of my brothers and mother, in my worried mind and haunted soul I referred every such event to my own "Abba." And the word's meaning wasn't even "Dad," but "Daddy," evoking the easy intimacy, and also worship, that surely I had felt for him once, years before. My nostalgia for a lost bond — before he was a general? before Joe got polio? — was like everyone's nostalgia for the Garden of Eden. We can never pin it down, when things began to go wrong, but we know it wasn't always so. When had "Daddy" become "Dad" to me? It hit me that the shifting away from the seamless bond implicit in "Daddy" had begun in Wiesbaden, where I'd admitted for a minute an ambition of my own that was not his.

By now the ground was moving everywhere I stepped — religion, politics, poverty, chastity, obedience, a stubbornly emerging sense of self. But beneath every rumbling fault line and every quake was the steady, subterranean shifting of the tectonic plates of my relationship with Dad. Daddy. If Jesus could feel forsaken by "Abba," what would that be to me? And if Jesus could still trust Himself to Abba, how could I? For finally this came clear. The message He offered was one of trust. How I longed to hear it. Trust in this life, this process, this history, wherever it takes you. Live without idols. As for religion, go about your eating and drinking and being together, and let *that* be the ligament binding you to God. Regard death — not only of the planet or of America or of Rome, but of ones you love and of yourself — as the ultimate moment of history, a fulfillment as much as a denial. Death would teach me a fuller lesson later, but here, in this discovery of His meaning, Jesus prepared me for it. The knowledge of death, that we all face it, is what enables us to live now in communities with each other, without arrogance. In *this* communion, the one I had with Paulists and with everyone, we affirm that death has moved from being the end of life, an absolute moment alone, to being a part of life, which is all any of us are. The whole of life belongs to God. It *is* God.

This was the religious education I received in the community it was my great good fortune to have stumbled into — and over a pair of penny loafers!

The message of our faith, what I'd begun to learn *personally* from Patrick Hughes on the ice, is trust. And here I was learning it *theologically*. But would it stand up? Three personal revolutions, I said before. The third was political, which in my case turned out to be the most personal of all, for I was about to undergo the loss of the only real trust I'd ever had. My father, my Abba, my Daddy, Dad. I was soon to find out that our bond of trust was not forever. Welcome to the earth, kid. Welcome to real religion. And welcome to politics, family style.

7

CAPERS IN CHAINS

WHEN MY FATHER was a brand-new FBI agent in Chicago, one of the targets of that field office was a man named Morris Chilofsky, an immigrant from the disputed region astride the Polish-Russian border. Chilofsky was a graduate of the Lenin School in Moscow. In Chicago throughout the 1930s, he'd been working as an organizer of the Communist Party. It is certain that my father would have known of him, and it is likely that, in the early 1940s, he'd have participated in surveillance of him. Not long after my father's transfer to Washington, Chilofsky himself, now known as Morris Childs, was transferred by his organization to New York, where in 1945 he took up the post of editor of the *Daily Worker*. But in 1947 Childs fell out with the Party and disappeared from its ranks. That should have been that.

In 1952, however, Morris Childs, together with his brother Jack, was recruited by the FBI as a secret agent. They reestablished their connection with the Party. For most of the next two decades, the Childs brothers, a duo code-named "Solo," would reveal everything the FBI needed to know about the Communist Party of America. It seems like a ludicrous project now, but beginning as it did in an era when Soviet spies penetrated, with disastrous consequences, the most rigidly guarded secret in U.S.

history — Klaus Fuchs et al. at Los Alamos — and in an era when war with Moscow was regarded as all but inevitable, the recruitment of the Childs brothers was considered a counter-intelligence coup. The secret of their FBI work would be protected, and the Childses would remain agents-in-place, for decades.

In 1954 Morris Childs's boss in the Communist Party was a New York lawyer named Stanley Levison. Together, Childs and Levison administered Party funds that the Kremlin smuggled into the United States, amounting to a million dollars a year. With Childs's help, the FBI was able to identify Levison as a key Soviet operative, and the Bureau put him under close surveillance. But in 1956 Levison's ties to the Communist Party evaporated. He quit, and had nothing more to do with the Moscow infiltration. Why? For the FBI, if for no one else, the answer would seem obvious when, within a year, Levison surfaced as an adviser, speechwriter and, eventually, trusted confidant to an until recently obscure Negro minister in Montgomery, Alabama. The minister had organized a transit boycott after a weary black woman named Rosa Parks refused to yield her seat on a bus to a white man. The minister's name was Martin Luther King Jr., and his close relationship with Levison would smolder, always threatening to ignite and obliterate the entire civil rights movement, until King's death in 1968.

One warm day in the summer of 1963, after a White House meeting of civil rights leaders, President Kennedy asked King to step out of the Oval Office into the Rose Garden. King would report to colleagues that he thought it odd to be asked outdoors for a chat, but now we know Kennedy was avoiding the hidden microphones that he'd had installed in his own office. In the garden, Kennedy warned King about Levison's background. If it became public that a one-time Communist Party official with proven ties to Moscow was at King's elbow, all chances of getting civil rights legislation through Congress would be destroyed.

King seemed not to believe Kennedy's assertions about Levison, but he later promised the Kennedy brothers that he would break with the lawyer. And for a time it seemed he had. But continuing wiretaps on Levison revealed that King was still secretly consulting with him. That was what prompted Attorney General Robert Kennedy, in the early fall of 1963, to authorize the FBI to tap King's phone and put listening devices in his offices and hotel rooms.

Like most Americans, I knew nothing about FBI surveillance of Martin Luther King until it was revealed in the 1974 congressional committee hearings chaired by Senator Frank Church. Even more pointedly, like most Americans I knew nothing of the serious reasons for that surveillance — Stanley Levison's history with Morris Childs, the Communist Party, and their Moscow money connection — until the distinguished civil rights chronicler David J. Garrow summed it up in his 1981 book *The FBI and Martin Luther King Jr.: From 'Solo' to Memphis*, which is my source for all that I assert about Childs and Levison.

When, in the early 1960s, open accusations were made or sly innuendos dropped about Communist influence in the civil rights movement and on King, I, an incipient liberal, refused to credit them. That there was a substantial, if ultimately mistaken, reason to suspect King, knowingly or not, of advancing plans laid in the Kremlin seemed the ridiculous fantasy of Red-baiting segregationists who blamed unrest on "outside agitators." But Garrow's scrupulous presentation changes the way those events must be understood. The facts of the "Solo" infiltration establishing Levison as a legitimate target of FBI concern now indicate that some questions about King's associations were proper. For the purposes of this account of my transformation from junior redneck to fellow traveler, the most noteworthy fact is that, unknown to me at the time, my father was privy to "Solo." He had known of Childs since the 1930s and, as a counterintelligence partner of J. Edgar Hoover's, was briefed on Levison and King until the end.

In the beginning, there was no difference in the ways we perceived such things. The first square on which I stood was his, and it was labeled with the three words of the FBI motto: fidelity, bravery and integrity. To me, my father embodied those virtues just as surely as, to him, by the time we began to argue about it, Martin Luther King embodied their antithesis.

If I had not become a Paulist, King would not have become the occasion of my first, tentative disagreements with my dad. The Alexandria of my childhood was still a pure Southern culture, undiluted yet by suburban interlopers from up north. Civic holidays, public rhetoric, and dozens of formal and informal rituals enshrined the victim-cavalier ethos of the Confederacy. Robert E. Lee was the patriarchal god. Stonewall Jackson was the slain Christ. The woods in which we played were haunted by John Singleton Mosby, the Gray Ghost.

My cousins in Chicago, on summer visits, called me "Jimmy Reb," but my Virginia classmates mocked me as a Yankee — an accusation the true sting of which I wouldn't feel until moving to Boston, where it would be efficiently made plain that I was anything but. It was doubtless this confusion about my identity that prompted an overcompensation. As I grew older, I embraced the local mores with a vengeance. As a high school freshman, commuting into Washington to a Benedictine prep school not in the least enamored of the Confederacy, I asserted my chosen loyalty on an otherwise uncelebrated Lee birthday by raising the Stars and Bars on the school flagpole. Father Austin's furious reaction stunned me — a first lesson in the true meaning of that symbol. I was expelled, and only my father's plea — he had to appear in person, time taken from the Cold War — satisfied the headmaster.

Now I recognize the contempt I saw in that priest's eyes as the judgment he'd made on an ignorant boy unaware of his own white supremacist assumptions. I had thought nothing of the balcony reserved for blacks — "Blue Heaven" — at the Richmond Theater on King Street. I had thought nothing of the separate parishes for black and white Catholics in Alexandria: our handsome St. Mary's Church made of chiseled stone, their flaking clapboard shanty church, St. Joseph's, on the other side of the tracks. Segregation by race was an even more ruthless fact of the world I grew up in than by religion. I not only did not question it; I did not notice it.

Until one day, ironically enough, at the FBI. I worked at Bureau headquarters for three summers, beginning in 1960, as a cryptanalyst's aide in the code-breaking section of the FBI laboratory. I recall the awe I felt sitting before stacked pages of computer printouts showing endless rows of numbers, encrypted messages to various Washington embassies originating not only in Russia and Cuba but in England and France. My job was to do a primitive arithmetical analysis of those numbers, counting certain digits, watching for patterns, making marginal notes, which my agent supervisor would review later. A word of plaintext at the top of each page — *Havana, Moscow, Vienna* — identified the source and kept the transcendent meaning of the effort at the forefront.

It was mind-numbing work that computers would soon be doing in flashes, and, not surprisingly, it all came to nothing. The only chance the Bureau ever had of reading those pure-random ciphers lay in obtaining their cryptographic keys, which was why the office's agents periodically pulled "black-bag jobs" on the Washington embassies of friend and foe alike. Burglary was against the law, of course, and the intrusion on allies was a violation of the diplomatic code. The ends don't justify the means, et cetera, but not for a moment, son of the Cold War that I was, did I regard such tactics as wrong. On the contrary, I was thrilled to have a part in them. My hope always was that the secret pattern of the numbers before me would fall open. I did as I was told. I saw things the way I was supposed to. The structure of my moral universe seemed immutable.

On the day in question, those of us who were summer employees were summoned to a special meeting of all the college interns working at the Justice Department. The attorney general himself was going to address us, making a Kennedy-style pitch for postgraduate careers on the New Frontier. Crossing into the southwest wing of the Justice Building and filing into the large, draped departmental auditorium, we FBI kids felt like a breed apart. For one thing, because of the Bureau's security requirements, we were all sons (not daughters) of senior agents, or, as in my case, of a former agent whose tie to Hoover held.

Another reason we felt like princes as we entered that auditorium was the FBI's role as the front line of Bobby Kennedy's own twin preoccupations: the fight against the Reds, for which he'd first become famous as an aide to Senator Joseph R. McCarthy, and his newly launched campaign against Jimmy Hoffa. Bobby Kennedy, we felt, would look on us as special allies in the struggles he took most seriously. So imagine my surprise when what Bobby — the hair, the teeth, the rolled-up sleeves — chose to speak about that day was neither Reds nor the mob but the rights of colored people. In my mind, the NAACP might as well have been on the attorney general's list of subversive organizations, though I knew as little about it as I did about the Lincoln Brigade.

I remember the shrill pitch of his voice and the open palm

of his hand slapping the podium. I remember his direct invitation to come back to Washington after graduation to join a new American crusade. "My fundamental belief," he said once, and I recall his saying something like it that day, "is that all people are created equally. Logically, it follows that integration should take place everywhere."

Fundamental belief? Powerfully faced with his, I had to admit that it was mine too. I remember, as it were, a light going on in my dull head: the flip side of "created equal" is "integration." It was an era when such lights went on all over the place. Arthur Schlesinger Jr. reports that after Bobby Kennedy and an aide took an early tour of the Justice Department, Kennedy asked, "Did anything occur to you as strange in our visit around the offices?" The aide referred only to how hard everyone seemed to be working. Kennedy replied, "But did you see any Negroes?"

There were 955 lawyers working at Justice, of whom 10 were black. At Kennedy's first staff meeting immediately upon taking office, he ordered the "thorough integration" of every departmental office, including field offices in the South. He personally recruited young black lawyers from the best law schools, and that day in the Justice Department auditorium I noted that a good number of the summer interns were black. But not one from the FBI side was, and to my astonishment, that now seemed a matter of deep shame. I was ambushed by two feelings at once, a first-time repugnance at the Bureau and a visceral attraction to Bobby Kennedy. We all knew that Hoover loathed Bobby, and until now I had not thought to choose between them. But if integration was to be a transcendent value . . .

J. Edgar Hoover, a Washington native, was an unapologetic segregationist. In response to earlier pressure to integrate the ranks of FBI agents, he had simply given his long-time chauffeur a badge — and kept him at the wheel of his car. In response to

Robert Kennedy's question, Hoover had told him there were five colored agents in the group numbering over five thousand. "He wanted me to lower our qualifications to hire more Negro agents," Hoover later told a reporter, which will, he said, "never be done as long as I'm director of this bureau."

I well remember how conditioned most of us were to deflecting challenges to the segregated status quo by such ready talk of lowered qualifications, as if all the white people around us in every situation had achieved the highest of standards. "Qualifications" were not Hoover's issue, of course, and they had never been mine.

I returned to the FBI side of the Justice Building that day — shaken, but also seeing something new. Not only had Bobby surprised me with his passionate endorsement of the civil rights agenda, but, in the receiving line after his talk, he had made it particular to me. We'd been instructed to shake his hand firmly, look him in the eye, and announce what college we attended and what we were majoring in. As I approached, I wiped the palm of my hand on my trousers, feeling awed and afraid and embarrassed at what I had to say. When he turned to me and took my hand, I told him I was about to go off to the novitiate and seminary to become a Catholic priest. He clasped my forearm warmly, an affirmation I longed for. He said, What a great time to be a priest! Then he said something to the effect that priests were urgently needed in the streets, where the ministers already were. Kennedy's words thrilled me, but their meaning was unclear. The racial divide was shifting, and here was a hint that the denominational lines would be shifting too.

One of the jokes we told in those days touched on both divisions. Little Caroline Kennedy went to the Oval Office and announced her intention to marry Martin Luther King's son. "Oh, no," the president replied, "you can't marry him." Beat. Beat.

"He's not Catholic." Laughter, which much later I would recognize as having been of the jittery kind.

When, near the end of that same summer, Bobby Kennedy sent federal marshals to Ole Miss to protect James Meredith, I had learned enough to understand that he sent marshals instead of agents because he could not trust the FBI. I also grasped by then that my beloved agents were not the only figures of mine absent from that first crucible. Its anonymous peacekeepers were the clergymen of the Southern Christian Leadership Conference. Ministers in the streets. Decidedly not priests. Catholics were nowhere to be seen in the early civil rights confrontations, and beginning with Robert Kennedy's comment, that came to seem anomalous. Later — I am ashamed to say years later — I would recognize Kennedy's words to me as a prophecy, and a conscription.

A few months after the crisis at Ole Miss, in November of 1962, while I was living in the hills of New Jersey waiting for a small lake to freeze, a headline appeared in the *New York Times:* "Dr. King Says FBI in Albany, Ga. Favors Segregationists." The article attributed this statement to King: "One of the great problems we face with the FBI in the South is that the agents are white southerners who have been influenced by the mores of the community." As a white man who had been influenced by such mores, I knew exactly what King was talking about, but I was still affronted by his open attack on the Bureau. How many episodes of *The FBI in Peace and War* had featured the decades-old crusade against the Klan? Hadn't the G-men put an end to the era of rampant lynchings in the South? Bureau tardiness on the issue was not the same as favoring White Citizens Councils. I was a connoisseur of bad guys, and I knew that in this case the bad guys were not, as I still thought of it, "us."

Martin Luther King was called a Negro militant, but his appeals to a philosophy of nonviolence were as unsettling as his stridency. Where would nonviolence get us with Moscow? And anyway, how could we take such rhetoric seriously when it came clothed in tactics designed to provoke violence? I accepted the assessment that Freedom Riders who courted arrest and the "direct action" demonstrators who defied redneck sheriffs did so for the sake of the now ubiquitous television cameras. Dr. King, in a phrase of the day, wanted too much too soon. Freedom now! How impatient the impatience of newly roused black people made us white people feel. I hated Bull Connor, but I also thought the demonstrators he seemed to take such pleasure in clubbing brought it on themselves. And when, in the summer of my novitiate year, 1963, Medgar Evers was assassinated in Mississippi, I was appalled by the deed but critical of Evers also. Only days before he had said, "I would die and die gladly." The vicious rednecks, I thought, gave him what he wanted. I did not know that Evers was a war veteran, and when he was buried at Arlington Cemetery I guessed it was because Robert Kennedy wanted him treated as a hero. To me, Evers had been a misguided man who'd made the plight of his people worse, not better.

And that's what King was. After Evers's death, anticipation and anxiety mounted as plans were laid for a massive march on Washington. Some of my fellow novices complained that we would be completing our program in New Jersey a few days after the rally at the Lincoln Memorial, just missing it. But I was not complaining. If we were in Washington, I, like other self-styled "moderates," would surely have stayed away. After the violence in Birmingham and the summer's carnage in Mississippi, President Kennedy and even his brother were making plain their opposition to the demonstration. The Kennedys wanted their civil rights bill, and a mass of militant, threatening black people descending on the capital would make its passage more difficult, not less.

At Mount Paul, on August 28, we watched the demonstration on television, as we'd watched Pope John XXIII's opening speech to the Council and then, nine months later, his funeral. Now we were watching the gathering of a quarter of a million people, the vast majority of them black. I remember images of the reflecting pool below the Washington Monument lined with Negroes soaking their feet. I remember Joan Baez and Peter, Paul and Mary.

I remember that, to my consternation, the Roman Catholic archbishop of Washington, Patrick Cardinal O'Boyle, was at the march as a participant. O'Boyle to me was a less charismatic version of Spellman. I had no appreciation for the fact, if I even knew of it, that he had anticipated the 1954 *Brown v. Board of Education* ruling by ordering an end to the segregation of Catholic schools and parishes in Washington in 1948, the year Truman did the same for the armed services.

And I remember the white pillars of the Lincoln Memorial, the brooding presence in its shadows, which served as backdrop to the podium to which Martin Luther King finally came. I had spent a lifetime being entirely unaffected by parish sermons. I had spent several years holding off the real meaning of the turmoil in the South. So how could I have anticipated what was about to happen?

He began by saying, "Five score years ago, a great American, in whose symbolic shadow we stand today, signed the Emancipation Proclamation. This momentous decree came as a great beacon light of hope to millions of Negro slaves who had been seared in the flames of withering injustice."

Slavery. King's starting point was slavery. "But one hundred years later, the Negro still is not free; one hundred years later the life of the Negro is still sadly crippled by the manacles of segregation and the chains of discrimination . . . one hundred years later the Negro is still languished in the corners of American society and finds himself in exile in his own land."

I had seen King in news clips before, had read about him repeatedly, and argued with my fellow Paulists about him. I had a rigid set of impressions, the very rods of which began somehow to melt as I listened to him speak. This was the first sustained attention I had ever paid to King, and it was obvious I knew nothing real about the man. Friends of mine at the FBI had called him "Martin Luther Coon," and I had never objected.

As his sonorous, musical voice rose, his words came to my ears clearly, but to my mind as if I were under water, or slowly emerging from a lifelong deafness. I had never heard language used this way before — and by a preacher, which is what I was preparing to become. But my idea of preaching was to tell people what they already knew. This preacher — by how he looked and sounded, by what he was saying from his first words on, simply by who he was, the word become a self — he was telling me something I had never heard before.

Slavery. Hard as it is for me to write these words or imagine how they could ever have been true, the evil of slavery had not dawned on me. I knew, of course, that the existence of slavery had contradicted American ideals from the start. Jefferson knew that — and kept his slaves. Perhaps, as a precondition of accepting the idea of cavalier Virginia, to claim a place with Jefferson, not to mention Lee, I had refused to move past the idea of the thing to the reality of it. For example, I had accepted the notion, perhaps breathing it in with the dust of slave-laid cobblestones in Alexandria, that despite the evident hardships, slaves were happy. Sambo was happy, wasn't he? And Uncle Remus? Wasn't the happiness I saw in the quick-stepping of Sammy Davis Jr. and the repartee on *Amos 'n' Andy* a vestige of slave happiness? The caddies at the country club, the janitors at St. Mary's, the orderlies who'd walked our dogs and cooked our meals and cleaned our houses in Wiesbaden and at Bolling — hadn't their smiles all been stunning? Wasn't their ingratiating deference a signal of an innate self-acceptance that permanently eluded, for one, me? And hadn't I embarked on a course, for comfort's sake, for security's, to make myself over into a slave of the Church?

Years later, in *A People's History of the United States* by Howard Zinn, I would read these words of John Little, a former slave: "They say slaves are happy, because they laugh and are merry. I myself and three or four others, have received two hundred lashes in the day, and had our feet in fetters; yet at night, we would sing and dance, and make others laugh at the rattling of our chains. Happy men we must have been! We did it to keep down trouble, and to keep our hearts from being completely broken: that is as true as the gospel! Just look at it — must not we have been very happy? Yet I have done it myself — I have cut capers in chains."

Martin Luther King was not happy. Martin Luther King was not smiling. There was not a hint of deference in him. His somber gravity weighed on me, and I recognized in it the weight of the recent murders in Mississippi and Alabama, of the cattle prods and fire hoses turned on schoolchildren, of the poverty of sharecroppers and the insult of segregation. As the camera panned across the upraised, mainly black faces of King's listeners, my mind opened finally to the fact that underlay all these other facts: slavery.

"Why am I a slave?" Frederick Douglass wrote in a version of the identity questions I had been putting to myself. "Why are some people slaves and others masters? Was there ever a time when this was not so? How did the relation commence?"

Slavery was not, as I'd willfully imagined, finished with a century before. Its freshly biting consequences had carried these people to the nation's capital, which was also my hometown. A television camera mounted in a helicopter shot the crowd from the air, and I thought of the view from the observation deck of the Washington Monument, a favorite perch. This was a *place* of mine, and here it was, filled with the bodies of those who'd danced capers in chains. But they were not dancing now. The camera gave us a shot of the monument itself. Years before, in our out-of-towner tours, my mother used to point to the line in the stone a third of the way up the obelisk that marked the place where construction had stopped during the Civil War. When building resumed after a decade, the granite no longer quite matched. The color break was an odd curiosity of my childhood, but now it seemed like yet another scar of slavery.

The color line cast in stone — King spoke directly to that assumption: "There are those who are asking the devotees of civil rights, 'When will you be satisfied?' We can never be satisfied as long as the Negro is the victim of the unspeakable horror of police brutality; we can never be satisfied as long as our bodies, heavy with the fatigue of travel, cannot gain lodging . . . We cannot be satisfied as long as our children are stripped of their selfhood and robbed of their dignity by signs stating, 'For Whites Only' . . . No! No! We are not satisfied until 'justice rolls down like waters and righteousness like a mighty stream.'"

The crowd broke into thunderous applause, and King wiped the perspiration from his face, and I stood there in the novices' common room. We watched the speech in silence, thirty white men, not moving our eyes from the face of the black preacher. I don't know about the others, but it seemed to me that I was there in that Washington swelter. It also seemed that I was in his presence alone. "I say to you today, my friends, so even though we face the difficulties of today and tomorrow, I still have a dream . . . I have a dream today. I have a dream that one day down in Alabama — with its vicious racists, with its governor having his lips dripping with the words of interposition and nullification — one day right there in Alabama, little black boys and black girls will be able to join hands with little white boys and white girls as sisters and brothers. I have a dream today! I have a dream that one day 'every valley shall be exalted and every hill and mountain shall be made low. The rough places will be made plain and the crooked places will be made straight, and the glory of the Lord shall be revealed, and all flesh shall see it together.'"

Martin Luther King was preaching the Word of God. Preaching! I saw that the conversion demanded by that Word is brought about not by words alone, but by words firmly rooted in the life of the one preaching. My reaction to King all at once took on a religious dimension — no, a religious substance. I who, since my childhood infatuation with the FBI, had been looking for a way to join my private impulse to a public crusade, was being shown it. I who, since Robert Kennedy spoke to me, had been looking for a way to match the timeless tradition in which I'd planted myself with the unprecedented energy of an inbreaking future, was being shown it. I who, since Pope John XXIII conscripted me, had been longing for a way the vocation I'd inherited from my father could feel like mine, was being shown it. King had stopped being a prophet of black liberation and had become, in a flash, a figure of my own.

". . . that day when all God's children, black men and white men, Jews and Gentiles, Protestants and Catholics, will be able to join hands and sing in the words of the old Negro spiritual, 'Free at last! Free at last!'" *My* freedom, I saw. He was talking about *my* freedom too. "'Thank God Almighty'" — King's eyes were awash in tears, and stupefyingly, so were mine — "'we are free at last!'"

"A powerful demagogic speech" was what he called King's oration — J. Edgar Hoover's top aide and an old friend of my father's, William C. Sullivan. The reaction indicates, perhaps, that he too had been moved, despite himself. That the black man who had dared openly to criticize the FBI should suddenly, through an act of rhetoric, lay claim to the American conscience would have been enough to prompt a resolve in Hoover to bring him down. In fact, by its own lights, beginning with Stanley Levison but not ending there, the Bureau had other, better reasons for setting out to do so. Which it did now.

When, days later, I arrived in Washington as a newly sworn Paulist seminarian, ready to begin my formal academic training in philosophy and theology, the changes in my circumstances were dramatic. Paramount among them was my reunion with my mother and father, a return to the city, into the New Frontier aristocracy of which they had themselves recently been initiated. My father was almost the exact age I am as I write these words. It is much easier now for me to imagine how things looked from his side. He was just then completing his second full year as head of the Defense Intelligence Agency. His assistant director was Lieutenant General William W. Quinn, whose daughter Sally would become a well-known writer and the wife of *Washington Post* editor Benjamin Bradlee. Dad would be reappointed as director four times, a record unmatched since, giving him tenure, unfortunately, through the worst failures of Vietnam.

As Air Force inspector general, in 1961, my father had impressed Robert McNamara with his investigation of leaks in U.S. intelligence, and particularly with his unraveling of the story behind the defections to the Soviet Union of two national security analysts, B. F. Mitchell and William H. Martin. But mainly, I believe, McNamara was drawn to my father because, owing to his eccentric history as an FBI man turned general, he was not bound by the narrow military loyalties, and had in fact set himself against many of the Pentagon orthodoxies that McNamara, as secretary of defense, had made it his business to terminate.

Now, in the year since the Cuban missile crisis in which DIA had played a pivotal role, my father's prestige, however discreetly manifested, was at its peak. His rivals within the military intelligence establishment had been defanged, and his turf-protecting counterparts at CIA, NSA, and the State Department had learned to work with him — a tribute to my father's skills as a bureaucratic infighter, and also a signal of the strong support he had from McNamara. I would later learn that only two months before this reunion in early September of 1963, my father had become the single representative of all military agencies on the U.S. Intelligence Board, where he shared the table as a peer with J. Edgar Hoover and CIA chief John A. McCone. Only a few days before my return to D.C., on the first of September, my father's reach within the clandestine side of government had been broadened significantly with the establishment of a separate DIA Office of Counterintelligence and Security.

It goes without saying that my father never spoke at home about his work, but I sensed his power, and my mother's satisfaction in it. I understood that in some unprecedented and unhoped-for way, President Kennedy had tapped my father. Only a few weeks from now President Kennedy would be dead, and as was true of so many men Kennedy had empowered, something in my father would from then on be dead too.

But not yet. Within days of my arrival from New Jersey, my parents came to visit me at St. Paul's College. My view of things was very narrow. I attributed the palpable difference I sensed in them not so much to their personal success or to the stunning communal arrival of their kind in the Kennedy era, but to the satisfaction they surely took in my recent act of self-sacrifice.

We went for a walk up Fourth Street to the National Shrine of the Immaculate Conception. They were on either side of me. My father was in a civilian blue suit, but I was in uniform, the distinctive Paulist habit. This was the garb my devotion to which, within months, Hans Küng and his ilk in their neckties would puncture, but that day I felt a neophyte's delight in appearing in public as a clergyman. I sensed my parents' pride, subliminally aware of the enormity of the occasion, a promised filling in of the ancient void around which they'd built their lives. A filling in, of course, with me. My mother slipped her arm inside mine. She was wearing white gloves.

We climbed the broad stairs to the entrance of the great basilica, with its brilliant blue mosaic beach ball of a dome. At the door, we glanced back toward the city spread out behind us, and now I imagine what we saw on that pristine early autumn day: the Capitol dome, the Washington Monument, the spires of my own Georgetown, and to the west, on the hill opposite this one, the towers of the National Cathedral (Episcopal), a pure Gothic masterpiece and a Protestant rebuke to the garishness of our church here. A seminarian's joke of the day described an apparition, the Blessed Virgin on the same top step, and her command, "Build me a *beautiful* church on this spot."

The interior of the Shrine is dominated by a huge floor-to-ceiling mosaic of Christ behind the high altar, a stern but effeminate face, the eyes of which follow everywhere. The Lord sitting in judgment was the idea, but to me that day and ever after, because of those eyes, and perhaps because of what began to happen between me and my father, the Lord sitting less in judgment than in merciless rejection.

Dad and I found ourselves alone. Maybe Mom had gone ahead to a bank of blue votive lights at the feet of Saint Mary, or red at the feet of Saint Joseph. She'd have been lighting candles for Joe's health and my vocation, the two main things she prayed for. Dad was a chain smoker, and we were in some marble-lined vestibule or corridor, out of sight of the apocalyptic eyes, where he could light up. And where, at last, I could tell him what was on my mind.

"Martin Luther King," I said.

We had never discussed King. I had not learned yet to dissemble with my father. Now that I had actually begun to shape my life according to the contours of the first one he'd chosen, I felt more desperately in need of his approval than ever.

"What about him?" he said curtly. I sensed at once how the mention of King's name displeased him.

My father listened in silence as I described my reaction to King's speech, how I'd recognized a dream of mine in what the Baptist preacher had said. And wasn't it amazing that in response to the viciousness of bigots in Alabama and Mississippi, he'd conjured up that vision of little black boys and black girls joining hands with white children? "He's right, Dad," I said. "Slavery won't be finished —"

My father was shaking his head, which made me stall.

I pushed on. "King said that if America is ever to be a great nation —"

"America already is a great nation. Don't be a sap."

"But King preaches nonviolence. He is the alternative to riots and rebellion, to Stokely Carmichael and Malcolm X . . ." How I longed for his ratification of the new feelings I had. I knew what fundamental shifts they implied, and my hope was that, since

Dad was one of Kennedy's men now, and since Kennedy himself was so clearly changing — after first opposing the March on
Washington, he had endorsed it — then wouldn't Dad be changing too? And couldn't he then encourage me to — ?

"Don't be taken in by King," he said. "The man is a charlatan."

"Come on, Dad. Maybe you disagree with him, but you can't
say he's not sincere."

"That's exactly what I'm saying."

"Not sincere? As in liar?"

"Yes. Take my word for it, son." The curl of bitterness in his
voice shocked me. "I know things about King that you don't
know and that I can't tell you."

"Like what?"

"Just don't be taken in."

"No, really, Dad." Now the curl was in my voice, which was
insistent, pissed off, as surprising to me as to him. "Like what?
You can't just stamp this 'classified.' This is important. I have a
right to know. Tell me."

Which of course he refused to do, on that occasion or any of
the other dozen times, each demand an escalation of the previous one, until I was screaming at him and he was ordering me
to silence as if I were an insubordinate aide.

For the rest of 1963 and all through 1964, through the trauma
of John Kennedy's assassination, the upheaval of Lyndon Johnson's campaign against Barry Goldwater, the steady release of
racial furies in the South, as well as through the seismic shifts of
religious meaning that jolted me in theology classes and in reading about the Vatican Council — through it all, every encounter
with my father was charged with the same voltage that flashed
around Martin Luther King — lightning, fire, the smell of car-
bon. But also plenty of illumination. My own instincts slanted
steadily in King's favor, but I was kept from acting on them, or

even voicing support in seminary debates, because my basic commitment still was to my father's instincts. Could I disbelieve his claim to having secret knowledge? And if I was building my spiritual life around my father's will, how could I defy it on an issue that was, as I'd have still said, merely political?

Yet when, in 1964, King was named winner of the Nobel Peace Prize, I went to Thanksgiving dinner at Bolling and gloated. "The Nobel Prize, Dad. Could they give that to a Communist? To a degenerate?"

Communist. Degenerate. Words my father, for reasons unknown to me, had taken to using about King. He choked on his rage and replied with his version of what J. Edgar Hoover said that same week: "Martin Luther King is the most notorious liar in America."

Decades later, David J. Garrow's book would lay out for me all that my father "knew," as a veteran of the ancient Chicago surveillance of Morris Chilofsky, a.k.a. Childs; as a participant in the rigid assessment of Stanley Levison's dual — but never simultaneous — role as a Moscow-sponsored operative and as King's confidant; as one privy to the bugging and wiretapping of King himself, which revealed no security breaches but a hidden life of illicit sexual encounters. Perhaps there is a kind of good news in the belated discovery that my father's furious rejection of King was neither the shallow racism nor the groundless paranoia I had concluded it was. Levison's history was a real issue. But in reading Garrow's account, I felt the simple shame of learning the terrible news that, in all likelihood, given his associations, my father had colluded in an FBI plot to destroy King — a true act of American fascism.

In the beginning, one half of all people eligible to vote in Dallas County, Alabama, were black, but only one percent of them were registered. Fifteen thousand eligible blacks lived in Selma, the county seat, but only 156 of them were registered.

For the last six months of 1964, the Student Nonviolent Coordinating Committee had been leading an effort to get the black citizens of Selma on the voting rolls. Among the obstacles to overcome were arcane literacy tests, poll taxes, the hostility of a registrar whose office was rarely open, a court order forbidding demonstrations and, most difficult of all, the dogs and electric cattle prods of a posse led by Sheriff Jim Clark. In January 1965, shortly after receiving the Nobel Peace Prize, Martin Luther King went to Selma too, seeking, as he put it, "to arouse the federal government."

King's presence drew the attention of the nation to Selma. In a courthouse confrontation, dozens of demonstrators were brutally arrested. "I hope the newspapers see you," one demonstrator said to Sheriff Clark, who answered, "Dammit, I hope they do." Photographs of Clark wielding his stick appeared all over the country. But then, as Juan Williams writes in *Eyes on the Prize*, "With speaking engagements elsewhere, King had to leave town for a while." It seems an odd moment for King's departure, and it prompts a digression from the narrative of Selma to consider what, besides speaking engagements, might have drawn King away at such a crucial time.

In October of 1963, within weeks of my first conversation with my father about Martin Luther King, Attorney General Robert Kennedy approved an FBI request to tap King's phone lines and place listening devices in his offices and hotel rooms. Rebutting common accusations and my own long-held conclusions that the request was part of a personal, essentially racist vendetta designed to punish a Bureau critic, David J. Garrow writes, "The origins of the King investigation lay in an honestly held FBI belief that Stanley Levison was a conscious and active agent of the Soviet Union, and that Levison's friendship with King was motivated by something other than a desire to advance the cause of civil rights in America."

But the effect of the bugs on King, especially of his hotel rooms, was to shift the FBI's preoccupation away from a perceived Communist threat and toward a puritanical repugnance at the perceived hypocrisy implied by his sexual behavior. For more than a year, FBI microphones gathered graphic information on King's secret life. Garrow states that Hoover, to the consternation of Bobby Kennedy when he learned of it, dispatched transcripts of tapes to the Pentagon — no doubt to my father. A puritanical, but also prurient, obsession with King's sexual restlessness fed Bureau rage, and when the civil rights leader won the Nobel Prize, Hoover decided to launch a covert campaign to discredit him.

Hoover recruited Cardinal Spellman, for one, to intervene with the Vatican, to head off King's meeting with Pope Paul VI. Spellman tried, but it is a measure of the inexorable tilting of the Church's axis that the pope ignored his warning and met with King — a fact I used against my father in our arguments. My father was forced to say, as he did one day to me — seismic shifts everywhere — that the pope himself was naive.

FBI efforts to discredit King became an effort to destroy him. On January 6, just as the climax of events in Selma was approaching, Coretta Scott King discovered a letter and a tape recording in the mail. The tape, compiled from more than a year's worth of bugging, contained "highlights" of her husband's encounters with other women in hotels in various cities. The accompanying letter contained an anonymous threat to expose King as "a colossal fraud . . . a dissolute, abnormal imbecile." The tape demonstrated that this letter was written not by a crackpot but by someone in the government. And then the letter went beyond a threat to expose the minister: "King, you are done . . . there is only one thing left for you to do. You know what it is . . . There is but one way out for you. You better take it before your filthy, abnormal, fraudulent self is bared to the nation."

How far the Bureau had come from Roger "Terrible" Touhy, when it took on its enemies directly, bravely, like men — my father's voice "the voice of doom." According to David J. Garrow, this cowardly poison-pen letter proposing suicide was written by Hoover's top assistant, William Sullivan, my father's old friend. It was surreptitiously carried to Miami and mailed from there by Lish Whitson, a counterspy legend and father of one of my cryptanalysis section chums. The threat to expose King was carried out when Deke DeLoach, another Hoover aide and family friend of ours, offered a transcript of the sex tape to Benjamin Bradlee. The editor refused to take it, and instead informed high Justice Department officials, who told the president of the plot. Instead of rebuking Hoover, Lyndon Johnson instructed his aide Bill Moyers, as Garrow writes, "to warn the Bureau that Bradlee was unreliable."

Martin Luther King was a tormented man. No one was more aware of the conflict between his public image and his flawed private life than he. The discovery that powers in Washington were also aware of that conflict and were using the threat to expose it as an inducement to suicide nearly crushed him. "They are out to break me," he said, referring not to Sheriff Jim Clark but to the very leaders — Hoover, the Justice Department, and Johnson — who alone could rescue him and his people from the bigots of Selma.

These were the likely thoughts of Martin Luther King at the time he "left town for a while." The man's greatness is nowhere more evident than in the fact that he returned to Selma, and on February 1 deliberately allowed himself to be arrested. "If Negroes could vote," he said, "there would be no Jim Clarks."

King's arrest riveted the nation, and white resistance in Selma grew more militant. At the end of February, state troopers killed a young black demonstrator, Jimmy Lee Jackson. At his funeral, King denounced a federal government that preferred a war in Vietnam to protecting "the lives of its own citizens seeking the right to vote."

The war in Vietnam? Hadn't we just elected Lyndon Johnson as the peace candidate? In fact Johnson, with my father's help in the Pentagon, was preparing to launch Operation Rolling Thunder, the bombing of North Vietnam, but who knew that? In my view, this first mention of the war by King seemed a huge mistake, one I hoped he would not repeat. The war was none of his business. On that front, Johnson's men, my father among them, knew what they were doing.

King announced a fifty-mile walk to Montgomery to protest at George Wallace's state capitol. Even SNCC opposed the idea as too provocative. The SCLC stood firm. The day of the march arrived, but King was in Atlanta. "Although he had promised to lead the march," Juan Williams writes, "he now said he needed to be in his own pulpit that day." At the Edmund Pettus Bridge, the six hundred marchers were attacked and routed. From Atlanta, King issued a call to the nation: "No American is without responsibility . . . Join me in Selma for a ministers' march to Montgomery on Tuesday morning, March 9."

It is speculation on my part to see in King's alternating presence and absence as the tension mounted in Selma evidence of a powerful internal struggle. My point is simply that the heroic role in which history has cast him does not do justice to the fierce and mostly secret conflicts — conflict of his own character and conflict with a fascist impulse of the federal government — he had to overcome in order to respond to the deepest call of his own conscience. Push had come to shove, and Martin Luther King was there. On March 9 he led fifteen hundred people onto Edmund Pettus Bridge again. That night one of the ministers who'd responded to his call, James Reeb, was fatally clubbed. Reeb was white. The nation that had been indifferent to the death of Jimmy Lee Jackson now exploded with demonstrations of support.

And at long last so did I. It took the death of a white man to break my inner — one could surely say Oedipal — paralysis. But more important to me than his race was the fact that Reeb was a minister. By then the effect of Hans Küng's advocacy of Christian reunion, and the Council's embrace of the ecumenical impulse, had undercut my sharp sense of the old distinction between ministers and priests. Hadn't Roman collars of all kinds — even on Unitarians — become ubiquitous at civil rights demonstrations? And James Reeb was a Washington minister at that. All Souls Unitarian Church, where he had served, was at a downtown crossroads I had passed through a thousand times. I can picture the church now, with its sweeping staircase, classic columns, and stately pediment rising on the corner of Sixteenth and Harvard streets. After Selma it would always seem like a monument, one of Washington's grave memories. Reeb was a man I might have known, and his death made the faraway events shockingly personal to me. It was a turning point, the occasion of a large and complete reversal in my life story.

SCLC organizers in Washington put out a call to ministers and priests who couldn't get to Selma to come to a sympathy demonstration on the street outside the White House, to demand that Lyndon Johnson intervene in Alabama. With a dozen other Paulists I went along, wearing black. The scene was alien and intimidating. Most of the demonstrators were young turks, Afro-haired and dashiki-clad. A commando-like contingent of youthful blacks organized by a — to me — inflammatory young preacher named Marion Barry frightened me and reinforced my instinctive rejection of provocative tactics. The militants wanted to draw police into violent overreaction, to discredit them. I remember how mutely I walked in the picket line, the steady long loop on the Pennsylvania Avenue sidewalk, while chants and shouted slogans broke the air above me. I was more afraid of my fellow demonstrators than of the police.

As a way of detaching myself from my threatening surroundings, I began to watch the blank windows of the White House, looking for movement. I wondered if Lynda Bird was in the mansion, peeking at us through the curtains. I had last seen her when she passed my spot on the avenue during her father's inauguration parade, a sad parade because it evoked Kennedy's funeral procession. But there had been consolation in it too, since LBJ, my own "Mr. Johnson," had defeated the warmonger — and reserve Air Force general — Barry Goldwater. The thought of Lynda Bird made me realize that I wanted her to see me on that street — she would never know how afraid I was.

And that thought put me instantly in mind of the one I hoped would never see me doing such a thing. The demonstration, as long as we obeyed orders to keep moving and stay on the sidewalk, was perfectly legal, but it was nevertheless for me an act of mortal transgression. I had until then opposed such activity, secretly afraid my father, who knew everything, was right about it. Even lawful protests — how I had argued this myself — lead to disorder. Which is what happened that day.

I was moving in the picket line behind a man who carried a sign that said, "God Is Love." I was acutely aware of him, as I was of everything around me — the cops on horseback, the plainclothes Secret Service agents, the White House guards, the cameras from which I kept my distance, shielding my face as if I were a mobster. Passersby stopped to jeer us. I heard the words "nigger" and "nigger lovers," which alone helped me feel some satisfaction with myself. This is all right, I remember thinking. I can do this.

But then the man in front of me and others drifted into the street. The policemen began to shove them back, and the horses bumped roughly into the line. The cops' harshness sparked resistance, and more demonstrators veered off the sidewalk into the avenue, blocking traffic. Orders were given through battery-powered bullhorns, which I'd never seen before. Sirens sounded, clubs were swung. People screamed, ran, shoved back against each other.

The pandemonium ended as quickly as it began. Those arrested were efficiently carried off, and the rhythm of the moving picket line was reestablished. I had never ventured toward the curb, nor moved to resist, and when someone had intoned the familiar anthem "We Shall Overcome," I could hardly bring myself to join in, though in the deepest part of myself I had longed for years to sing those words in exactly such a setting.

Next morning, the front page of the *Washington Post* carried a photograph of a protester hitting a policeman on the head with his hand-lettered sign, "God Is Love." I nearly fainted at the sight of it. It took me a long moment to focus so that I could study the photograph and make sure — oh, Christ, what if Dad sees this? — I wasn't in it. What a hero I was to myself then. A familiar self-contempt, bile in my throat.

What happened to me that weekend was nothing compared to the electric bolt that linked Selma to D.C. The next day, Lyndon Johnson said that he saw in the struggle in Selma "the heart and the purpose and the meaning of America itself." I like to think the demonstrators outside his window played a small part in it — Lynda Bird fetching him to watch? Pointing at me? That day the president stopped being J. Edgar Hoover's ally and became Martin Luther King's. That night, in one of the greatest speeches ever given by an American president, Johnson proposed the Voting Rights Bill. I saw the speech on the television in the Paulist common room. LBJ concluded with a stirring report of his own, as I'd learned to call it, *metanoia*. Then he leaned toward us, his "fellow Americans." He peered above the rims of his glasses, like an old man hunched over a steering wheel. With a sharp intake of breath, he said in that redneck drawl of his, "And we *shall* overcome!" The words, I would later read, brought tears to the eyes of Martin Luther King. They certainly did to mine.

In support of the Voting Rights Bill of 1965, I helped organize a round-the-clock seminarians' vigil at the Lincoln Memorial, teams consisting of a Protestant, a Catholic, and a Jew. One rainy spring night during a shift of mine, at about two in the morning, a car pulled up to the curb in front of us and stopped abruptly. The doors slammed open. Lincoln's Doric temple loomed behind the figures who approached aggressively. They wore trench coats with swastika armbands, a melodramatic sight it was impossible at first to take seriously, but which then made us all afraid. They came right up to us, cursed us, and spat at our feet. "Nigger lovers!" one said, and to the Jewish seminarian, "Kike!" I recognized one antagonist as George Lincoln Rockwell, the crackpot head of the American Nazi Party. He would later be assassinated. Instead of getting back in their car, the three Nazis took up positions down the street from us, a countervigil. Oddly, their presence was a kind of triumph, making our small part in the struggle seem more real.

That spring and summer, the Voting Rights Act passed in both

Joseph F. Carroll, as an FBI agent in the early 1940s, fires his weapon on a practice range. After capturing the notorious Chicago gangster Roger Touhy in 1942, he would become a member of J. Edgar Hoover's Washington inner circle.

Mary Carroll holds me outside our Chicago apartment building. It is 1943, the year the family moved to Washington.

Over objections of the brass, Joseph Carroll was commissioned directly to the rank of brigadier general in 1947, the youngest general officer in the U.S. military.

J. Edgar Hoover and General Hoyt S. Vandenberg, Air Force chief of staff, watch as Air Secretary Stuart Symington presents the Legion of Merit to Brigadier General Carroll in 1949. By then Carroll's Office of Special Investigations had proven its worth despite its Pentagon critics.

35890

Mary and Joe pose in the living room of the house in Hollin Hills, Virginia. They are on their way to a White House reception in the early 1950s.

Joe and Mary welcome Francis Cardinal Spellman to Wiesbaden, Germany, in 1958. To Mary's left is Colonel (Father) Edwin Chess, chief chaplain of the Air Force in Europe. Next to Joe is the cardinal's secretary.

Pope John XXIII receives the Carroll family in January 1960. I am standing behind my mother. Next to General Carroll is his mother.

I have just preached my first sermon, in the chapel at Bolling Air Force Base, Washington, in February 1969. To my right is Major General (Monsignor) Edwin Chess, by now the Air Force's chief chaplain.

Weather Forecast

District and vicinity—Clear and cold tonight, low middle 30s in the city and middle 20s in the outlying suburbs. Increasing cloudiness tomorrow and continued cool. High, 55 at 1 p.m. today; low, 36 at 4:15 a.m. today.

Full Report on Page B-4

The Evening Star
WITH SUNDAY MORNING EDITION

Guide for Readers

Amusements B-6-8	Editorial Articles ...A-7
Business, Stocks A-14-16	Feature Page B-4
Classified C-4-12	Food D-16
Comics B-9-11	Obituaries B-5
Crossword B-10	Society-Items D-17-19
Dining and Dancing ..B-7	Sports C-1-4
Editorial A-6	TV-Radio B-11

110th Year. No. 305. Phone LI. 3-5000 ** WASHINGTON, D. C., THURSDAY, NOVEMBER 1, 1962—60 PAGES Home Delivered: Daily and Sunday, per month, 2.25 10 Cents

8 Rail Lines Sought in Area Transit Setup
$793 Million Plan Sent to Kennedy Asks Road Cuts

By LEE FLOR
Star Staff Writer

A report recommending a $793 million, eight line rail rapid transit system for Washington area residents was handed to President Kennedy today.

The report recommends a regional highway construction program of $628 million by 980, a cutback from present proposals of $814 billion, the National Capital Transportation Agency said.

If the recommendations are accepted, Washington area residents will have a rapid transit system by 1973 that "will be greatly superior to any existing system in North America," the report states.

The report said the controversial Three Sisters bridge would not be needed, and also recommended against several key Inner Loop highway projects. It said the north and east legs should be eliminated. The center leg from 3rd street N.W. to the downtown area, should be retained. So would the Baltimore & Ohio railroad.

The report recommended building a freeway along the "Wisconsin avenue corridor," but did recommend approving a road from Benning-down to the road network along the Potomac River.

The recommended eight rail lines would be 83 miles long, with 65 stations for passengers, the 16 stations in the downtown area to be located so that all, or 80 per cent of all downtown employes will be within minutes' walking distance from transit service.

The report said that trips to work will be from 25 to 50 per cent faster for travelers using rapid transit and riders switching from buses, to trip will be from 30 to 40 per cent faster.

Lower Than Bus Fares

The complete system will be cheaper for suburban residents, compared to present bus use, the report said.

For example, the Rockville resident now pays 82 cents to use or bus in the District. With the rapid transit system a would pay 54 cents. But to cost all long trips by system, fares would then they are today, it said.

It also said that the cost of the $793 million rail would be repaid in proper if the agency recommendations are accepted by Congress and governments in the area.

The transportation recommending a transfer plan that is almost one recommended. Instead of four rail transit program per rail line time. The 1959 used eight express and today's report reconsidered.

Fewer Displacements

The NCTA recommends call for displacement residents, compared would be displaced 1959 plan, the report at The yearly tax loss NCTA recommendation is $300,000, compared million.

Annual operating costs would $2.5 million under the NCTA, versus $5.1 million in the earlier plan.

All these estimates by the transportation agency are highly controversial and are subject to various interpretations.

See TRANSIT, Page A-2

Shea Plans to Probe Reliefer Credit Buying
Full-Scale Inquiry Begins in 10 Days; Some Known to Get Luxury Items

By BETTY MILES
Star Staff Writer

Gerard M. Shea, District public welfare director, said today he will launch a full-scale investigation of credit buying among relief recipients. The probe will begin within 10 days.

Mr. Shea yesterday received a report on a special welfare check of credit accounts held by a Montgomery County loan firm that showed only half of those investigated here for further relief.

Of 132 families involved, 69 were to continue on the rolls. 38 were removed, 24 had their checks held up and 11 had been approved tentatively but were being studied further. Two applicants for relief were denied and five were approved.

Credit Accounts Disclosed

Luxury buying among relief recipients took the spotlight last August when an employe of the Montgomery County firm showed reporters usable credit accounts men and women on assistance had run up for buy television sets, stereo phonographs and other such items.

The Welfare Department asked and was granted permission to check the firm's records.

Mr. Shea said he hopes to get similar cooperation from various Washington firms which sell to recipients on credit. He estimates investigators can spend six weeks checking out accounts with each firm, with the investigation continuing into the summer. It has not been decided whether Baltimore credit firms, where some recipients have accounts, will be questioned.

Other Action Planned

Mr. Shea will take two other steps to clarify rules on credit buying:

1. The section of the welfare manual dealing with credit buying and possession of luxury items will be clarified.

2. Social workers will be given clear-cut guidelines to help recipients plan acceptable purchases.

Only one Washington store has been involved to any extent in the probe of recipients whose accounts were held by the Montgomery County firm. That is the New York Home Furniture Co. at 1215 Seventh street N.W., which had sold scarce items.

some of its accounts to the firm.

Milton Meckler, manager of the furniture store, has complained that welfare's handling of the case discriminated against him and against some relief recipients.

The credit company buys accounts at 22 per cent less than their full value and takes over the collection. Mr. Meckler said that while recipients whose accounts had been sold to the Montgomery County firm were investigated, others whose accounts happened to be held in his office had never been checked. Nor had other loan stores selling on credit been asked to reveal their records, it was said.

There is no money earmarked for furniture in the relief grant. Possession of luxury items, such as television sets and stereo phonographs is not forbidden, but if these are found in a home the department wants to know if the recipient has another source of income besides relief.

Cheaters Discovered

Disclosures of credit buying came in the midst of welfare budget hearings before the Senate District Appropriations Subcommittee, whose chairman is Senator Robert C. Byrd, Democrat of West Virginia. Special investigations of possible cheaters on the rolls ordered by the Senator revealed a high percentage of ineligibility. Many recipients were found to have another source of income drawing relief checks from the public fund.

The 1963 welfare budget includes money for a vastly increased investigative force.

26 Whoopers Counted

A record number of 26 whooping cranes have been counted this winter on the winter grounds on the southeastern Texas coast. Earlier reports had accounted for 20 of the birds.

25 TO 55-CENT FARES ASKED

It would cost from 25 to 55 cents for a ride on the rail transit system proposed today for the Washington area.

U. S. Restores Blockade, Air Survey of Cuba Bases

BARRICADING KEY WEST

Soldiers string barbed wire along the Key West beaches facing Cuba. Military installations in the background were hustled into place during the Cuban crisis.—AP Wirephoto.

Red Missiles Are Going, Thant Told

By GARNETT D. HORNER
Star Staff Writer

The United States arms blockade of Cuba went back into effect today and air surveillance was ordered renewed to guard against sneak continuance or resumption of the Soviet missile buildup in the absence of United Nations inspection.

The President had suspended the blockade against offensive arms shipments into Cuba and aerial reconnaissance flights over Cuba for the last two days while acting United Nations Secretary General U Thant was in Havana trying to work out inspection arrangements.

Mr. Thant flew back to New York last night and reported that he was informed that dismantling of Soviet missiles in Cuba was in progress, and should be completed by tomorrow.

Snags on U. N. Inspection

But some snags developed in efforts to arrange for U. N. inspectors to check on the carrying out of Soviet Premier Khrushchev's promise to Mr. Kennedy Sunday that work would stop on Soviet missile sites in Cuba and the missiles would be dismantled and shipped back to Russia.

The President insists upon establishment of adequate arrangements through the U. N. to insure that these commitments are carried out before he sees through with the part of the bargain to endorse the arms blockade and give assurances against any U. S. invasion of Cuba.

Mr. Thant said nothing was said today on the dismantling of the Soviet jet bombers in Cuba which are an additional factor in the situation.

While officials made clear that aerial surveillance would at once be resumed, it was not clear whether it had already started today. There was no word at the White House on this.

Missile Spotting Resumes

While officials made clear that aerial surveillance, to check on whether work had stopped on construction of Soviet missile bases in Cuba, would be resumed, they refused to say exactly when the aerial picture-making flights would be made.

The White House continued its tight silence today on developments in the Cuban crisis. Even Secretary Pierre Salinger would say only that the arms quarantine was resumed and daybreak as the President had ordered last night.

He refused any comment on Mr. Thant's report that he had been reliably informed in Havana that dismantling of the Soviet missiles in Cuba was underway.

Won't Discuss That

Asked if the United States has any evidence of its own that the Soviet bases are being dismantled, Mr. Salinger said he was not prepared to discuss that.

There are a similar answer when asked what orders American reconnaissance planes had if they were attacked over Cuba.

Mr. Salinger said the President

See BLOCKADE, Page A-4

4th A-Blast Fired Over Johnston Isle

HONOLULU, Nov. 1 (AP)—A fireball flashed across the Pacific today as the United States set off its fourth high-altitude nuclear device in eight attempts above tiny Johnston Island.

A brilliant orange ball of colors visible here, 750 miles from the test area, lighted the skies for about a minute before fading into the darkness.

The fireball wasn't expected to be visible here and observers were surprised by the sudden brilliance of the day. The flash of last Friday's blast barely was visible through the clouds.

The device, sent aloft an estimated 30 to 40 miles last night by a Thor booster rocket

Castro, Irked at Khrushchev, Rejects Inspection by U. N.

UNITED NATIONS, N. Y., Nov. 1 (AP)—Fidel Castro's annoyance over being bypassed by Soviet Premier Khrushchev caused the Cuban leader to reject a U. N. inspection plan that would have cleared with a high U. N. source said today— the source said that Mr. Castro was irritated because Mr. Khrushchev had not consulted him before agreeing with President Kennedy that U. N. inspectors could be sent to Cuba to verify the dismantling of Soviet missiles.

These disclosures came as acting Secretary General U Thant plunged into a new series of diplomatic talks in an effort to get the Cuban peace effort back on the track.

Informed sources said Mr. Castro had given him an outright rejection at their first meeting in Havana Tuesday, but had been much more agreeable yesterday.

Acceptance Seen

The belief was expressed in high U. N. circles that Mr. Castro might accept the U. N. inspection plan after his present mood passes.

Diplomatic informants in Havana said Mr. Castro had delivered a bitter tirade in his talks with Mr. Thant and accused Mr. Khrushchev of having sold him down the river. A spokesman for Mr. Thant said this was "completely unfounded." The spokesman also denied Washington reports saying Mr. Thant had had a most unpleasant trip to Cuba.

The secretary general's first

appointment today was with the current president of the Security Council, Mahmoud Riad of the United Arab Republic and with Ghana's Quaison-Sackey, U. N. delegate. Later Mr. Thant was to confer with India's V. N. delegate, Zafrulla Khan, who flew back from Panmunjom last night. Mr. Lechuga arrived to present his credentials, but it was possible also that he and Mr. Thant would meet with the Cuban situation.

United States Ambassador Adlai E. Stevenson had an afternoon appointment to see Mr. Thant. Mr. Thant said on his return from Havana last night he had been reliably informed

CUBAN STORIES ON INSIDE PAGES

Red 'Intellectual' Apathy Seen As Factor in Crisis. ... Page A-4	
Pentagon 'White Paper' Explains Crisis Action. ... Page A-4	
Mikoyan, Seasoned Diplomat, to See Castro. ... Page A-4	
U. S. Trouble Shooters Sent to Meet Mikoyan. ... Page A-5	
U. S. Officials Reject Thant Snag in Cuba. ... Page A-5	
Pravda Ignores Peiping Criticism Over Cuba. ... Page A-5	
U. S. to Receive Body of Flyer Killed in Cuba. ... Page A-5	
Pro-Castro Brazilians Rap Missile Buildup. ... Page A-5	

the bases would be dismantled by tomorrow and the Soviet equipment shipped out of Cuba soon afterward.

Mr. Thant said today nothing was said on the dismantling of the Soviet jet bombers or the removal of the Soviet 42,000-man force. The purpose of his trip. This mission, plus the return with him of the military aides he had taken as a nucleus of the inspection group, was taken as evidence Mr. Castro's position had hardened on his refusal to permit any inspection.

The United States announced that it was resuming its naval blockade of arms shipments to Cuba at dawn today and that aerial surveillance of the missile sites also was being resumed. Both had been suspended during Mr. Thant's company peacemaking visit to Cuba.

Soviet First Deputy Premier Anastas I. Mikoyan was due in New York this afternoon just a round of conferences before going on to Havana for talks with the adamant Cuban Prime Minister. Western observers in the Soviet capital interpreted his sudden visit as an attempt to bring Mr. Castro into line with the Kennedy-Khrushchev agreement to dismantle the missile bases and send United Nations personnel to Cuba to verify fulfillment of the agreement.

Without mentioning the missile situation, Mr. Castro's aide, Havana Radio said Mr. Castro is standing firm on his demand that the United States give up its naval base at Guantanamo and call off all

See CUBA, Page A-4

DAYS THAT SHOOK THE WORLD
Gen. Carroll Saw Something

By RELMAN MORIN
Associated Press Staff Writer

Shortly after 7 o'clock on the night of Monday, October 15, a general of intelligence picked up the "hot line," a security telephone in the Pentagon, and put through an urgent call.

He said he had "seen something." His voice was taut.

This call, although nobody realized it then, was to unleash a swift and fearful train of events and raise the specter of nuclear war. The climax would come in another telephone call, to President Kennedy, early last Sunday.

In between were the days that shook the world.

It was Lt. Gen. Joseph Carroll, director of the Defense Intelligence Agency, who made that telephone call October 15. He told Deputy Secretary of Defense Roswell L. Gilpatric had seen something disquieting in a new set of photographs of that's's home. It carried Cuba.

A reconnaissance mission had flown over the island on the previous day, Sunday.

Analyzing the pictures, experts detected some scars in the earth, along with evidence of construction work.

Minutes after Gen. Carroll's

LT. GEN. JOSEPH CARROLL
AP Wirephoto

and the rest of us at 7:30 in the morning," Mr. Gilpatric told them.

The experts worked all night. Mr. Gilpatric went to a dinner at the home of Gen. Maxwell Taylor, chairman of the Joint Chiefs of Staff.

By coincidence, Gen. Taylor's guests included most of the men who later participated in the decision-making conferences leading to the "quarantine" of Cuba—members of the Executive Committee of the National Security Council, and authorities from the Defense and State Departments.

Mr. Gilpatric told them about the photographs.

At 7:30 Tuesday morning, these same men met at the Pentagon with Mr. Gilpatric. The photo analysts reported their findings. The evidence of the construction of actual Soviet missile-launching sites still was not regarded as conclusive.

But Mr. McNamara did consider it sufficiently "hard," and disquieting, to call the President. About an hour later a reconnaissance mission was in the President's hands.

Later that day, Mr. Kennedy examined the photographs himself.

His first step was to order a

See EVENTS, Page A-4

BULLETIN
Teachers Vote Option

The Virginia Education Association today voted 591 to 350 in favor of allowing local affiliates to integrate their own membership if they choose. The vote rejected a VEA committee report recommending against local option. The convention then began debating a motion to implement the local option by a constitutional change. (Earlier story Page B-1.)

LOVE'S MEANING; A POINT OF VIEW

LOVE AND ALL ITS splendor means two different things to the teen-ager and the adult. For the former, it's usually infatuation; for the other it can be called love. Eugene Gilbert, writing in today's chapter of Making Marriage More Rewarding, on Page 5-6.

A MELLOW 'SPREAD' is the approaching harvest-time and December holiday season is a red-letter-holiday season is a well-spiced fruit cake, whose The Star's Food Editor, Vitel Faulkner, in an article with recipes on Page D-1.

Have The Star Delivered Daily and Sunday. Dial Lincoln 3-5000.

What the general saw, in reconnaissance photographs of Cuba, were suspicious signs of construction. The discovery of missile-launching sites brought the world to the brink of nuclear war.

Heavy solid lines show the eight rail rapid transit lines recommended by the National Capital Transportation Agency. Dashes show the main bus routes, plus the bus route to Dulles airport which may become a rail line.

Lieutenant General Carroll's official portrait, taken in the late 1960s, at the peak of his power as director of the Defense Intelligence Agency.

General Carroll, grand marshal of the Chicago St. Patrick's Day parade, marches with Mayor Richard Daley in 1970. *(Jeff Lowenthal/© 1970, Newsweek, Inc.)*

At a peace demonstration at Pease Air Force Base in Portsmouth, New Hampshire, I wore a Vietnamese peasant-style hat with the words "Orphaned Boy." A few moments after this picture was taken, the demonstrators fell to the ground, miming a napalm attack.

At a retreat center in 1972, I preach on the theme of a believer's obligation to resist the war.

In an act of passive resistance, I am carried off by police at Hanscom Air Force Base in Lexington, Massachusetts. Scientists at Hanscom had developed electronic sensors that, when used in Vietnam, called in B-52 strikes on civilians and soldiers alike. (*Lexington Minuteman*)

In the early seventies I celebrated Mass at Marsh Chapel, Boston University, with Reverend John F. Smith, BU's Episcopal chaplain.

Joseph Carroll in the mid-1980s, photographed
when the new DIA building was dedicated
in Washington. In 1995 the Air Force named
the OSI building at Andrews Air Force
Base in his honor.

Mary Carroll receives the flag from her husband's coffin at his funeral at
Arlington National Cemetery. The flag is presented by Lieutenant
General Harry E. Soyser, the director of the Defense Intelligence Agency.
It is January 1991, the week the Persian Gulf War began.

houses of Congress. Senator Hubert Humphrey praised the religious community for making the difference in its passage. Lyndon Johnson, with Martin Luther King at his side, signed the act into law. Within months, nine thousand blacks had registered to vote in Dallas County, Alabama. In the next election, Sheriff Jim Clark was voted out of office.

My father, with his steady access to a series of secret Bureau briefings, each called "Martin Luther King: A Current Analysis," had gone from denouncing him as a Communist or Communist dupe, which I'd never credited, to calling him a degenerate, which I'd refused to believe, to labeling him a radical who wanted to overthrow the system — which came to seem the exact and proper truth.

"America is deeply racist and its democracy is flawed both economically and socially . . ." This is King talking to an interviewer in 1968. "The black revolution is much more than a struggle for the rights of Negroes. It is forcing America to face all its inter-related flaws — racism, poverty, militarism and materialism. It is exposing evils that are deeply rooted in the whole structure of our society. It reveals systemic rather than superficial flaws, and suggests that radical reconstruction of society itself is the real issue to be faced."

What Hans Küng had showed me about my Church, Martin Luther King showed me about my country. Finally, in seeing King as a revolutionary figure, my father and I agreed about him. About the desirability of King's "revolution," as about the desirability of Küng's "reform," we disagreed.

By the spring of 1968, I was a local SCLC organizer in Washington of preparations for the Poor People's Campaign. The plan to bring massive numbers of poor people of all races to Washington represented King's shift from the quest for racial equality to the demand for economic justice. The government and the media had been cooperating in the portrayal of the coming of anti-poverty demonstrators as, in David J. Garrow's phrase, "a re-enactment of the Vandals' occupation of Rome." King's broadening of the civil rights agenda to include issues of class, income, and employment, especially paired with his by now strident condemnation of the war in Vietnam, frightened even many of his supporters. There was an edge about King, an open anger and an off-putting impatience, but by now I myself had learned to trust him.

And I trusted the movement too. My own dear Paulist confreres were part of it, even in Memphis, where lately King had been using the Paulist parish, St. Patrick's, as an organizing center for the sanitation workers' strike. My boss in the campaign in Washington was a rotund Italian-American curate named Gino Baroni, a gruff street priest around whom I'd constructed a new idea of what I hoped to become. More than once he tapped me, with others, to help a young SCLC preacher who'd come ahead of King to see to final preparations. His name was Andrew Young.

My main job, again, was to organize teams of seminarians — Protestant, Catholic, Jew — to go out to suburban congregations to soothe fears and drum up support. We collected donated supplies — bedding, tents, camping equipment, cooking utensils — that the tens of thousands of demonstrators would need in Resurrection City, the tent settlement that was going to sprout alongside the reflecting pool. It would not be a one-day affair, or even a week's. The citizens of Resurrection City, a people's lobby inspired by the Bonus Army of the Depression, were going to stay until the government showed signs of hearing them.

The coming Poor People's Campaign was the occasion of my one glimpse of Dr. King in the flesh, when he spoke from the pulpit of a packed National Cathedral. I was standing in the far rear of the elegant structure I'd grown up thinking of as a Protestant rival, but which I now cherished for its Gothic — high Catholic — purity. Even at that distance, the light reflected off King's glistening forehead. His cadences rolled down the nave, filling even the alcoves of the buttress chapels. His appearance there on the last Sunday in March may have been for the scheduled service, but I remember it as a robust gathering of supporters who'd been working so hard to prepare Washington for the campaign. We held each other and rocked the place, singing "We Shall Overcome." I have no specific memory of King's remarks, although I recall catching a distant sense of his gravity, a hint of which had impressed itself on me five years before, when I'd craned toward his televised image in the novices' common room in the New Jersey hills.

Now I know what a period of despondency this was for King. Though my work for him was exhilarating, I recognize that the movement itself, like the country, had developed an air of desperation. Garrow identifies a peroration that King often attached to his remarks during this period: "[The Lord] promised never to leave me, never to leave me alone, no never alone, no never alone. He promised never to leave me, never to leave me alone."

The feeling I had that day was that *I* would not leave him. King was the first public figure, more than either Kennedy, to whom I felt personally devoted. He was the first to whom I was attached as if he were mine — again unlike the Kennedys, who belonged, after all, to my parents. He represented so many elements of a world I was choosing for myself, in contrast to the world into which I was born. Thus, despite King's mood, and despite my bare glimpse of him in the cathedral, I felt a vivid happiness at last to be in his presence. Like Elvis's, in an odd way. And Pope John's. And Hans Küng's.

My father did not know I was there. However much he knew about the world's secrets, Dr. King's, or those of Morris Chilofsky, I'd made sure he knew very little of mine. Coward that I still was, I had not openly proclaimed, to the only one I had to, the content of this new loyalty of mine, this new love.

Five days later — I always think it was Good Friday, but it was the Thursday evening before Palm Sunday — I was patiently explaining to a worried congregation at a Catholic parish in Bethesda, Maryland, that Dr. King's followers were all committed to *satyagraha*, the truth force of nonviolence. Therefore, I assured them, nothing bad would happen at Resurrection City. A nun interrupted us with the news that Dr. King had been shot in Memphis, was reported dead. On the radio they were saying that parts of Washington were already on fire, that fires had been set near the White House.

Later that night, I watched from the roof of the St. Paul's College castle tower as flames lit the night sky only a mile or two away. Smoke obscured the spotlit Washington Monument. Drifting cinders stung my eyes. I heard sirens near and far, and bursts of what I took for gunshots. When I was unable to stand it anymore, I went inside. Despite myself, in grief, I called home, wanting the consolation of a word with my mother. In her way, she was as devastated as I was. Washington was her Jerusalem. The city aflame was an end of the world to her. She described with a shaking voice the air policemen, in battle gear with fixed bayonets, who were posted along Generals' Row. Jeeps were patrolling the base, machine guns mounted on their hoods. Helicopters were landing and unloading more troops. My mother told me to be careful, and she said she loved me, which was what I'd called to hear.

When my father came to the phone, I sensed that he too was staggered. But all he could bring himself to say to me was "See?"

8

HOLY WAR

"IT WAS LIKE paradise at night," my mother said. As she described the scene, I could almost see the flashbulbs amid the sea of candles held aloft by the tens of thousands, as if reflecting the unseen stars above in the balmy autumn night. Ninety thousand people sang and swayed together, a wonder of the faith to this savvy South Side Irish Catholic, a display that marked our true arrival, she said, not just in this country but, after the events of that day, in the eyes of all the nations of the world.

My mother was Cardinal Spellman's personal guest at the Mass at Yankee Stadium on the night of October 4, 1965. The Mass was celebrated by Pope Paul VI, at the end of his historic day-long visit to the United States, the first ever by a sitting pontiff. If, in our audience with Pope John XXIII in the Vatican in 1960, Mom had never felt more proudly Catholic, now, commissioned by Spellman as one of the welcomers of His Holiness, she never felt more proudly American. Present for the pope's warm salutation at St. Patrick's Cathedral that morning, and among the select to receive the Communion bread consecrated by His Holiness that night, my mother was herself the object of true arrival — a woman whose dream, unlike Spellman's, was not in the least defiled by what the pope had said that day.

The purpose of the pope's trip was to address the General Assembly of the United Nations as it celebrated its twentieth year. His speech had stunned the president of the United States, Cardinal Spellman — and also me, watching, as always, on the common room television in Washington. Later I would learn that my father, too busy to make the trip to New York, also watched on TV, in his Pentagon office. My mother would tell me that the pope's words hit Dad like a truck, but when I would ask him about it, he would brush the speech off as if I had given it.

"Peace!" Paul VI said, such a striking figure in white at the green marble rostrum in the hall of the General Assembly. "It is peace which must guide the destinies of peoples and all mankind."

Everyone present knew that he had just come from a private meeting with Lyndon Johnson at the Waldorf-Astoria, and everyone was attuned to the new meaning the word "peace" had acquired in that season. Here was the world leader of Catholicism announcing that he had come to speak in the name not of God or of the Church but "of the young who legitimately dream of a better human race . . . and of the poor, the disinherited, the suffering; of those who hunger and thirst for justice." "Justice" too had acquired new meaning. The pope was not sounding like a pope. Where was his emphasis on order? on tradition? on proper respect for authority? Why was he speaking for the young and the poor? And what about Communism?

His visit took place seven months after the launching of Operation Rolling Thunder and less than three months after the first massive infusion of GIs into South Vietnam. By now Lyndon Johnson and Robert McNamara, relying on intelligence provided by Richard Helms at CIA and by my father at DIA, had dispatched nearly 200,000 troops, with another 100,000 soon to follow. I was quite aware of the fact that my father had traveled to Vietnam only months before, in July, to form his own impressions of the conflict. He had refused to share them with me.

Others were less reticent about making their views known. A "Declaration of Conscience" opposing the bombing had appeared, signed by hundreds of people including Martin Luther King, Benjamin Spock, and Linus Pauling. Only two recognizably Catholic names appeared on the list: the Reverends Daniel and Philip Berrigan, one a Jesuit, the other a Josephite. The "Declaration" was followed by an event that amounted to the birth of the antiwar movement. On a spring day in 1965, twenty-five thousand people gathered at the Washington Monument. The day's climax came when a throng marched eighty abreast down the Mall to present a "Petition to Congress." "We call upon you," it read, "to end, not extend, the war in Vietnam." It was a respectful act of democratic appeal, although the political establishment mostly agreed with Senator John Stennis, who denounced the demonstration as "shameful and deplorable."

Cardinal Spellman denounced the Berrigans for participating in the public protests, and he led the chorus of support for the military escalation, declaring, "Less than victory is inconceivable." But the peace movement grew. Within days of the pope's appearance in New York, more than 100,000 Americans would demonstrate against the juiced-up war in nearly a thousand cities. Already people crying "Peace!" were being labeled traitors. Even the liberal Hubert Humphrey said that the "international Communist movement" was behind the antiwar campaign, and establishment voices like James Reston of the *New York Times* charged that second-guessing U.S. military initiatives was "not promoting peace, but postponing it."

It was into this maelstrom that Paul VI stepped when, to his host's horror, he deliberately chose to make a single unambiguous point before the General Assembly. He felt, he said, "like a messenger who, after a long journey, finally succeeded in delivering the letter that had been entrusted to him." He raised his fist above his head. He was speaking in French. As I recall it, the droning low voice of the interpreter hesitated, as if to let these words leap unmediated from the pontiff's mouth. Even I could understand: "*Jamais plus la guerre! Jamais plus la guerre!*"

"War no more," the interpreter put in then. "War never again."

I thought of my mother in the pope's presence. That night at Yankee Stadium, as if to be sure he was understood, he said, "First of all, you must love peace. Second, you must serve the cause of peace." My mother, with her heart wide open, already afraid for her sons, three of whom were home still, heading for the draft — how could she not hear such words with gratitude? If the pope was calling for peace, then how could peace not follow?

I thought of my father, and immediately imagined him deflecting the pope's words by pointing out that they were not spoken *ex cathedra*. "If you wish to be brothers," His Holiness said, "let the arms fall from your hands. You cannot love while holding offensive weapons." Within weeks, I would quote these words to my father, not in any spirit of defiance — I was yet miles from defiance — but in a state of genuine confusion. In that first year of the war, I worked to bend my mind into the shape required to support it, not just for my father's sake but for Lyndon Johnson's. He was our hero of the Great Society and "We shall overcome." I worked to support the war for my own sake too. The Air Force was my dream city. "Off we go into the wild blue yonder" was still music to me.

But I had sensed, with the onset of Rolling Thunder, that the order of my moral universe was at stake, and I wanted to protect it. So contrary words from the pope's mouth, unlike anything from, say, Senator Fulbright's or Rabbi Heschel's or even Martin

Luther King's, shook me to the core. Who was the pope if not the avatar of the order I had, at my father's invitation, put at the center of my life? Not the center, actually, for the operative symbol was a pyramid, but the top.

That is why, not long after the pope's appearance at the United Nations, I found an excuse to get permission to visit my parents out at Bolling. My brother Joe was away at graduate school, and Brian was at college in Massachusetts. Dennis, a dayhop at a local Catholic high school, was already yanking our parents' chain with the length of his hair. At dinner, it was apparent that a new and unpleasant mood had settled over the family, and what seemed remarkable was that not even the pope's visit could be casually discussed. After dinner, Dennis and Kevin disappeared, then so did Mom. Though I was due back at the seminary, I went with Dad into the living room. To my surprise, the orderly, without being asked, followed with a glass of Scotch on a silver tray. My father hadn't made a habit of drinking after dinner, but things were changing. The orderly offered me a drink. As required, I declined. When Dad and I were alone, I asked him, finally, what he'd made of the pope's speech. He answered smoothly, "His Holiness wants what we want. We are all working for peace. His Holiness said, 'Drop your weapons.' But in the real world, our weapons keep the peace. That's what deterrence is all about."

"But Vietnam —"

"His Holiness does his job by holding up the ideal. We do ours by seeing how it applies in a specific situation, which assumes information and expertise His Holiness doesn't have."

I was incapable at that moment of hearing it, but my father's dispassionate response included the seeds of dissent from papal teaching that would infuriate him a few years later when the issue had shifted to birth control.

My father's authority overrode the beginning of my doubt, which was what I'd hoped would happen when I came home. But then he cast his head in the direction of our neighbor's house, where Curtis LeMay had lived when he was vice chief of staff. "'Peace Is Our Profession,'" Dad said, citing LeMay's SAC motto. But the reference to LeMay stopped me. "I never asked you," I said. "What did you think when he said we should just drop the H-bomb on Hanoi?"

My father stared at me. His blue uniform shirt was open at the collar, his blue tie loosened, his steel-gray hair not a strand out of place. Smoke wafted up from the cigarette between his fingers. I focused on his shiny Rolex watch. He looked at me in silence for a long time. I had to stifle the urge to bring up something else — the White Sox, Jack Nicklaus, whatever. I had no idea what he would say, but I knew from the rare intimacies of a few years before — Berlin, Cuba, not Vietnam — that he was no more able than I to contemplate that manmade sun, its mushroom cloud, vaporized cities, radioactive dust swirling around the globe, the incineration all at once of millions, including, as he'd put it to me that night driving home from the Pentagon, "Mom and the boys." Fear of the Bomb, when he'd let me see his, had made us friends, friends forever. He was like me in this, not like Curtis LeMay, of that I was certain.

Finally he answered: "You never tell your enemy what you're going to do or what you're not going to do. If they think we might use the Bomb against them, good."

"But —"

"Jimmy, you know these are things I can't talk to you about."

"But you *have* talked to me about it." I wanted to add, And you made me afraid — I'm still afraid.

I think my father knew what was in my mind. Sadness clouded his eyes, and he said, "Well, I shouldn't have."

To which I wanted urgently to reply, But Dad, I loved you

when you spoke to me of these things, and I felt your love for me.

I said no such thing, of course. And if once I had caught a germ of fear from him, what I caught now was that sadness. Neither he nor I would ever shake it.

After returning from the papal spectacle in New York, my mother told me all about it. Cardinal Spellman, she said, had asked about me — Jimmy Carroll. "He's still counting on ordaining you." And I was still capable of being thrilled at the prospect. Alas, she reported that he was looking awfully frail. The pope had even taken him by the elbow as they mounted the sanctuary stairs at St. Patrick's. His Holiness had called the aged Spellman "our beloved son." From gossip in the seminary, I had picked up the undercurrent of something entirely other flowing between the pope and the archbishop of New York. And there was the LBJ-insulting content of the pope's speech. My usually alert mother was focused on her own particular agenda, Spellman's ordaining me. She had chosen to ignore the humiliation the cardinal surely felt.

Within weeks the pope would embarrass Spellman again by rejecting his advice to ignore Martin Luther King. I knew nothing of those machinations, but certainly, given my father's access to Bureau information, his assessment of papal naiveté could only have been reinforced when Paul VI granted an audience to King. J. Edgar Hoover would say, "I can't believe the pope would meet with that degenerate." My mother, like many other Catholics wary of civil rights, would take the pope's meeting with King as an endorsement she could not ignore.

The pope was taking his people by surprise again and again, but there were no surprises between him and Spellman. They had known each other for thirty years. As Montini, and now as Paul VI, the pope knew very well things that others did not know. The full drama of papal defiance on Spellman's own turf cannot be appreciated except in the context of a larger story. It was untold at the time, although the pope surely knew it and so, probably, did the New York priests named Berrigan. It was the story of how, before it was Lyndon Johnson's war, or even Robert McNamara's, the war in Vietnam belonged to my mother's friend, my father's ally, my brother's "enema," and my own designated godfather in the priesthood. The Vietnam War began as Spellman's.

Among the many cursed moments that led to the American tragedy in Vietnam, none looms more fatefully than the meeting in 1950 between Cardinal Spellman and Ngo Dinh Diem, an obscure Vietnamese mandarin exiled because of opposition both to the Communists — Ho Chi Minh's Vietminh troops had killed one of Diem's brothers — and to the French. Another of his brothers, Ngo Dinh Thuc, was a Roman Catholic bishop, and it was he who introduced Diem to Spellman.

Diem was a Catholic mystic who had taken a lifelong vow of celibacy. At the time, he lived at the Maryknoll seminary in Ossining, New York, just up the Hudson from the city. He had also lived in seminaries in Belgium and, upon first coming to America, in New Jersey. Spellman was immediately taken with Diem. Shortly after they had met, still in 1950, the cardinal arranged a meeting of the Vietnamese exile and the head of the Asia desk at the State Department in Washington, a young official named Dean Rusk.

Catholics in Vietnam were disillusioned with French colonial rule, but they could be counted on as opponents of the Communists, who had taken the lead in the anti-French revolution. Thus, though Catholics amounted to less than 10 percent of the country's population, they seemed a potential base for a "third way" between colonialism and Communism. Such an innovation could be the key to solidifying Western influence throughout the postcolonial world. This humane wish was the beginning of America's interest in Vietnam. Through Spellman, Ngo Dinh Diem seemed a potential guarantor of U.S. influence.

By the time of Dien Bien Phu, in May of 1954, Diem was the beneficiary of an elaborate, mainly Catholic network of American support. Spellman had recruited to his cause Joe Kennedy and his son the senator from Massachusetts; "Wild Bill" Donovan, the former head of the Office of Strategic Services; and Henry Luce, husband to the most famous Catholic convert in America. Diem had met with editorial boards at the great newspapers and lectured at prestigious universities, especially Catholic ones. When the U.S. government proposed him as prime minister to the Vietnamese emperor Bao Dai after the French defeat, Diem's support ran from Eisenhower's Washington to Pius XII's Vatican.

In June, Diem returned to Vietnam as the head of government. His brother Thuc became archbishop of Saigon. That August, Spellman addressed the American Legion convention in Washington, and he made the first major American declaration of support for the new regime, saying that its failure would be "taps for the buried hopes of freedom in Southeast Asia . . . bartering our liberties for lunacies, betraying the sacred trust of our forefathers, becoming serfs and slaves to the Red rulers' godless goons."

Tom Dooley, a Spellman favorite and a Navy doctor operating out of Haiphong, soon began describing the plight of Catholic refugees being driven by the Reds from their homes in the North. A pious Catholic, Dooley was instantly taken as a hero of the Cold War. His best-selling books, which described the torment of Vietnamese Catholics, and his broad-based appeal for funds made Dooley famous. Not incidentally, his reports caused most Americans to believe that Vietnam was a Catholic country under Communist siege — an Asian Poland, you might say. Later, Robert McNamara would accept this fiction — he said so at Harvard in 1995 — and so would others of the best and the brightest as they stepped onto the slippery slope leading down to an endless, lightless tunnel. Dooley, who died in 1961 just as John Kennedy ignited the torch of freedom, would be put forward for sainthood by Spellman, but his candidacy would later be swamped in revelations of the secret ties between his efforts and those of the CIA. The post–Dien Bien Phu exodus of "terrified Catholics" from North Vietnam to South had in fact been deliberately staged by American intelligence agents, not caused by the vicious Reds. The CIA wanted the hundreds of thousands of Catholics in Haiphong and Hanoi to move because Ngo Dinh Diem needed them as a political base in overwhelmingly Buddhist Saigon. Tom Dooley, whether as a dupe or a villain, had engineered the first big lie of the United States in Vietnam.

By 1956 Spellman had succeeded in solidifying the commitment to Diem of the liberal establishment. Robert McNamara, in his memoir *In Retrospect*, would cite a speech that year by Senator John Kennedy as determinative. "Vietnam represents the cornerstone of the Free World in Southeast Asia," Kennedy said. "It is our offspring. We cannot abandon it, we cannot ignore its needs." Formerly French Vietnam was by no stretch of the imagination our "offspring," but Ngo Dinh Diem certainly was. Early American support of his regime was channeled through Spellman, with millions of dollars in U.S. aid being disbursed by the Catholic Relief Service. The Church was the rock upon which America intended to build its new kind of Free World nation.

Unfortunately, whatever the merits of America's romantic search for a "third way" between Communism and colonialism, the concrete form it took was an embrace of a dangerous illusion. Instead of leading a democratic government, Diem ruled through his malevolent family: his brothers Thuc, Ngo Dinh Can, and Ngo Dinh Nhu, the conspiratorial head of the secret police, and his wife, the nefarious Madame Nhu. Lyndon Johnson would call Diem "the Winston Churchill of Asia," but he was more like its "Papa Doc" Duvalier, only far more heavily armed and funded by his U.S. patrons. While the American government credited Diem with cracking down on Communists and jailing dissidents, he was mainly waging an ever more vicious war against Buddhists. He had the Catholic faith of the Inquisition, and he sought to impose it especially on rural peasants, who unlike city dwellers were not beneficiaries of lavish American aid. Diem was the Vietminh's dream, driving more and more of the populace into its arms. Americans expected him to be a democrat, but he was a true medieval Catholic of the kind that even the Vatican knew only in nostalgia. Diem believed that he ruled by the will of God.

McNamara cites the U.S. support of Diem as the critical first mistake. "That he had studied at a Catholic seminary in New Jersey in the early 1950s seemed evidence that he shared Western values. As we got closer and closer to the situation, however, we came to learn otherwise . . . We totally misjudged that."

Buddhists staged a huge demonstration on May 8, 1963, in Saigon to protest Archbishop Ngo Dinh Thuc's edict banning Buddhist flags on Buddha's birthday. Nine people were killed when the Catholic-led army fired at the protesters. The unrest only mounted, culminating in early June, when Thich Quang Duc, a Buddhist monk, set himself on fire on a Saigon street. Douglas Pike wrote that he could see "the whole fabric of Vietnamese society coming apart." Around the world, and even in Washington, the immolated monk — Madame Nhu's infamous "Barbecued Bonze" — was seen as a true sacrament of Diem's failure. A few months later, in what McNamara would call "the fateful fall of 1963," Diem and his brother Nhu, abandoned even by Spellman, were killed in a coup the Kennedy administration tacitly approved of, if it did not outright engineer it.

Diem and Nhu died on All Souls' Day, wearing the cassocks of Catholic priests — a putative disguise, but also an epiphany of the entwined relationship between their brutal failure and their religious hubris. Their brother Archbishop Thuc escaped by having gone to Rome for a session of the Vatican Council. He would never return to Vietnam. Thuc had not been reprimanded by the Vatican for the fascist Catholicism, the blood of which greased the skids of the coming American war. However, when he later dared embrace the cause of radical traditionalist Archbishop Marcel Lefèbvre, rejecting, for example, the use of the vernacular in the liturgy, Thuc was excommunicated.

By the time Diem was dead, and in large part because of the way he died, the United States, according to McNamara, had forfeited its freedom to stay out of the quagmire. Diem had been, in JFK's word, America's offspring. Alas, so had been Diem's murder. In his last days, Kennedy was haunted by it, and when three weeks later he himself was killed, Madame Nhu said now we're even. Lyndon Johnson and his advisers shouldered the burden of the war in Vietnam, trying to bring order to chaos, for a number of reasons — not the least of which was that we had caused that chaos. Washington hoped to cancel the moral debt of America's central, if misguided, role in the rise and fall of Ngo Dinh Diem.

Cardinal Spellman, meanwhile, had not allowed himself a second thought. As the war became Americanized, he became even more devoted to it. He became Curtis LeMay in a red soutane. He traveled to Vietnam frequently: early to dedicate a Marian basilica he had funded; later, armed with "Holy

Smokes," to spend Christmases with grateful GIs. It was during a Christmas visit to Vietnam that he made his famous statement of faith, "My country right or wrong." The grunts who cheered him for his unthinking loyalty to the mystery of what had put them there had no more way of knowing than I did, as I looked forward to his ordaining me, that central to that mystery was Spellman himself. If some Catholics went on to act as if they bore special responsibility for ending the war, perhaps it was because they did.

Less than a month after the pope's visit to the United Nations, on November 2, 1965, two years to the day after the murders of the Ngo brothers, a thirty-one-year-old Baltimore man set out for a drive with his infant daughter. Saying goodbye to his wife, he added the question, "What can I do to make them stop the war?" As a new father, the man had been particularly upset by the deaths of Vietnamese children caused by American bombs. From Baltimore he drove to Washington, and then across the Potomac into Arlington. It was rush hour when he pulled into a parking lot at the Pentagon. Still holding his daughter, he poured kerosene onto his clothes. At the last moment he put the baby aside, then struck a match on his shoe, igniting himself. His name was Norman Morrison. He died quickly.

Immediately above Morrison was the third-floor office of Secretary of Defense Robert S. McNamara, who, according to his biographer Deborah Shapley, noticed when "a column of orange flame leapt twelve feet high." McNamara went to his window and, realizing what had happened, was stunned. Years later, he told Shapley that the suicide was "a personal tragedy for me."

In his memoir, McNamara would write about Morrison's death: "I reacted to the horror of his action by bottling up my emotions and avoided talking about them with anyone — even my family. I knew Marg and our three children shared many of Morrison's feelings about the war, as did the wives and children of several of my cabinet colleagues. And I believed I understood and shared his thoughts. There was much Marg and I and the children should have talked about, yet at moments like this I often turn inward instead — it is a grave weakness. The episode created tension at home that only deepened as dissent and criticism of the war continued to grow."

I cannot read McNamara's words now without wanting to take them as an expression of my father's feelings — even if he never admitted to them. My father's office was down the hall from McNamara's, so perhaps he saw the pillar of fire too. At the time, I wanted to call my father, as much to console him for the shock he must have felt, I think, as to seek help in dealing with my own. But I was afraid to call. "Kook" was a word I'd heard Dad apply to protesters, and, confused as I was by Morrison's act, it would have been unbearable to hear him dismissed as that, even if my father were to do so out of his own version of McNamara's bottled-up emotion.

Much was made of the fact that Morrison was a Quaker, as if his membership in that heretofore benign but exotic sect kept him at a remove from the rest of us, as if he were a saffron-robed Buddhist. As with those earlier Saigon immolations, I was incapable of reading such news, or of seeing reports of it on television, without thinking of my father. I always thought of him at such times with the deepest feeling of love. My father was the best man I knew, and to me he was always watching from the sidelines of whatever field I was playing on. We were arguing about civil rights by now, but not about Vietnam. My father was no warmonger. Hadn't I heard his voice shake with fear at the thought of war? The course being set in Vietnam was being set, in some small part, by him. So it had to be right. Despite a visceral, if horrified, sympathy, I convinced myself in a snap that

Norman Morrison was a victim of his own naive assumptions. After all, Quaker or not, wasn't suicide an act of violence? And wasn't this particular form of it, in the presence of a child, an act of savagery?

The distance between me and the likes of Morrison was one thing, but then, a week later, no doubt in response to the self-immolation at the Pentagon, the thing happened again. On November 9 Roger Laporte, twenty-one, set fire to himself at the United Nations buildings in New York, the site of the pope's speech the month before. Laporte was a member of Dorothy Day's Catholic Worker community on Chrystie Street near the Brooklyn Bridge — a soup kitchen I had visited myself. The Catholic Workers were our heroes, and news of this one worker's act was shattering beyond anything that had preceded it. I recall standing in the front hallway of the oldest wing of St. Paul's College, reading the *Washington Post*. It was very early in the morning, and I had stopped here intending only to catch the headlines on my way to chapel. Then I saw the front-page story about Laporte. "I am a Catholic Worker," he said before dying. "I am antiwar, all wars. I did this as a religious act."

Religious act? A Catholic? I carried the question into morning prayer with me, feeling a new level of anguish. Jesus on the wall above me had never seemed so wretched. What did Laporte know about war, about religion, that I didn't know? I remember furious arguments among my fellow Paulists after Laporte's death. The very men who'd reacted to Norman Morrison with a detached horror responded to the young Catholic with extreme feeling. Some denounced the suicide. Others denounced the war. The conflict that began that day would go on for years, and I realized soon enough from my place on its margin that I could make the arguments for either side better than anybody. Inside I was screaming: I am antiwar, all wars! And: I love the U.S. Air Force! But to all appearances, I was numb.

I was already writing poetry and taking cues from poems I read. George Starbuck's poem "Of Late" would stun me: "Norman Morrison, Quaker of Baltimore, Maryland, burned what he said was himself. You, Robert McNamara, burned what you said was a concentration of the Enemy Aggressor." Starbuck would be my teacher years later. Everywhere I turned, it seemed, the formerly pallid art of poetry felt subversive. My ideal of priesthood had been the Jesuit poet Daniel Berrigan. His first collection, *Time Without Number*, had won the Lamont Prize in 1957. Marianne Moore had called his work "literary magic." Berrigan was the rare Catholic writer, cleric or not, who'd established a serious reputation outside the narrow subculture, and that alone had drawn me to him. I had imitated his poems with poems of my own. I had used his writing as focal points of my religious meditation. I already thought of Berrigan as our living Gerard Manley Hopkins. When I studied with Allen Tate in the summer of 1966, he would tell me that Daniel Berrigan was "one of our best poets."

Berrigan's emergence as the first Catholic of the antiwar movement had already disoriented me. Because of him, even before the war began to cloud my dream of the future, the image of the military chaplain had begun to bow in my mind before that of the priest-poet. "The priest calls to the poet" — these lines from Karl Rahner I'd taped to my mirror — "The poet calls to the priest." And also this, from Goethe: "To the true poet God has given the mission to say what he suffers." I could not know it, but in Daniel Berrigan, meanwhile, the priest-poet was bowing to the image of the prophet.

Roger Laporte, it turned out, was a friend of Berrigan's. I was in no way prepared for it when I read that the Jesuit, during a funeral Mass offered at the Catholic Worker house, defended Laporte's suicide. "His death was offered," Berrigan said in a eulogy, "so that others may live."

I thought Berrigan's statement was terribly misguided. What, we were now to have a rash of self-immolations? How would that advance the cause of peace? The great Thomas Merton rebuked Berrigan, and so, far more predictably, did Cardinal Spellman. He was in Rome, at the Council, but he ordered Berrigan out of New York. The Jesuit authorities complied, effectively banishing Berrigan, although purportedly sending him on a tour of mission outposts in Latin America. The news of this disciplining caused an uproar among as yet unmobilized Catholics, which confused me even further.

At that time, the severest critics of LBJ, the war, and now Spellman were so full of certitude and self-righteousness that I found it impossible to identify with them. The arguments raged around me. Laporte was criticized or defended, and then so was David Miller, another young Catholic Worker who became notorious that season — for immolating his draft card. Daniel Berrigan's brother Philip called Miller's act "the highest expression of loyalty" to his country, but if that was so, what expression of loyalty was it that kids like us were offering by the tens of thousands already — the ones who'd shipped out and now were stepping on shit-encrusted punji sticks and homemade land mines? What would Laporte, Miller, or either Berrigan be to them?

That fall of the unprecedented events was not over yet. Catholic Americans reacted with outrage to the disciplining of Daniel Berrigan. Much in the way that Spellman had made the film *Baby Doll* an overnight sensation by condemning it, he had made the Jesuit an instant national figure. Hunger strikers protested at a cathedral in New Hampshire and at Notre Dame. Pickets carried signs outside St. Patrick's Cathedral which read, "Merry Christmas, Dan Berrigan, Wherever You Are" and "End Power Politics in the Church." There were demonstrations near my own St. Paul's College, over at Catholic University, but — this was nine months after I had first picketed for Martin Luther King at the White House — I could not bring myself to participate.

Neither could I ignore the seismic jolt it was to open the *New York Times* on December 12, 1965, and see a full-page ad criticizing Cardinal Spellman and demanding Berrigan's return. The ad was signed by nearly a thousand people, many of them priests. The real shock came when they forced Spellman to back down. Berrigan returned from his exile. He and others like him had only just begun, while — and here was what Berrigan's victory meant — the likes of Spellman were finished. The bold people who took out the ad identified themselves as the Committee for Daniel Berrigan, and despite my welter of reservations and disagreements, I felt physically sick that morning not to be one of them.

A few weeks later, at Christmas, I went to Generals' Row again. I'd already had one turkey dinner at midday, but I got the special permission needed to leave the seminary afterward. Mom delayed the family meal for me. As the orderly began to serve us, my four brothers and parents and I laughed about my second supper, but a somber mood inevitably fell over the table. Our thin chat — the bowl games, the Redskins, Paul Hornung, Sam Huff — subtly underscored the thick subject of which no one knew how to speak. Joe was well along in a Ph.D. program in psychology. Still severely crippled from his polio, he was decidedly classified 4-F. As always, Joe made me feel uneasy, and I had not quite grown up enough to understand that my uneasiness was coming from me, not him. Brian was home from college. He'd found his niche as an athlete and all-around fun guy. His girlfriend, Vicki French, was a nursing student in Washington. She was the daughter of an Air Force colonel, a classmate from Wiesbaden. They'd fallen in love forever back then and made a match that would outlast the one their classmate Priscilla Beaulieu had made with Elvis. Priscilla and Elvis had recently announced their engagement, proving that the wildest rumors can be true.

Dennis was a senior in high school. His hair was too long for my parents' taste, but he had quietly defied their orders to cut it. And today no one was going to make an issue of it. At this meal he was reserved and unforthcoming, the brother who had changed the most since I'd been gone. He was the one I felt I knew the least. But he was also the one who would ask me, after we left the table, if I had read Camus. We would discuss *The Rebel* briefly, and I would offer to send him a paper I had written. Kevin, the youngest, with his red-haired happiness, gave us all a point of unity. He was in early high school, but he could have been an infant for the uncomplicated affection in which we held him. Kevin alone, then and always, had no curves aimed at him, and none came from him either. When he was part of the gathering, we were a family.

Presiding at one end of the table was Mom, and at the other, Dad. The two multipaned windows opposite the table opened out on the river valley. But the curtains were closed, and so it was my mind's eye that saw the blue runway lights of the airstrip and, in the far distance, the lights of National Airport. I pictured planes landing and taking off, landing and taking off. Magnificent machines. Cruciform objects of my love.

At this dinner table, in the past, back when Berlin was its flashpoint self, we would sit arrayed like this, and occasionally the Red Telephone in our parents' bedroom would ring, with its shrill auxiliary bell sounding in the kitchen. The sergeant would push open the swinging door, an alert new blade of light in his eyes — no cook now, no servant, but an aide de camp, a general's man. Dad would touch his napkin to his mouth and get up without a word. The hot line to the Pentagon rang for only one of two reasons: to announce the start of war or to test the system. When the phone rang at dinner time, Dad would disappear and a stark silence would settle on the table. Even little Kevin seemed to know what was never more than an inch below the surface of this life.

Me? Especially after that night in 1960, I always expected Dad to reappear for a moment, kiss us each quickly, then go away forever. What always happened instead was that Mom would break the silence with a simple order: "Eat your potatoes, Jimmy." "Elbow off the table, Kevin." Saying, in effect, Eat, live, be alive.

That's what she was doing now, helping the orderly put the heaping platters on the table. When the sergeant had disappeared into the kitchen again, my father looked over and asked me to say grace. A first. Heat rushed to my face, but I bowed my head and recited the rote offering. Improvised prayers had come into vogue, but I knew better than to try that here. Nevertheless, the familiar words I spoke unleashed other words, and despite myself, especially despite my mother's clear though unspoken wish, I turned to my father as we all finished crossing ourselves — all but Dennis, who had not touched a hand to his forehead or heart. I blurted, "Dad, what did you think when that man died at the Pentagon?"

His eyes filled with the sadness I'd seen before. They were hard on me. I felt the weight of his judging disappointment.

Mom, serving plates, broke in sharply, "We're not discussing that."

"We don't need to discuss it, Mary. But Jimmy has a right to an answer." Dad stared at me and spoke slowly. "What do we all want? The end of the war, right?"

"Right." I was grateful that his voice sounded so calm and even, which seemed a concession. Already, without knowing it, I'd accepted the hateful stereotypes of the peaceniks. This was no warmonger, this was Dad.

He leaned toward me to make his statement. Not a discussion, not an argument. A statement. "The war will end," he said, "when the Communists see it's futile to resist us. That's why we've gone in so strong. A quick, strong attack. A bloody nose. Bang. Now — and here's the point — protests like Norman Morrison's, however sincerely motivated, or like the kooks who burn the flag —"

"I don't believe in burning the flag, Dad."

"— the *kooks* who burn the flag — they send exactly the wrong message to Hanoi. They give the Communists reason to keep fighting. Does that promote peace or postpone it?"

"Postpone it, I guess."

"So does that answer your question?"

"Yes, sir," I said, convincing myself that it had.

And that was it — Christmas dinner, 1965, on Generals' Row, also known, coincidentally, as Westmoreland Avenue. Except for this. In the silence after my father's efficient statement, Mom began to serve a plate for Dennis. He reached across and stopped her. "No turkey, Mom," he said.

"What do you mean, no turkey?"

"I'll have potatoes and the beans. I love your beans. I don't eat meat."

"You what?"

We all stared at him. I was amazed at how cool he was, sitting with his hair down nearly to his collar, not even blushing.

"I'm a vegetarian," he said, so simply. A first-time declaration, devoid of anger. Yet it was a firm response, I saw at once, to that season of blood. So clear. So uncomplicated. So true. And so unlike me. How I envied him. Dennis would not eat meat again, ever. I would envy him often. Me? I was eating turkey for the second time that day.

Once, at such a meal, we discussed Robert McNamara. I had met him a few times when I went to the Pentagon to pick up Dad. There was the time, one summer during college, I was stopped for speeding by an air policeman on the main road of the base. The AP was hardly older than I was. He blanched when he saw my ID, tagging me as a general's kid. Only then — dope — did he notice the stars on the bumper. There was no speed limit on base for this car. But the AP had started something, and I sensed his making up his mind to finish it. He wrote the ticket and gave it to me.

"Now what?" I asked.

"It goes to your CO," he replied. In that innocent time, CO meant commanding officer, not conscientious objector.

"My old man?"

"No, I mean, I guess it goes to *his* CO."

"That's the secretary of defense."

The AP stared, and I felt sick as I realized that he wasn't backing off. A few nights later, Dad came home steaming. He took me into the side room and told me how, at a meeting with the brass, McNamara had announced a grave crisis. After a weighty moment, he'd produced the traffic ticket. Laughter all around. But it was no joke to my father. He grounded me.

At a family dinner, another time, somebody said, "McNamara's Irish, isn't he? Why isn't he Catholic?"

We all looked at Dad, who had no answer.

From her end of the table, Mom said, "He's a souper."

"What?"

"Someone in his family took the soup."

Dad laughed. "Go away, Mary."

"No, really." She seemed serious. She explained that during the Potato Famine the British offered soup to starving peasants, but only if they converted to Protestantism. Those Catholics who did so were called soupers. Mom finished the story by fixing me in her stare. "And a curse settled on the village of anyone who took the soup. From then on, no son of that village would ever receive the grace of a vocation to the priesthood."

Jesus Christ, enough! Enough already! And what a blusher I was. The heat in my face, Jesus! But I remember that my father rescued me by cutting my mother short. "Never mind that, Mary," he said. "The point is that Mr. McNamara is a good man."

Mister. It was the only way I ever heard my father refer to McNamara. The formality that this implied, and the subservience, did not disguise what I'd sensed early on in my father's feelings for his boss, what would only deepen as the years went by, and the wound opened — an admiration, a pride of association, an absolute loyalty that eventually would repulse me, which was how little I knew.

In September of 1966, in a ceremony with my classmates, before the superior general of the order, I took my final promises as a Paulist, a lifelong solemn commitment to poverty, chastity, and obedience. I moved through the paces in the sanctuary — kneeling, standing, genuflecting — showing, I am certain, no sign of the inner anguish I felt. If I could take such vows at all, it was only because of the fervor with which I assented to the superior general's rubrical prayer for me: "What God has begun in you, may He bring to completion." Amen.

My mother and father attended the evening ceremony on their way to a reception at the White House. Dad was resplendent in dress whites, three silver stars gleaming on his shoulders. The seminary chapel gleamed too: floor stripped and freshly waxed, statues dusted, every pew polished that afternoon. What zeal we had! When the service was completed, having handed over to my religious superior, if not to God, what I was sure was the rest of my life, I sought out my parents, who didn't have time to stay for our collation, since they had to get to Lyndon Johnson's. But my father, at least, would remember what his son had done that day, because his magnificent white uniform, in which he'd sat on our magnificent oak benches, was stained from the shoulders to the seat of his trousers with cherry-hued furniture polish. After a terrible moment, my mother defused the situation by saying, "Thank God the president is a Democrat." My father, who I would before long associate only with stony rage, reacted with a crack about his long-standing bad luck with uniforms. To my knowledge, President Johnson never mentioned the stains.

Increasingly, though, I found it impossible not to mention that other stain. On some holiday or other I sat at the dining room table and dropped the words "Bach Mai" on the sheen of our chatter. The *New York Times* correspondent Harrison Salisbury sent dispatches back from Hanoi in 1966, the first solid reports that the American government's denials of widespread civilian casualties were false. Bach Mai was the name of a hospital that had been bombed.

"What about it, Dad?"

"You think our flyers *deliberately* targeted a hospital?" I see his fork suspended in midair.

I push against him. "But you said —"

"No." He cuts me off. "If one of our pilots *deliberately* bombed a hospital and I found out about it, what would happen?"

I do not know anymore, so I say nothing.

"What would happen?" He is really angry now. He clutches the fork in a fist.

I lower my eyes, as if the shame is mine. "You'd have him court-martialed."

"You're damn right I would. You're goddamned right I would. Bach Mai was a tragedy. Don't use those poor people as a ploy. And while you're at it, tell your friends that the North Vietnamese put an airfield near that hospital, right next to it. The airfield was the target! The hospital was hit because the NVA put the target there. Tell your kook friends that!"

"I don't have any kook friends, Dad."

"I don't want to hear 'Bach Mai' from you again. Is that clear?"

It was, and he wouldn't. By the time Bach Mai hospital was bombed again, during Nixon's Christmas bombing of 1972, when far more than any mere airfield was targeted, Dad was out of the war, and we weren't talking anyway.

Years later, as the twentieth anniversary of the war's end approached, I happened to meet a pair of pediatricians from Hanoi who were visiting Boston. I asked them about Bach Mai. A man and a woman, they exchanged a wary glance. "That was our hospital," the man said.

"You were there?"

The 1972 raid came at twilight, they said. Neither was at the hospital at the time, but on hearing of the attack, they rushed to help. One American historian reports that doctors at Bach Mai had to amputate the limbs of some of the wounded in order to free them from debris.

The Christmas bombing, beginning December 18, went on for eleven days and nights. A hundred thousand bombs were dropped in three thousand sorties, mainly of my once beloved B-52s. The raids were the highest concentration of firepower in the war, a penultimate savagery whose motive — our surrender agreement was already worked out and would be signed within weeks — was simply to punish the Vietnamese for defeating us.

The "Vietnamese." In the presence of those doctors, who did not really want to speak of this, the ancient abstraction of that word became the particular children who had been their patients. I thought of Maya Lin's piercing black memorial in Washington, how it had helped soothe America's pain. But that wailing wall is carved with not one single name of the three million Vietnamese who died.

On an impulse I asked the doctors to walk with me the few blocks to Boston Common. When I explained that I wanted to show them something precious, they agreed. A few minutes later we were standing on the side of one of the Common's graceful hills, below a young but stalwart oak tree. It was a mild spring afternoon. Passersby moved swiftly along a footpath, unaware of us. The tree's twigs and branches were tipped with greenish gold, the early buds of its rebirth. I had often stopped at that tree since witnessing its planting twenty years before, with fifty veterans of the antiwar movement.

Now I said almost nothing in explanation, but the woman pressed my arm firmly. She told me she would bring the tree's image home and keep it always. The man drew close to me on my other side. He insisted on being photographed with a branch of the tree by his solemn face.

At the base of the tree is a plain stone marker that reads, "For Hai and Sacha, Age 9. For All Vietnamese Children Who Died in the War. And for Ourselves. 1975."

I knew so little. To me, my father was a general, pure and simple. But to his fellow generals, he was anything but. Ever since 1947 when he'd been forced on them by Stuart Symington and Harry Truman, generals had looked askance at my father, a general who had not served in World War II! An Air Force general who could not fly a plane! A general who had not been tempered by the hazing of rising through the ranks! Those who associated with Dad as colleagues in security or intelligence work had always come to revere him, but more broadly in the Pentagon he had remained a kind of pariah general. His standing as such had only intensified with the arrival of Kennedy and McNamara.

Among the new administration's first problems was one of its own making. Candidate Kennedy had been taken in by dire Air Force warnings of a "missile gap," a U.S. inferiority to Soviet ICBMs. Moscow, after all, had beaten us in the race to put a man in space. Kennedy had made the most of the gap in his campaign, but on taking office he learned that if a missile gap existed in 1960, it was in America's favor.

Air Force intelligence estimates that had been leaked to Kennedy had never reflected that. The "missile gap," like the "bomber gap" before it, had been cooked to square with Air Force budget ambitions. McNamara wanted to eliminate such service bias from Pentagon intelligence estimates, and after the Bay of Pigs fiasco, Kennedy wanted a second intelligence source as a check on the CIA. Thus, in 1961 McNamara ordered the establishment of the Defense Intelligence Agency, to consolidate and objectify all military intelligence activities.

Doubtless aware of my father's background as a Pentagon maverick, McNamara appointed him the first director of DIA. (According to a 1995 article about my father in the *American Intelligence Journal*, "McNamara believed that Carroll's integrity and civilian background, which had kept him out of the internecine battles of the Pentagon, would enable him to influence the production of reliable and objective NIEs [National Intelligence Estimates].") Once again my father's role was to challenge the assumptions and power of the brass, only this time his opponents in turf battles would be Navy admirals and generals of the Army and the Marines as well as of the Air Force. From now on, and for the first time, there would be Pentagon intelligence estimates from an agency that owed first loyalty neither to a service branch nor even to the Joint Chiefs of Staff, but directly to the secretary of defense and the president. As for the CIA, it had to reckon with its neophyte counterpart when in September 1962 the DIA, not the CIA itself, provided the first hard proof that the Soviets were putting missiles in Cuba.

The American war in Vietnam was characterized from start to finish by misunderstanding, ignorance, confusion, illusion (Vietnam a Catholic country!), deception, and contradiction. My father's direct experience of the war, running from its effective beginning until his retirement in September 1969, was and remains unknown to me.

But I have read declassified military histories that describe, for example, the furious interagency argument over how to define, and therefore count, the enemy. DIA argued that the Communist order of battle should not include the Vietcong's so-called self-defense (SD) and secret self-defense (SSD) forces because, in fact, those terms were VC designations for old people and children who were not brought into regular forces. They were often, literally, in the last ditch.

The CIA wanted SD and SSD numbers included in estimates — but wouldn't that in effect have obliterated the distinction between combatant and civilian, a distinction that the DIA position implicitly wanted to maintain? Of course, the actual "counting" was mainly of dead bodies. Defining success in the war by body count was itself disastrous, because it meant that everyone in the chain of command, from NCOs to HQMACV, had a motive for exaggerating the count. Odd numbers were always rounded upward, and dead civilians were almost always tagged as soldiers. The end result of all this was that GIs went on missions with only the haziest notions of the opposition they might face. What the grunts had learned in shadows, the whole world saw in clear light during the Tet Offensive, in January 1968. That explosion of Communist forces, which U.S. military historians still insist on describing as a victory for our side, laid bare the harsh fact that every American intelligence estimate, DIA and CIA and all, had grievously undercounted the enemy. Tet was vivid proof that U.S. intelligence in Vietnam, across the board, had failed.

My father never spoke to me of his sense of failure, but for years after the war, as he sank through hellish circles of depression into senility, I saw it plain. What I did not imagine at the time was that his own failure could have consisted not in a myopia he shared with the brass, but in a newly developed inability to stake out influential positions that were different from the other generals. Had they finally intimidated him? It seems clear that my father influenced McNamara, whose confidence he had. But the generals were something else. If my father disagreed with them, why hadn't he argued his case with a clarity and force that had an effect? And then, after he and McNamara each left the Pentagon, each refused — wasn't this the gravest failure? — to try to influence the public. Knowing full well, by the time of his retirement in 1969, that the war was futile, my father, like McNamara, said nothing to challenge Nixon, Laird, and Kissinger as they continued to send boys to kill and die.

From various sources, such as the Pentagon Papers, the revelations of the Westmoreland-CBS libel trial, which was an argument about counting the enemy, and from numerous other accounts, particularly McNamara's memoir, I have come to some appreciation, if not full knowledge, of the frustrations of my father's position. It should not have surprised me, but it did, when I learned from McNamara's testimony what had never been authoritatively stated before — on the contrary, it had always been denied — that the generals were actively contemplating the use of nuclear weapons.

The Bomb. Referring to secret planning sessions held in November 1964, while Curtis LeMay was still Air Force chief and not long after LBJ's campaign ads depicted Barry Goldwater as dying to use the Bomb, McNamara writes, "The president and I were shocked by the almost cavalier way in which the Chiefs and their associates, on this and other occasions, referred to, and accepted the risk of, the possible use of nuclear weapons."

McNamara reports that in 1966 and again in 1967, the Joint Chiefs made proposals that involved "utilizing the nation's full military capability, including the possible use of nuclear weapons." If China entered the war, the Chiefs were ready to use the Bomb against it. McNamara claims to have regarded the consideration of such strategies with abhorrence, and I believe him. And I also believe that my father, whom I knew to lack even an ounce of cavalier swagger on this question, would have been equally appalled. Kooks? On this subject I am sure that, to him, Curtis LeMay was the kook. But could he say so?

As I stepped gingerly into the ever expanding circle of the antiwar movement, I was surrounded by people who thought they knew all there was to know about the generals running the war. But my constant experience, as I heard generals first chastised for stupidity and then condemned as baby burners, was that such critics knew nothing about them. I was wrong. Now I would say, more simply, they knew nothing about my father. What kept me paralyzed long after the immoral savagery of the war became clear to me was the mystery of my father's commitment to it. How could the war be what William Sloane Coffin, Abraham J. Heschel, Martin Luther King, Daniel Berrigan, and even the pope said it was — what I thought it was — if Dad thought otherwise? What I couldn't know was that all the conflicts then surfacing in our society about the war were conflicts deeply buried inside certain individuals charged with managing it, one of whom, I see now, was surely my father.

For example, from his early days at the Office of Special Investigations, Dad had opposed the mentally enslaving effect of
the military's sacrosanct chain of command. He had succeeded
in creating one agency, OSI, that defied it, and he tried but failed
to do the same thing at DIA. The problem seems obvious. Since a
military man's success depends solely on the good opinion of
his immediate superior, the system punishes any impulse to dis-
please that superior by telling him what he does not want to
hear. The prescribed military answer to the question "Can you?"
is "Can do."

General Bruce Palmer Jr. served as a corps commander in
Vietnam in 1967 and went on to become Army vice chief of staff.
He wrote, "Not once during the war did the JCS advise the
Commander-in-Chief or the Secretary of Defense that the strategy being pursued most probably would fail and that the U.S.
would be unable to achieve its objectives . . . [The Chiefs] were
imbued with the 'can do' spirit and could not bring themselves
to make a negative statement or to appear to be disloyal."

To men like that, my father had often appeared to be negative
and disloyal. After McNamara's memoir appeared in 1995, Louis
G. Sarris, a former State Department analyst, wrote an op-ed
piece for the *New York Times* in which he listed critics of early
military involvement in Vietnam, including "even the Defense
Intelligence Agency." For a controversial 1963 report in which
Sarris challenged the generals, he drew on DIA assessments,
among others. This report, in the words of David Halberstam,
writing in *The Best and the Brightest*, "showed that the war effort
was slipping away."

McNamara's position in those early years remains in dispute,
but I confess the relief it was to read in his memoir of an early
and direct DIA intervention, which was in effect a first shoe
falling. As a summary of American prospects following Diem's
assassination, it was a flat contradiction of reports from the

U.S. mission in Saigon, which had touted up to then our "progress in Vietnam." McNamara goes on, "But on December 13, 1963, I received a memorandum from the Defense Intelligence Agency stating that, while the Vietcong had not scored spectacular gains over the past year, they had sustained and even improved their combat capabilities. The report added that unless the South Vietnamese Army improved its operations, Vietcong activities would probably increase." This "new and gloomy assessment," as McNamara calls it, was later confirmed by the CIA's John McCone, who told the president, "It is abundantly clear that statistics received over the past year . . . on which we gauged the trend of the war were grossly in error."

Grossly in error: for the next ten years, that would be the one consistent characteristic of Vietnam assessments and reports reaching the top echelons of Washington. "Wars generate their own momentum and follow the law of unanticipated consequences," McNamara writes. "Vietnam proved no exception." The miserable, cursed, futile, impossible effort to find out what was happening in the jungles, along the supply routes, on the bomb-cratered plateaus, in the alleys of teeming cities, along the electrified demilitarized zone, and in the hearts and minds of the Vietnamese people eventually drove American decision makers, including my father, past distraction and into a kind of madness. My father's fellow Air Force generals should have been able to count on him to support their cause by reporting that the bombing of the North was working, but according to the Pentagon Papers, the DIA consistently offered up analysis — data, not argument — that the bombing was having no significant effect on Hanoi's capacity to wage war.

By August 1967, before executive sessions of the Senate Armed Services Committee, McNamara was in a feud with the Joint Chiefs over the winnability of the war. At that point, there were more than 525,000 GIs in Vietnam. General Westmoreland was asking for another 200,000, and the Chiefs wanted another 400 bombers for a massive expansion of the air war, which until then had focused on supply lines. They wanted harbors mined and dikes destroyed and the flow of traffic on the Red River stopped. They wanted $10 billion more per year, above the $30 billion already being spent. They wanted, as Curtis LeMay had put it two years before, "to stop swatting at flies and go after the manure pile." McNamara, in his testimony before the subcommittee chaired by Senator John Stennis, opposed all of this. He rebutted the generals and admirals by citing the monthly DIA report, "An Appraisal of the Bombing of North Vietnam," which "invariably concluded" — here was the second shoe falling — that the air campaign was not working.

McNamara had come to the conclusion — and in this as well as other secret councils was arguing for it — that the war could not be won and should not be expanded. A suspension of the bombing and earnest negotiations to end the war were what was needed. "Mr. Secretary, I am terribly disappointed with your statement," Senator Strom Thurmond replied. "I think it is a statement of placating the Communists. It is a statement of appeasing the Communists. It is a statement of no-win."

McNamara denied Thurmond's charge, but it was true. Many Americans hated McNamara then, and when his memoir appeared on the twentieth anniversary of the end of the war, accompanied by his tears on camera, many felt a fresh bolt of rage toward him. At a Harvard lecture, when an angry questioner demanded to know how McNamara could have maintained his public silence about a war he'd concluded could not be won, he responded by evading the question. When pressed, he replied sharply, "Shut up!" — an efficient reminder to everyone of why they'd despised him.

McNamara's memoir generated other feelings in me. We thought that the main argument going on in America in those years was between hawks and doves. But among the hawks themselves, the argument was far more deadly. However much liberals and aging peaceniks continue to hate him, it was the right wing that truly threatened McNamara in the 1960s, not the left. It was the right wing that broke him. To hawks, both at the time and when his memoir appeared, McNamara represented the failure of the government to pursue the war "manfully." His crime was not the violence he unleashed, but his unwillingness to ride it all the way. In a memo to the president dated May 19, 1967, he warned again that nuclear weapons "would probably be suggested . . . if U.S. losses were running high while conventional efforts were not producing desired results." He concluded that memo, "The picture of the world's greatest superpower killing or seriously injuring 1000 noncombatants a week, while trying to pound a tiny backward nation into submission on an issue whose merits are hotly disputed, is not a pretty one."

McNamara's lack of enthusiasm for the war led to the announcement of his resignation on November 29, 1967. Although McNamara coyly says that he remains unsure whether he resigned or was fired, it seems clear that LBJ forced him out. To all appearances, Johnson was prepared to give Westmoreland and the other generals what they wanted. At stake was the very survival of civilization in the northeast corner of Southeast Asia. At stake was the possibility, readily acknowledged by the Joint Chiefs, that an expanded war could draw in China and even the Soviet Union. At stake — the generals admitted this — was World War III.

McNamara's "collapse of will" came at just the worst time for Lyndon Johnson. To support his decision to tough it out in Vietnam, the president had just established that fall a White House "psychological strategy committee" under Walt Rostow to nurture support among the American people. The New Deal's Wise Men were all on board. That season's selling of the war to the public included General Westmoreland's statement "I have never been more encouraged," and his promise to the House Armed Services Committee that victory would come in two years.

Opponents of "McNamara's war" brought their efforts to a climax too. On September 14, in a famous letter to his constituents, Congressman Tip O'Neill broke with the war, one of the first establishment pols to do so. On October 21, 100,000 people marched on Washington. Of that number, 20,000 went on to the Pentagon itself, Norman Mailer's "Armies of the Night." In the same month, Father Philip Berrigan and others committed the first of the acts of Catholic war protest, pouring blood on draft files in Baltimore. Also in that month, Tom Hayden and others visited Hanoi. Taken alone, these acts of so-called radicals and the mass demonstrations by ordinary citizens could have strengthened the hawk position, but in the convoluted politics of the day, they had the effect of making more moderate acts of dissent all the more powerful. The day after McNamara announced his resignation, Senator Eugene McCarthy declared his candidacy against Johnson on an antiwar platform. Long-time opponents of the war must disparage McNamara, but we must also see how his decision led to McCarthy's.

In Vietnam itself, the Communists launched the January Tet Offensive, which, by the numbers, they lost. Far more important, however, Tet laid bare as an illusion every hope for an eventual American victory. In February, during a regular evening newscast, Walter Cronkite rejected the war, predicting it would "end in stalemate." LBJ told an aide, "If I've lost Walter, I've lost the support of Mr. Average Citizen." On March 12, 1968, Mr. and Mrs. Average Citizen voted for Eugene McCarthy in the New Hampshire primary. By the numbers — like the Communists of Tet — he lost, but by polling 42 percent to LBJ's 48 percent —

AN AMERICAN REQUIEM • 192

a surprise showing against a sitting president, like the North Vietnamese Army's showing against the U.S. war machine — McCarthy transformed loss into victory. Thus, on March 30 Johnson announced his rejection of the escalation plans of the Joint Chiefs of Staff. He said no to Westmoreland's wish to "clobber the enemy once and for all." He said no to any possible use of nuclear weapons. He suspended the air war over the North. He asked for an immediate start to negotiations with Hanoi and the Vietcong. And he renounced plans to seek reelection. Remembering my slight encounters with him years before, and thinking of his earlier alliance with Martin Luther King, I reacted with an overwhelming gratitude and affection. I thought his decision meant now the war would end and I could get my father back. I wrote the president to thank him. In due time, I received from the White House a printed acknowledgment.

In these crucial months, the war at home was waged for the "hearts and minds" of "average citizens." Nixon would defy them by endlessly prolonging the war. Two months after McNamara resigned, the U.S. high command reported 16,459 American dead; Nixon, Kissinger, and Laird would add 41,676 to that number. Under McNamara, U.S. forces had dropped one and a half million tons of bombs; six million more tons would fall. Nevertheless, a cold stop was put right here to the generals' inexorable escalation. That had been the goal of the march on the Pentagon in October. No one who participated in that demonstration had counted it a success. Yet it was.

"I watched the whole thing from the roof of the building," McNamara writes. "Years later a reporter asked if I had been scared. Of course I was scared."

So was I. It was a Saturday. I had slipped away from the seminary without permission and alone. By now some Paulists were as vociferous in opposing the war as I was silent about it.

But it was unthinkable to me, at last, that I not attend the demonstration. I arranged to meet up with the only other person who could understand the complicated feelings I had: my brother Dennis, the vegetarian. He was then attending George Washington University, a few blocks from the White House. His hair was yet longer. He was tall and lanky. With his wire-rimmed glasses he looked like John Lennon. We hardly ever saw each other except in the house on Generals' Row, but, alone among our brothers, we had learned to find each other's eyes in the terrible awkwardness of family gatherings.

On that Saturday, we met near the Washington Monument and then hovered at the margins of the demonstration while it was centered at the Lincoln Memorial. There were speeches, we were told, by Norman Mailer and Robert Lowell and Dr. Spock and William Sloane Coffin, but we did not get close enough to hear them. Small groups formed around signs reading "CORE," "SNCC," "RESIST," "The Catholic Peace Fellowship," and dozens more. But Dennis and I stayed clear of every group.

When a sizable part of the crowd began to move from the Lincoln Memorial into Virginia and toward the Pentagon, we folded ourselves into it. In the front lines were the small number of defiant protesters who challenged the soldiers ringing the Pentagon. Arrests were made, and for a few moments it seemed the demonstration would become a riot — a prospect that horrified Dennis and me. At one point, we heard that some of the crowd got into the building, but what we saw was troops in battle gear filing steadily out. We didn't get close to the building, and we never stood apart from the crowd. We knew exactly which window was his, and we stood there staring at it for a long time. Mute. Ashamed.

It has long been my conviction, widely shared, that the antiwar movement stopped the escalation by making it politically untenable for Johnson. That is not the whole story. Like all peaceniks, I was ignorant of the conflict going on inside the Pentagon — which we took to be the ultimate monolith. In fact, it was as sorely divided an institution as the nation itself. Now I realize that of all the events that made a Johnson choice in favor of the generals untenable, none can be ranked above Robert McNamara's loss of faith in the military solution. One week after this demonstration, on November 1, 1967, he sent a secret memo to Johnson proposing a halt to the bombing for the sake of negotiations. McNamara's loss of faith in bombing resulted not from the protests, even though members of McNamara's own family participated in them, but from his conclusion, based on evidence, that the enemy we were fighting in Vietnam was simply not going to be defeated. No matter what we did to them, short of reducing their part of the subcontinent to a radioactive graveyard, the Vietnamese Communists would not surrender. And of all that went into that conviction of McNamara's — his critics on the right still regard it as the true moral collapse of the war — my father's analysis is duly credited as a factor, early and late, by McNamara himself. "A factor" to them, but something more than that to me.

The fact that McNamara, my father, and others like them did not go public with their conclusions about the war when Nixon and company continued it with a considerable, if secret, escalation of bombing, in Cambodia especially, means they bear an additional, horrible responsibility. They thought, as McNamara puts it in his book, that their highest duty was to the commander in chief. Perhaps they thought they "wouldn't have had much influence," which seems dubious at best. My father remained in his position at DIA through the rest of Johnson's term and long enough into Nixon's to have an independent falling out with the new administration. Whatever his convictions had become, he forever maintained his silence, which, given everything I know about him, was the only thing he could do. As events would show, Dad had more capacity for a public break with his superiors than I'd have expected, but he was entirely unable to say aloud that the boys he'd helped send off to die had died for a mistake. Alas, his silence helped send off even more. Silence. By October 21, 1967, his silence toward me and Dennis was already deafening.

When I think of Dennis and Jimmy, those two frightened young men standing in a crowd, staring at a window, a blank eye, in the largest building in the world — the largest tombstone, there, by Arlington — I want to reach back through time and hug them both, that John Lennon, that freckle-faced, big-eared Alfred E. Neuman. I want to comfort them, but, thinking of that man inside the Pentagon who was then only five years older than I am now, and of the deadly moral choices still ahead of him, I also want to shake those two, slap them, wake them up, make them see through the haze of their anguish. I want to yell, Don't be afraid of demanding of him that he explain himself to you! Don't let him down by assuming *already* that he is lost. Indeed — how I wish I could get this message back to Dennis and Jimmy — he needs your challenge! He needs your love!

For the first time, here, in the writing, I see my own responsibility for what followed. It's a bit of a narcissist's fantasy, perhaps, but here it is: the son will shake the father, who will then do the right thing, and the world will be a better place. Still, it seems true. As my father failed to find a way to influence the generals, I failed to find a way to influence him. My failure compounded his. My failure, then, contributed to what Nixon did.

A few weeks later, at Thanksgiving, I went to dinner at Bolling for the last time. Convinced that my father thought the war was good, I almost dared to tell him it was evil. But the most I could bring myself to say was that he had no right to call Phil Berrigan a kook. Hell, *I* thought pouring blood on draft files was a kooky thing to do, but I had come to despise that word. "He is not a kook!" I cried, which reads now like a comic anticipation of Nixon.

My mother told me to lower my voice, and I said to her, "Tell him to stop saying that. Phil Berrigan is a priest!"

My father leaned toward me and hissed, "Which makes it all the worse." He banged his fist on the table, pushed himself away, and left. A few minutes later, I told my mother at the door that I wouldn't be coming for Christmas. I'd be doing the holidays at St. Paul's, where I belonged. I remember heading out into the night, glancing back at sullen, stunned Dennis, and feeling the sting of guilt I'd felt previously only in relation to polio-stricken Joe. I was abandoning Dennis.

A few days later, McNamara announced his resignation. The day after that, McCarthy announced his candidacy. And with what grave relief did I listen to his speech on television. McCarthy's forthright, brave denunciation of the war moved me to tears, which I desperately hid from the other seminarians. McCarthy was a serious Catholic who had himself once studied for the priesthood; who wrote poetry, read Teilhard, and could quote Jacques Maritain; who could make his points against Johnson by appealing to Saint Augustine and Thomas Aquinas and the Just War tradition that I had mastered; who, unlike the radicals, wanted to work within the system, to change it; and who conveyed through humor and self-deprecation an astounding lack of hubris. Watching him that day was like seeing a log drift by before going down for the third time. My gratitude would keep me loyal to McCarthy even after Bobby Kennedy declared for president.

Having been raised with a hero in the house, I had slowly but surely lost him as such. I still needed heroes, and had made sure to have them. Hans Küng was one. Martin Luther King was another. Daniel Berrigan, perhaps. But Eugene McCarthy was something else. He seemed to offer me a way to stand against a hostile world, defining myself in opposition, and actually to change that world. Eugene McCarthy was running for president! He made me believe that Americans, as true Americans — lovers of our country! — could end the war. Patriots for Peace. For a time, I gave myself entirely to him.

I went to work at once, putting the basic organizing experience I'd gained on civil rights vigils and demonstrations actively to work to oppose the war for the first time. I would settle in as a recruiter of college students, getting them "Clean for Gene." But the initial effort was to help organize, along with a dozen other Paulists, an early rally for McCarthy. It took place in the ballroom of the Mayflower Hotel, a raucous celebration led off by a group of singing seminarians, the Roamin' Collars, led by my own Patrick Hughes. They performed the Simon and Garfunkel hit "Mrs. Robinson." As I watched the packed ballroom sway in rhythm with the song, I felt proud, relieved and like myself at last. I also felt strangely consoled by the line "Jesus loves you more than you will know."

Later, in a corner of the crowded room, I met Senator McCarthy. When I told him I was a seminarian, he pressed my hand warmly, as years before Bobby Kennedy had, and for the same reason. It was a version of the small affirmation Catholics habitually gave their chosen ones, and to which, frankly, we felt entitled. Between me and the senator, a handclasp could be a brief signal of comembership, a seal, and a hint that because of my vocation I could be especially valuable to the cause. To *la causa*, as we, with Cesar Chavez, were calling it by then.

I returned to the seminary that night feeling energized and hopeful. Pat Hughes and I and a few others watched the late news. When the TV screen suddenly filled with Pat's round face, we hooted. He was grinning happily above his banjo, singing, "Jesus loves you . . ." Then the film cut to McCarthy, and as the camera panned across the crowd, my heart stopped. God, what if the camera shows me? I turned cold with fear — again. He'll see me. He'll know. Today my children hold their breath whenever we drive past a cemetery: otherwise they will die. That is what I did. I held my breath, a magic act that made the camera miss me.

It was perhaps that very week, and as if because of what I'd begun to do — the spirit of the movement encouraged such grandiose self-reference — that Francis Cardinal Spellman died. My classmates who knew of his interest in ordaining me offered wry condolences, but I felt only relief that he was dead. Free at last, I thought. But of course I wasn't. When I called my mother, a storm front of complicated emotions rolled in, as much hers as mine. She reminded me that while so much else in her life as an uneducated, "unfinished" woman who'd been conscripted into the role of a general's wife had aimed to undercut her, Cardinal Spellman had only affirmed her. Recognizing a rare esprit, and freeing it, he gave her ways to feel proud of herself. Through Catholic councils of military women in Europe and in Washington, he gave her ways to exert leadership and express herself. As we spoke, I sensed that, on the other end of the line, she was close to weeping. She fell silent. I imagined her fingering the gold medal at her throat embossed with Spellman's seal. He had given it to her for service to the Church. Years later, dying, she would ask us to put that medal on her for the viewing at her wake.

I told her that I would pray for Cardinal Spellman. She did

not reply. I told her, out of a sudden and ancient feeling of desperation, that I loved her, knowing that what she really wanted to hear at that moment was that I'd loved him.

"And now," she said, "he'll never ordain you."

"I know."

"He'd be as disappointed about that as I am," she said. Then she forced a laugh. "But he's in heaven, where disappointment is forbidden."

"Forbidden disappointments." The phrase struck me. It would be the title of my volume of poems. I thought of a crack with which to reply: You'll be disappointed, Mom, even there. But I didn't say it. I don't remember what I said.

A few weeks later came Tet, when even I began to grasp that our country's failure belonged in some special way to my father. And within weeks of that came My Lai, which, when we later learned of it, would seem to Americans both outrageous — Lieutenant Calley tossing an infant in the air, spearing it with a bayonet — and not all that different from what, less personally, our B-52s were doing from the air.

When Cardinal Spellman's successor, an agreeable Irishman named Terence Cooke, was installed as archbishop of New York and vicar of the American military, his first words from the episcopal throne in St. Patrick's were spoken to Lyndon Johnson, sitting in the cathedral's front row. As I had in my letter to the White House that very week, Cooke thanked the president for his search for peace. In fact, the real search was being conducted by 549,000 GIs, many of whom would never find peace again. Reflecting Cooke's position, the American Catholic bishops issued a statement, implicitly defying Pope Paul VI, in which they said, "It is reasonable to argue that our presence in Vietnam is justified." Not much was made in the press of Cooke's friendly words to the beleaguered president that day, because a few hours after the episcopal installation, Martin Luther King was shot.

On May 17, 1968, Philip and Daniel Berrigan led a Catholic raid on a draft board office in Catonsville, Maryland. They burned records with homemade napalm. Daniel Berrigan's statement began, "Our apologies, good friends, for the fracture of good order, the burning of paper instead of children . . . We could not, so help us God, do otherwise." I taped it to my mirror, where once Lacordaire's pious hymn to the priesthood had been. I would have Berrigan's words on my mirrors or bulletin boards in a sequence of rooms for years. The consequences of Catonsville would give shape to my priesthood.

And in that same hard season that ended with the murder of Bobby Kennedy, two other things happened in my family. My brother Dennis decided that, in conscience, he could no longer cooperate with the Selective Service System. He renounced his student deferment, then told our father he had done so. Dad stormed away from him in fury. Mom served Dennis his dinner, a casserole that, though meatless, he could not eat. He would be leaving the house on Generals' Row, and then the country. Dennis would be a draft exile for more than a year, working in a leper colony in India, a kind of self-imposed alternative service. And our brother Brian, out of college and married now to Vicki French, would resolve a youthful restlessness about future and career, if not also about a place in the universe, by applying to become an FBI agent. Upon receiving his badge and gun, he would be assigned to track down draft fugitives. When they went underground, Brian would be given the job of finding the Berrigans, and then other Catholic resisters. It would be reported that he tried to penetrate the Catholic left through me.

9

THE IMPOSITION

ST. PAUL the Apostle Church is on the West Side of Manhattan, across Sixtieth Street from Lincoln Center. It was designed by one of the first Paulist fathers, a hundred years before my ordination, at a time when Midtown was the edge of wilderness. Father Deshon had been an Army engineer, and indeed, to me, the church resembled nothing so much as an armory. Its stunted twin spires seemed like the crenelated towers of a fortress. St. Paul's vast interior was mystically dark, except for a few pillar-mounted lights that shone on the ceiling vault, a midnight-blue canopy on which was painted the night sky showing the stars and planets exactly as aligned on the night of the conversion of Saint Paul. That never made sense to me, because Paul's experience — knocked from a horse in bright daylight on the road to Damascus — had made him blind.

We saw nothing. My classmates and I, halfway through the ordination ceremony, were lying flat on the cold stone floor, prostrate. Our faces were buried in our arms. We were blind, knocked down, but converted? Meanwhile, the boys' choir in front of us, alternating with the congregation behind us, sang the transfiguring Litany of Saints. Its strains ricocheted between the high-pitched precociousness of the boys and the ragged happiness of the amateur throng.

Lord, have mercy.
Christ, have mercy.
Lord, have mercy.
Holy Mary, Mother of God.
Mom. I thought first of her, what a dream come true this was. The reward to the people of her father's village in Ireland for never having taken the soup; her guarantee of a special place in heaven; proof that she had done the right thing in marrying Joe.
Pray for us.
Saint Michael the Archangel.
Pray for us.
On the refrains rolled, like heaven's chariot rolling over us. The litany is an arcane Who's Who — Athanasius, Sebastian, Agatha, the arrow-pierced eunuchs, the virgins whose breasts were crushed with the paving stones of the Roman Forum.
All ye holy men and women, saints of God.
Pray for us.
Lord, be merciful.
A prayer for mercy was one I had no trouble making mine. Only moments earlier, I had knelt before Terence Cardinal Cooke with my folded hands inside his, like a blade inside a scabbard. He'd looked me in the eye and asked, "Do you solemnly promise to respect and obey me and my successors?"
All around were witnesses, not only my Paulist brothers and my family and the families of my dozen classmates, but Air Force chaplains, five of them, or ten, or fifteen — I kept seeing more. They were present because I was the son of a general, the first son of an active-duty Air Force officer subject to the military ordinariate to be ordained. They came to show a pious solidarity — and to be seen doing so by Cardinal Cooke. They wore their blue uniforms, standing behind me like sponsors. Slim priestly stoles draped their necks, stoles of the kind meant to be worn on

a battlefield, evoking Mass on the hood of a jeep. The stoles across their epaulets blanked out the silver bars, leaves, eagles, and stars of their rank.

"Do you solemnly promise to respect and obey your ordinary?"

Ordinarily.

"It depends, Eminence," I wanted to say. This man and others like him had just sheepishly endorsed the war. And only months before, he and others like him — ordinary indeed — had bowed to the pope's demoralizing edict on birth control, *Humanae Vitae*, published in July 1968. I knew that if, in that season, B-52s had been dropping condoms on the hills and valleys of Vietnam, Cardinal Cooke and Washington's Cardinal O'Boyle and all the other "ordinaries" would by now have solemnly condemned the war as intrinsically immoral, forbidding Catholic participation. But instead, they called it justified because the B-52s were only dropping napalm.

The cardinal had put my hands in his when, at that moment, despite myself, what I'd wished for was to put my hands inside Dad's. The image I had of myself was of that little boy in boots, chaps, and a cowboy vest, standing hand in hand with his Air Force father, equally awkward in his general's uniform. Cowboy? Didn't my lying here on the cold stone floor equal elevation to the status of the Lone Ranger himself?

"Monsignor, take this one aside," I imagined His Eminence saying in response to my mute paralysis. But mute paralysis, only rarely broken by the poems I'd tried to write, was my true condition. I had begun this process of handing myself over to God, if not the Church, years ago, wanting only to be like Dad. And then what happened?

In the crushing months before, with the assassinations of Dr. King and Bobby, with the pope's reform-killing encyclical, with the debacle at the Democratic National Convention — the Chicago riots took place within blocks of my birthplace — I had tried one last time to hurl myself from the ecclesiastical express, to get out of becoming a priest. That summer I'd been a pastoral counseling intern at a clinic for alcoholics in Atlanta. For three months I lived and worked in a becolumned mansion, once the home of the Coca-Cola Candlers, a family of notorious liquor drinkers. Now their stately house was the refuge of a ragtag collection of drunks and therapists. The solarium had become an arts-and-crafts center. The ballroom was the cafeteria. In the former master bedroom were bunks for twelve. My bed was in the corner of a small room. I loved the work, my first independent taste of the pastoral ministry. But I was challenged, to say the least, by my collegial closeness with female nurses and social workers, as well as partnership with Baptist and Methodist ministers. As a Catholic, I was a mystery to the mostly redneck patients, who, with edgy good humor, called me "bull nun." I handled it all with apparent equanimity, but I ached with loneliness and uncertainty. Visions of myself as a defeated whiskey priest woke me in the night, and I would lie there in the dark trying to remember how any of this had happened. One minute I am a laughing boy with a girlfriend in a gala room, waiting for Elvis, the next I am an avowed eunuch in a narrow bed alone.

I hitched a ride one weekend up to Sewanee, Tennessee, site of the University of the South, where Allen Tate now lived in retirement. I hadn't seen him in two years, but I had continued to send my poems to him, and he had faithfully sent them back, properly defaced. His support had seemed an ongoing miracle to me. Slowly I accumulated a collection of finished poems, some of which would appear, with his imprimatur, in *Forbidden Disappointments*. In Atlanta, thinking of my approaching ordination, I panicked, fearing among other things that Tate's interest in me depended on my status as a priest in training. But, I argued with myself, even as I drove into Sewanee, hadn't Mr. Tate been the one to warn me with his demurral about my "two vocations"? Priest and Poet — not you, kid. How about Priest and Poet and Prophet. Maybe Daniel Berrigan could do it, but I couldn't.

My spiritual director had recently told me that, in the final evaluation of my candidacy for ordination, one priest faculty member had observed disapprovingly that I had a "soft middle." Like the earth? I wanted to ask. Like bread? But it was true. I was soft where all the heroes, from Cardinal Cooke to Daniel Berrigan to my father, wanted me to be hard. On this at least those three would agree. Priest and Poet, I can't be both? By now I am concluding I can't be either. When I quit, they will think it's the war, and I may even say as much. They'll think it's birth control, or that I want a woman. All of which will be true, but only partly so. I drive into Sewanee knowing that the unidentified faculty critic has seen right through me. Addressing a reflection in the windshield, I rehearse what I will say when I resign: "Three reasons: poverty, chastity, and obedience." But the truth will be something else, and "soft middle" is as good a term for it as any I know.

Soft middle — the place, above all, in which the silence becomes words, giving me poetry. Wasn't I coming to Sewanee now to tell Mr. Tate that he'd been right? That summer marked the end of my hope of becoming a Catholic priest of the kind my father wanted. If there was another kind — Thomas Campion the resister, not Thomas à Kempis the pious fool — what would that be to Dad? Therefore, what would it be to me? The choice seemed clear. As I arrived in the small Tennessee hill town in which Allen Tate had first made his reputation, I realized that in coming here I had already made the choice. I was coming to declare myself to Allen Tate, to announce my determination to make a life as a writer. He would bless me, calling me out of the priesthood, and out of prophecy too. Yes, Allen Tate would be my new father in the Word, but lowercase.

I found his house, a surprisingly modern split-level with redwood siding set off by large panels of glass. It was in a tony section of the remote academic town, a hip faculty enclave. In Minneapolis, I'd been entirely focused on Tate's meaning for me, but now I knew that the summer of 1966 had been a momentous one in his life too. Only months before, he'd divorced the poet Isabella Gardner, and in July, while patiently tutoring me, he had married a young woman who had been a student of his. Her name was Helen Heinz, and she was a nurse. Tate's first wife had been the writer Caroline Gordon; that his third was a young nurse made their marriage a choice tidbit on the literary gossip circuit. That she had been chief nurse in a large Catholic hospital in Minneapolis made it gossip among Catholics.

Her youth was reflected, I sensed, in this bright, appealing house. So was the fact — he'd told me this in his letter — that they had recently had twin sons. When I'd read that, I'd pictured the young poets in Dinky Town taverns back at U of M, elbowing each other about the old man's virility. Tate was sixty-eight. For a change, as I approached the front door I was not carrying a sheaf of poems, but I did have a pair of small wrapped boxes, crib toys for the twins. I rang the doorbell, aware of myself as the latest in a long line of would-be poets who had come to him like this, seeking a literary laying on of hands. Even Robert Lowell and John Berryman had done so, and years later my friend Robie Macauley would tell me that so had he. In an instant, had the image occurred to me, I knew that I would have put my hands inside Tate's, promising to respect and obey him. But now I realize that the reason I felt inclined to do so was that he'd have never let me.

The door opened and a shockingly small, frail old man in a short-sleeved white shirt stood there, red-eyed and slack-jawed. His huge forehead — it was Tate's most distinctive feature — was crimson, as if he'd just been running. I hardly recognized him. He stared blankly back at me. He seemed the opposite of virile. To my horror, I realized he had no idea who I was. In his letter, he'd appointed this hour for my visit, but clearly he'd forgotten.

"Paul?" he said.

"It's Jim Carroll, Professor."

He leaned toward me. I was wearing a blazer and a dark cotton turtleneck, despite the summer heat. I had abandoned the necktied Hans Küng as my clerical sartorial ideal in favor of Daniel Berrigan. I would hardly ever wear a Roman collar, but at that moment, to help Tate recognize me, I wished I had. I saw that his eyes were wet, as if he'd been crying, or as if he were drunk. I assumed drunk.

"Oh," he said suddenly, "James!"

When, in Minneapolis, I had asked him to sign his book to "Jim," he'd written "James," and I've used the name as a writer ever since.

"Forgive me," he said now, opening the door wide and stepping aside for me. "Forgive me," he said again, bowing slightly, the Southern cavalier. Tate ushered me into the spare, modern living room with its high flagstone fireplace, its Scandinavian furniture, its slate floor. I sat on the couch and, to my surprise, Mr. Tate sat next to me, close. I looked around for his bourbon glass and did not see it. I heard the faint sounds of someone else stirring in a distant part of the house.

"Oh, James," he said then, leaning toward me. "I could have used you yesterday."

"Why?"

A startled expression crossed his face. "You don't know?" The sharp edge of inquiry in his eyes told me he was not drunk at all. But his eyes . . .

I forced a big smile. "You mean about your twins? Yes, sir. You wrote me about it." I held my boxes out.

He shrank back. "Oh. Oh." Then he simply shook his head. Tears fell from his eyes. Finally he said, "My baby died. One of my babies died. Michael . . ."

He explained that one of the boys, Michael Paul, in the care of a nanny, had vomited while sleeping and choked to death. His wife, he said, was devastated. So was he. He looked off toward the part of the house from which I'd heard noises. Now, thinking of that collapsed face of his, I find these lines from his much earlier poem "Death of Little Boys":

> When little boys grown patient at last, weary,
> Surrender their eyes immeasurably to the night,
> The event will rage terrific as the sea;
> Their bodies fill a crumbling room with light.

"I could have used you yesterday," Tate said again. "I needed a priest like you."

"What?" I asked, fearing that I'd misled him, since I wasn't a priest yet.

"The Catholic priest here in the local parish — he would not let us have a Catholic funeral. Helen —" Tate began to sob. I touched his arm. "Because of me," he said. "The priest refused to bury Michael because, he said, my marriage was notorious."

"Your marriage?"

"My divorces. I am a bad Catholic."

"Oh, Christ!" The words rushed from my mouth ahead of a bitter bolt of disgust.

"We buried Michael in the Protestant church."

I heard in Tate's voice not bitterness or anger but despair.

Religious despair. I knew that Tate had become a Roman Catholic, with his wife Caroline Gordon, in 1950. While other poets had embraced the Church as an act of faddish aesthetic self-expression, Tate had grappled for decades with the figure of Jesus — his 1928 poem "The Cross" is a religious masterpiece. His conversion to Roman Catholicism was the result of a lifelong spiritual quest and was a deeply transforming event. Jacques Maritain would cite him as an influence. But to the Sewanee curate, Allen Tate would have been the wrong kind of Catholic from the start. Not long after his baptism, writing in the *New York Times,* Tate had denounced Cardinal Spellman's censorship of the 1951 film *The Miracle.*

Bad Catholic — the phrase meant as little to me as "good Catholic." What had I spent six years learning except that Jesus Himself had been labeled bad. Who had killed Him? Not the Jews, I had learned by then, but the curates. The monsignors.

In his urbane and knowing lectures, Professor Tate had seemed beyond the cruel pettiness of the Church. But he wasn't beyond it at all, and that was a revelation to me. The Church gives us our faith. Later I would read that all of Tate's poems were about the suffering that results from disbelief. It was Tate who'd made me love "Pied Beauty," by that other convert Gerard Manley Hopkins, but now I saw that the Holy Ghost hovering over us with "Ah Bright Wings" had razor talons, which were sunk deep into this man's soul. Later I would learn how deeply they penetrated mine.

I pressed his hand and said inane things about God's love for Michael, about the real meaning of our communion, about the importance of Jesus' own experience of such a rejection. Even as I spoke, I could not imagine that what I was saying could relieve his obvious pain, but when I fell silent, he asked me to say more, and I did. In the end I told him that I would pray for his dead baby.

And with the most direct gaze ever to pierce me, he said, "Thank you."

"I think I should go."

He nodded. Then we stood and he went with me to the door, where he put his hand on my shoulder. "Your visit helped, James. More than I can say."

Embarrassed, I turned his remarkable statement aside with a laugh. "If you can't say it, Professor, no one can."

He smiled thinly. We shook hands. And I departed. I would never see him again, although I would continue to send him poems and he would continue to be kind about them. As I left, the irony hit me. From one point of view, it seemed I'd gotten the opposite of what I'd come for. But it didn't feel that way. Allen Tate, who'd given me permission to be a writer, had just given me permission to be a priest. Yes, I would pray for his infant Michael, at my first Mass.

And so, six months later, there I was on the floor of the sanctuary of St. Paul the Apostle Church, with all these images floating like motes through my willfully distracted mind. I thought at one point of the war protesters who threw themselves down to the ground like this, miming the roles of napalmed Vietnamese. Several of my classmates and I had discussed the possibility of refusing to exchange the kiss of peace with Cardinal Cooke as a protest against his support of the war. The idea was that, immediately after he had made us "priests forever according to the order of Melchizedek," one of us would go to the microphone and explain our act of conscience. I remember how, in our grave discussion, we all fell silent, staring at each other. Actively contemplating such an act of defiance was enough to make it impossible even for my peacenik friends. As for me, why not just ignite myself with candle wax?

So no, I was not miming the part of a napalmed villager, although one day, at the main gate of Pease Air Force Base in New Hampshire, I would do just that — conical hat and all. But neither was I dead to the secular world, as the sacramental theology intended with this symbolic prostration, nor was I about to be resurrected into the spiritual realm. The great irony of my time in training for the priesthood was that, forcing my participation in the revolutionary events of the day, it had made me more alive to "the world" than I'd ever have been as a gung-ho fighter jock. Holiness had ceased to be an ambition of mine, which may have been the problem. To me, Jesus was not holy. Why should I be?

By the time the Litany of Saints was ending, I may not have been dead, but the feeling was, my life had flashed before my eyes. And in truth, for all my worry and obsessive self-doubt, it was a life I felt grateful for. Even more, I felt grateful that it was far from over. Finally I relaxed into the last of the music, accepting where I was, what I was doing, and who was with me.

From all evil . . .

Lord, save your people.

From every death . . .

Lord, save your people.

By your death . . .

Lord, save your people.

Bless these chosen men and make them holy.

Lord have mercy, yes. When they called my name, I stood and said in a firm voice, "*Adsum*," which a soldier would say means "Present," but which at that moment in my life meant, "Here I am, Lord. Send me." That too was Isaiah's statement, and what was he — trouble coming, for sure — but a prophet?

Uncoerced and with a clear mind, I accepted the chasuble of charity upon my shoulders. Touching the chalice and golden paten with the sacred host upon it, I received the power to change bread and wine into the body and blood of Jesus. When the cardinal anointed my hands with the oil of kings, and then wrapped them in fine linen bands, I had the only gift my mother ever wanted, for as tradition required, I would give that oil-stained linen to her. She would treasure it, unlaundered, and when she died, her own hands would be wrapped in it so that at the gate of heaven angels would recognize her at once as the mother of a priest.

At the kiss of peace, Cardinal Cooke greeted me with such genuine warmth — his own son! a son of the military! — that it appalled me that I had ever thought of insulting him. When he said, "I hear you are going to be an Air Force chaplain," I was too surprised to respond. Before I could deny it, he was hugging me again. And then, having donned his golden miter and his jeweled crozier — the shepherd's stick they use on their sheep — he was gone. There was nothing for me to do now but turn and go down the stairs to the altar rail, for the moment toward which my whole life had been building.

The ritual is that, immediately following the ceremony, the newly ordained priest imposes his first priestly blessing upon his mother and father. An imposition of hands. An imposition.

Thirty-five years before, Joe and Mary had risked everything to be together. In the last hour, he had refused his own ordination, defying his own cardinal, his mother, the Church, and, by all lights, God. Then Mary had stared that act of sacrilege in the eye and found a way to second it. They had married, leaving the parochial world behind. They were free, they thought, of the fishmonger's curse. But then their first-born son, like some biblical Egyptian, was touched by plague. It was impossible, despite an otherwise magical ascent, ever again to feel out from the shadow of the spoiled priest. Until now.

"May the blessing of almighty God . . ." My kneeling mother's head was bent before me. She was wearing the black mantilla, what she'd worn each of her two times in the presence of a pope. Her hands on the altar rail clutched the rosary.

". . . the Father, the Son, and the Holy Spirit . . ." I am quartering the air above her. In a million years, she would not look up at me, and I do not want her to. This is not about her Jimmy, I tell myself. This is about God. Jimmy does not exist here. It is not Jimmy who brings his hands together, palms downward, and lowers them to her bent head. It is a priest. ". . . descend upon you, and remain with you forever."

There, Mom. For you.

When I reach to touch her chin, she startles me by grasping my hands and pulling them to her mouth. My mother kisses my hands, as if she is an Irish peasant, as if I am the pope.

Before I can say, "I love you," she is turning away, then gone.

I take one step along the rail. In those vestments I feel like a float in a parade. My father in his dark civilian suit is kneeling there with his head bent, his face in his hands. What I notice is his hair, and I am shocked to see how white it has become. He is fifty-eight years old, but I have never thought of him as anything but young and powerful.

If I could have looked into the near future, I would have seen the two of us sitting alone on the terrace of the Officers' Club at Ramey Air Force Base in Puerto Rico, the SAC base where, years before, he'd confessed his dread of the Bomb. We are there again the week after my ordination, a priest's honeymoon, a vacation with the folks. Mom is back at the bungalow. Dad and I are having breakfast before heading out for golf. The sun is warm already, glinting off the green-flecked Caribbean. Things have been awkward between us since my first sermon at Bolling, my use of the forbidden word "napalm." We cannot talk about the war. I know that. Yet I am determined to break through the wall of silence the war has built between us. So, suddenly, because it is the only question I have ever really had, I ask him, "Dad, why didn't you get ordained?"

He puts his fork down, thinks for a minute, and seems to decide it is time to answer truthfully. His eyes meet mine. "Because I wasn't worthy."

"Worthy?" I am mystified, and to my horror, I feel a jolt of anger. Worthy? What the hell does *worthy* have to do with it? Who the fuck is *worthy*? I am here at a SAC base with you, with B-52s swarming like gnats, pretending they are not in my fucking nose, pretending not to be a hypocrite and liar. "Worthy?" I say again. I hear the pitch of my voice rise. "I was just ordained, Dad. You think *I'm* worthy?"

My father stares at me, thinking. At last he answers. "Yes, I do."

How I wish I could note this moment as the magnificent affirmation he may well have intended it to be. But I see it as something else. I am worthy because I have immolated my will. He is unworthy — here is the very definition of his life — because he would not.

"May the blessing of almighty God . . ."

I raise my eyes toward heaven, but what I see are the stars as they were the night Saint Paul was knocked from his horse.

". . . the Father . . ."

I bring the blade of my hand up in front of my own face. Behind my kneeling father are my brothers, a line of relatives from Chicago, and the blue-uniformed chaplains waiting to kneel to me. Not me — a priest.

". . . the Son . . ."

I lower my hand toward my bent-over dad. My eyes follow and are caught by something, a motion in his shoulders.

". . . and the Holy Ghost descend upon you . . ."

I put my hands on my father's head, pressing that gray hair, the first time I have ever touched him there. I am so grateful to have this way to press into him at last all my thwarted love. But as I do, it is as if an electric current flows through me, because instantly his body convulses. The movement in his shoulders explodes into quaking, and I fear at once, though I cannot imagine what it is, that some awful breach of nature has occurred.

And so it has. I have never seen a hint of such a thing in him. My father is racked with sobbing. Crude guttural sounds come from inside the hands that remain closed upon his face. He is loudly weeping now, and — as if he is my own Allen Tate — I press my love onto his head. Oh, what gratitude for the raw physical sensation it is to touch this man to whom I can no longer speak. I want to fill the abyss inside him, and I do not care if what I fill it with is myself.

Myself. At the time I thought his weeping was all about me, my fulfilled priesthood balancing the scale of his failed. At the time I thought he was weeping because he was finally released from the curse. I was the ransom paid to God. Now I see what a narrow self-reference all that was. My father had far more to weep about than me, the Church, and even God. Fifteen thousand dead GIs, for one thing. Was he making contact through me with feelings for all those lost sons? The extremity of the sobs that broke and broke and broke again, long after I had said, ". . . remain with you forever," should have told me. I knew so little.

Less than a month before, Richard Nixon had become president. Melvin Laird had become secretary of defense. Among Laird's first messages was one sent to the Joint Chiefs of Staff: the era of breakdown between civilian and military leadership would now end. The Nixon administration was intent upon winning the war. Henry Kissinger announced that we would "prevail." He wanted, in particular, to reinvigorate the JCS, and indeed its recommendations for escalation, long thwarted by McNamara and his successor, Clark Clifford, were already being implemented. By mid-March, less than a month after my ordination, Nixon ordered a major expansion of the air war and began a series of secret and illegal raids by B-52s against North Vietnamese Army sites in Cambodia. This expansion would lead to the ground "incursion" into Cambodia in the spring of 1970, which in turn prompted the shootings at Kent State, sealing the alienation of an entire generation. Nixon's escalation would be partial, giving the Chiefs their air war in exchange for gradual troop withdrawals beginning in mid-1969. But Nixon's escalation would work no better than Johnson's had.

I have no idea if my father objected within Pentagon councils to Nixon's expanded air war, although I doubt that renewed reliance on bombing could have been justified by his DIA estimates. Controlling the flow of military intelligence, my father would have been acutely aware of the other unpublicized development of that season: the psychological and moral unraveling of the U.S. fighting force. The full horrors of the massacre at My Lai, which took place in 1968, were just being uncovered by the high command, although the story would not become public until November of 1969. More and more GIs were committing "refusals to fight." Hundreds of officers were being assaulted — "fragged" — by their own troops. Up to a third of the Army was using drugs. What the Vietnamese could not do to the American military, it was doing to itself.

The war inside the Pentagon was acrimonious too. Nixon's people hated Johnson's, and they especially hated those associated with McNamara. Under Kennedy, McNamara had launched an effort to unify the services as a way to end their turf fighting. His attempt to reassert the civilian control that had been lost in World War II marked the beginning of his conflict with the Chiefs. But my father's role in that struggle predated McNamara, going back to Symington in 1947. As a way to win the loyalty of the Chiefs, Laird retreated from the goal of restoring civilian primacy. "Laird Gives Back Key Budget Role to the Military," read a headline in the *New York Times*. No more would the office of the secretary of defense design force structures or impose weapons programs. Coordination of the services' planning and procurement would be deemphasized. With the McNamara impulse toward unification undercut, my father's efforts at the Defense Intelligence Agency were doomed. Under Nixon, the various competing intelligence operations would sprout again, like mushrooms after a spring rain. That my father's dream of a cohesive military intelligence system turned into yet another bureaucratic nightmare is succinctly revealed by the fact that in fiscal year 1995, as I write, the DIA budget is $600 million, while the combined intelligence budget of the separate services — what DIA was established to take over — stands at $12 billion.

Thus conflict between Laird and my father must have been inevitable. In any event, it came. I assume there were serious differences between them about the air war, but their public break resulted from something else. In the late summer and early fall of 1969, while I was learning the ropes as a peacenik priest, Melvin Laird was trying to get the U.S. Senate to appropriate funds for an antiballistic missile, the Sentinel. His case for the ABM depended on his unprecedented assertion that the Soviet Union had recently begun developing a "first-strike capability," the ability, that is, to so completely wipe out our nuclear arsenal that we would be unable to retaliate. If true, this represented a major shift in the balance of terror that depended on Mutual Assured Destruction, MAD. Nothing in Robert McNamara's or Clark Clifford's assessments had warned of this shift in Soviet intentions.

My father was called to testify before the Senate Foreign Relations Committee, chaired by Senator William Fulbright, whom I'm sure my father detested. He stated that he was reluctant to testify before that committee, even in executive session, because its highly politicized atmosphere would make it impossible to keep secret what he said. That was true, which is why I read about his testimony in the newspapers. Otherwise, I would never have had this context for concluding why his life of public service came to such an abrupt and ignominious end.

The hated dove Fulbright was the committee chair, but in a strange twist, another leading opponent of the ABM was Senator Symington, my father's former mentor. They still held each other in high esteems and who knows how that influenced what happened? The climax of the debate came when Fulbright produced a report entitled "Intelligence and the ABM," which purportedly cited CIA analysis that undercut Laird's claim. Then Symington produced what he called a secret Pentagon report that drew the same conclusion. It was one thing for Laird to be contradicted by CIA chief Richard Helms — but by his own man in the Pentagon? Later I asked my father about this, and he told me that he and Helms were in complete agreement, seeing no change in Soviet strategic planning. When the senators put the direct question to my father — whether, as the director of DIA, he had been the source of Laird's information about the new Soviet intentions — he replied (I see him doing so) coldly that he was not. He was then asked if he had intelligence data that supported the testimony offered by the secretary of defense. My father answered no. When pressed, he stated that he saw no evidence anywhere that what Laird had said was true.

This was in late July. Within days — my mother once told me it was the next day — my father was notified that he was being transferred and demoted. He was nearly sixty years old. My mother told me how stunned he was by this clear consequence of his divergence from a line that the defense secretary and the Joint Chiefs had drawn. He was instantly shunned, a betrayer after all. Until then he had been healthy, but exactly at that point — a classic psychosomatic reaction — he was immobilized by a savage attack of sciatica. Within a week he was in the generals' wing of the Andrews Air Force Base hospital undergoing surgery on his lower back. It was not successful. For most of a year, he would be crippled. Like his son Joe had been. He retired from the Air Force, having never returned to his Pentagon office.

Secretary Laird, meanwhile, unable to produce credible backup for his claim about the USSR, shifted the argument. He began to define the ABM as protection against China. Though he won that summer's vote, he ultimately had no better luck with that rationale. The ABM, which would have amounted to a U.S. move away from Mutual Assured Destruction, never got off the ground. I do not know if he meant to, but my straight-arrow father, bound by a need to say only what he saw, had in fact ended his career by striking a blow against the nuclear madness. I believe his unsung act contributed in some small way to the momentum that led in 1972 to the ABM Treaty with the Soviet Union, the beginning of the end of the arms race.

When, as a young man trained since childhood to be a priest, Dad said no to the cardinal archbishop of Chicago, everything in his Irish-Catholic culture then said no to him. When he and my mother left Chicago, they were surely under the curse of his defiance, and they would fail. But for many years, spoiled priest or not, they had seemed, as it were, to beat the devil. For a time they bore the suffering — my mother openly, my father mutely — of their eldest son's polio. But that sadness lifted too, as Joe junior, despite his endless surgeries or because of them, grew into a sensitive, accomplished student whose graduation with a

Ph.D. in psychology prompted one of the few unclouded family celebrations of the late 1960s.

Yet here he was before me — my father in the prime of life, a man of power and prestige, the proud father of five good sons, the faithful husband of a still handsome, witty woman — here he was sobbing like a baby. What could those others have made of this? What did he see behind those hands of his? A career that begins in defiance must end in defiance? To himself, I see it clear at last, my father was already a failure. And the awful truth is that to me then, too, he was a failure. The war was wrong. He knew it. Despite his image as a truth teller — the thing Symington and McNamara had prized him for — it seemed to me he knew less about the truth than I did. This was months before I had a hint of his other war, the one in the Pentagon. The only war I knew of was Vietnam, which was a brutal crime against GIs and Vietnamese both. A terrible piece of me thought of him as a war criminal for his part in it. Yes, I felt the old emotion as I pressed my hands onto his head, but I felt something else as well. For the first time in my life I was ashamed of him. His weeping made me think that my almighty father — Roger Touhy's "voice of doom" — was a weakling and a coward.

Within a year he would be an almost entirely broken man who would, over the next twenty years, never recover. He would sink from chronic depression into stroke-related dementia or Alzheimer's disease, into complete senility. Oh James, young James, could I but shake you now! Wake up, you smug bastard! If I could only press into your head what I saw years later when I took him to the Vietnam Veterans Memorial on the Mall. He was half demented by then, with snow-white hair and a stooping, lumbering physique. I watched as, with increasing frustration, he tried to find on that black wall the names of men he'd known. He ran his fingers over the etched granite, lost, shaking his head. He became frantic in his searching, but refused my offers to help. As he explained later, he thought the names were arranged alphabetically, instead of in the order in which they'd died. His beleaguered mind was stuck in that mistake.

Something in the intensity of his feeling made me see *my* mistake. I had thought he'd kept his silence about the war not because he believed in it, especially the phase that began with Laird, Kissinger, and Nixon, but because, as McNamara would put it in his memoir, he had felt slavishly obligated by a code of loyalty to his superiors. Not a good enough reason, and as the ABM debate demonstrated, not true of him anyway. But now, watching him finger the names of grunts and pilots and Seabees and leathernecks, I saw the far more compelling obligation that bound him, an officer's obligation, a general's. How could he ever have said about these dead men that their sacrifice had been offered for a stupid mistake? Once he had helped dispatch thousands of young men to their deaths, certainly he'd have seen any subsequent denouncing of the war as breaking faith with them — his other sons.

And then I thought, with horror, that my father, running his fingers over that granite, was looking for another name, his own. I wanted to cry out, Only the dead are recorded here, Dad! But suddenly I saw him as one of those who'd died in Vietnam. Certainly, he had died to me. But now I saw that he had died to himself too. His name might as well have been carved there by Maya Lin.

". . . descend upon you and remain with you forever." Finally I withdrew my hands from his head. My father made it to his feet and staggered back to his pew. He continued to hide his face. I went on blessing people, my brothers, relatives, and the blue-suited chaplains. Many wet eyes. Much pride. Much admiration for me. I took almost nothing in. My ordination to the priesthood meant so much to all these others. What did it mean to me?

Only now do I understand. During the preceding seven years — Hans Küng, the Vatican Council, Martin Luther King, protest at the Pentagon, the assassinations, *Humanae Vitae*, the return of Richard Nixon — I had stopped believing in my father's God and all that went with it: a God more American than Christian, more Roman than Catholic, a God of orthodoxy, conformity, sexlessness, and patriarchy. Even as I swore to be a priest forever, I was afraid that I was losing my faith.

Yet even at that moment of my infinite distance from the pieties that were expected of me, I was finding my faith. I was discovering the God of Jesus Christ, the blasphemer, the heretic, the criminal, the disgrace. In Jesus Christ, passion, doubt, uncertainty, anguish, despair even — all the emotions breaking in me while I was prostrate on that cold stone floor — were signs not of moral failure but of human life. As I looked forward to a priesthood of which I knew already that neither the cardinal nor my parents would approve, my spine was stiffened by the knowledge that Jesus, in keeping bad company, had been disapproved like that. The Gospels recorded a way of life that, from what I could see, had little to do with the life these others expected me to lead. I was very much afraid, but I did not feel alone. I had as friends and comrades Patrick Hughes and a few others, heading out with me from exactly such a place. And I had a vivid sense of the presence at my elbow of Jesus Christ. By some miracle of a transformed faith, despite all the reasons not to, I trusted Him. I wanted to speak of Him to others. The truth is, I still do.

Erasmus defined happiness as the wish to be what you are. By that definition, on the complicated day of my ordination to the priesthood, I was happy.

10

A PRIEST FOREVER

THE WAR would be at the center of my life as a priest, even if I was always on the margin of the movement to end it. After ordination — it was 1969 — I was assigned to the campus ministry at Boston University. At first, after all those years in the seminary, I was intimidated and mystified by the freedom and rampant joy — by Jansenist standards, true hedonism — of the students I encountered. BU was one of the capitals of the student antiwar movement. For a moment in history, *they* were the teachers. In fact, BU students gave form to instincts and impulses I already had myself. Being with them freed me.

The Catholic Student Center, also known as Newman House, became controversial. I permitted a group to open a health food restaurant in our basement, and when they asked me to suggest a name, I offered "Hedgeschool," for the Irish resistance. To my surprise, Hedgeschool became a left-wing organizing center. The sheep of my flock were not the timid Catholics, the puritans and patriots, I'd been sent there to serve. They were radicals, Jews, feminists, gays, SDS kids, draft dodgers, resisters, misfits, and wackos. Not sheep at all.

I became a draft counselor, helping kids avoid induction. With colleagues who were already in the Berrigan network, I became part of the underground — the self-styled East Coast Conspiracy to Save Lives — helping to get conscripts and deserters to Canada before FBI agents could find them. My brother Brian, operating out of the Philadelphia field office meanwhile, was on the fugitive squad, tracking draft dodgers.

The greatest fugitive of all, beginning in April 1970, when he disappeared rather than turn himself in to serve time for the Catonsville action, was Father Daniel Berrigan, S.J. He played cat and mouse with the FBI, traveling incognito up and down the East Coast with the help of hundreds. J. Edgar Hoover was enraged as Berrigan, popping up at rallies and giving interviews, made fools of the Bureau. That I was moved by the Jesuit's courageous witness to deepen my involvement in antiwar activity was hardly unique. Thousands of us were recruited. "We are summoned to act in unison with our friends," he wrote, and I heard the words as addressed to me, "to join in conspiracy, in jeopardy, in illegal nonviolent actions, to hotten up the scene wherever we are."

We tried to hotten up the scene at BU. Several professors, including some Jewish professors who were less likely to draw FBI notice, were part of the underground network hiding Berrigan, and he often seemed close at hand. We held celebrations and rallies, always evoking his name and always hoping he would show up. We helped stage sit-ins to block military recruitment. On Good Friday we picketed the Brighton residence of Cardinal Humberto Medeiros, asking him to denounce the war. "Another Crucifixion in Indochina," read the sign I carried. As his priests and nuns, we asked to see His Eminence. When he admitted us, he said sadly how tormented he was about the war. But his torment, compared to that of the Vietnamese, seemed beside the point. I was not rebelling against authority. I was in search of it.

Daniel Berrigan became my authority. In relation to him I'd

found a voice, and I used it against the war as forthrightly as I could, while he was underground and then when he was in prison. One day I received a phone call from a producer at *The Dick Cavett Show*. "Frankly," she said, "it's Father Berrigan we're interested in interviewing, but he's not available." She laughed, and I didn't. "We're told you could speak for him."

"Me? I don't even know Dan Berrigan."

"Look," the producer said impatiently, "Mr. Cavett is trying to get your guy's point of view on the air. They've approved you. Don't say no."

With a sinking feeling I thought, Christ, they know about Dad. They want me because of Dad, the sensation it will cause. But then, exactly because I'd thought of him, I realized I had to do it. In the early afternoon of the day of my appearance on the Cavett show, the street outside the Catholic Student Center was blocked with demonstrators trying to keep a Marine recruiter from entering the nearby BU placement office. Invited, even goaded by the university president, John Silber, Boston police swooped onto campus and savagely attacked the students: "Ho, Ho, Ho Chi Minh my ass!" Cops invaded Newman House, threatening my secretary and shoving me aside to get at the fleeing kids. By midafternoon I was hoarse from screaming at police, taking badge numbers, stalking the sergeants and captains. "If you're with them, Father, fuck you!"

I was still trembling with anger and frustration by the time I arrived for the early evening taping at the ABC studios in New York. The producer greeted me and showed me to the green room, where Cavett's other guests were waiting. They were the comics Jack Klugman and Henny ("Take my wife — please") Youngman, the singer John Sebastian, and, looking very sexy, the actress Elizabeth Ashley, soon to appear on Broadway as Maggie in *Cat on a Hot Tin Roof*. When I entered the small sound-proof room, no one looked at me. The other guests continued their hushed chatting with their handlers and agents. There was nothing to note in my appearance. I was wearing, as usual, black chinos, a black turtleneck, and a dark J. Press tweed sportcoat that I'd bought at an Episcopal church rummage sale.

I began to wonder where Dick Cavett was, and, sure enough, just before showtime the producer put her head in the room to say Dick was ill. My heart sank when she asked Jack Klugman if he would sit in as host. The goofy Klugman? What about Cavett's impulse to put in a word for Berrigan? What about the solemn agenda that had brought me here? Klugman hurried out.

More than an hour later, after all the other guests had done their self-promoting shticks, the producer came for me. I had just poured yet another cup of coffee. I carried it along, as if I were an old hand at this. When I stepped out into the backstage area, the unmuffled sound of the show's band jolted me, and just as the announcer was speaking my name — "Father James Carroll, an antiwar priest" — I spilled the coffee all over the crotch of my pants. Numbness gave way to a feeling of nausea, and even as I heard the dutiful applause of the studio audience, I frantically wiped at my pants. Only at the last second did I determine that the coffee stain was invisible. Thank God for black.

John Sebastian and Henny Youngman greeted me warmly, as if we hadn't ignored one another in the green room. Then Elizabeth Ashley kissed me full on the lips, a wet kiss that drew hoots from the audience. Take that, Father. I was to be their straight man. Very straight.

When I'd taken my place on the couch, nearest Klugman, who was at Cavett's desk, the comic's opening line to me, aimed at my turtleneck, was, "Where's your dog collar?" The audience gasped pleasurably at the gibe, then waited for my reply. Oh, this could be fun.

"I'm sorry?" I stalled, trying to think of something to say.

"Your dog collar, Father. You know, woof-woof." *Ba-boom* went the drummer. More laughter. Get with it, Jimmy.

I stared at him. The audience grew silent. The hapless Klugman was a Boston cop, his nightstick at my throat. I said, "Is it priests in general you want to insult, or only me?"

Klugman made a hammy face at the audience, but the scattered applause was for me.

I smiled as broadly as I could, still aware of my wet pants. I reached across to put a friendly hand on Klugman's arm. "We aren't dogs anymore, Jack. But we still bite." More applause, an advantage to be pressed. "Now can we talk for a minute about something serious?"

"Oh, now, Father, if we —"

I cut him off. "That's why I came here. I want to tell these folks about a police riot I just left. Not three hours ago, I was roughed up by cops myself."

The clean statement, the start of a narrative that had to be completed, stopped him. He glanced at the audience, saw their interest, and so sat back and let me talk. Which I then did. Beginning with a description of the clash at BU, including a swipe at Silber's outrageous encouragement of police brutality, and moving on to state my appreciation and concern for Daniel Berrigan, I spoke uninterrupted for what seemed like a long time. I called on everyone present and everyone watching to do what they could to oppose the war. Then I stopped.

There was a moment of awkward silence. Klugman was nonplused. He looked toward Henny Youngman, who for once had nothing to say. Then some members of the audience began to applaud. The floor manager waved at Klugman from behind the camera. He stammered, "I guess we'll take a break." During the commercial, no one on the set spoke to me. Klugman huddled with the producer. After the break, in an unheard-of departure, the band played an entire number and the show ended.

I learned from my mother the next day that my parents had not seen the show, but that she had heard about it from friends. "What did you hear?" I asked.

"That your hair is too long, and you wore sandals."

"My hair is fine," I said. "What did Dad say?"

"I didn't tell him, and I'm not going to. He doesn't need to know that you've deliberately embarrassed him."

"Embarrassing Dad had nothing to do with it."

"Don't be ridiculous. They only asked you onto their program because of him."

"That's not true, Mom." To my horror, I heard the whine in my voice. How I'd feared at first that it *was* true. "They didn't even know about Dad. He never came up."

"Then why did they ask you?"

My question too. "I don't know, Mom. I've been writing things. I've given speeches."

"Come on, Jim. You really think a national TV show asked you because of *you?*"

"I guess I do, Mom."

She said nothing for a long time, then broke the silence with her sternest voice. "Just don't you embarrass your father. And don't embarrass Brian."

"Wait a minute, Mom. Wait a minute. What if they're embarrassing me?"

There was no answer. I heard the click when she hung up.

Later that year, "Philip Berrigan and seven others," as the press always referred to them, were charged with plotting to blow up steam pipes under the Pentagon and to kidnap Henry Kissinger, the architect of Nixon's air-war escalations. Phil was in prison in Lewisburg, Pennsylvania. He had trusted another inmate, who had study-release privileges, to smuggle letters to and from Sister Elizabeth McAlister, a radical nun at New York's Marymount College, where I'd met her. The inmate was an FBI plant. In fact, the McAlister letters did contain reports of conversations about antiwar strategies, including a proposed "Citizens Arrest" of Henry Kissinger. The letters also provided the FBI with the crucial clue to Dan Berrigan's hiding place on Block Island, where he was finally arrested. The FBI vendetta against the Berrigans continued with indictments and the trial of the so-called Harrisburg 8.

The by now broad Berrigan network, which was centered on but not limited to Catholics, used the trial as another mobilizing event. I helped organize support. At one point my campus ministry colleague, a former nun named Anne Walsh, was subpoenaed to testify about Phil's activities, which she refused to do. She was charged with contempt of court, and I traveled to Harrisburg to testify as a character witness for her. I wore the Roman collar when I took the stand.

At an outdoor rally in Harrisburg one night, I gave a speech and read my poems. It may have seemed to others that I was successfully reinventing myself on the model of Daniel Berrigan, a priest-poet at last. But the truth was, inwardly I was terribly frightened all the time. That night, after my appearance, while I stood on the edge of the crowd listening to another speaker, a derelict approached me. Repelled by his stink, I sidled away, but he followed. His shabby beard and matted hair and soiled clothing made him seem half mad. I moved again, but he stayed with me, drawing close enough to whisper, "If you don't tell your friends about me, I won't tell mine about you." He flashed a shit-eating grin. Brian. Before I could answer, my FBI-agent brother melted back into the crowd.

Jesus told his disciples, "You will have trouble," and when I did, I tried to take it as a mark of the faith to which I was clinging. I was raised to be obedient, polite, and good. Yet I had become someone I did not recognize — defiant, angry, and irreverent. There were good reasons for the changes, of course, but I did not like myself that way. I got in trouble with John Silber for denouncing him on the Cavett show. I got in trouble with the cardinal when parents complained that I was advising their sexually active college-age children to use birth control. The cardinal heard rumors that I was concelebrating a weekly midnight Eucharist with an Episcopal priest, that we'd merged our congregations. It was true. The cardinal received objections about sit-ins organized at Newman House. Ultimately, he heard hysterical reports that my colleague — a nun! a woman! — had said the Mass in my absence. It was true, all true.

Once I even got in trouble with my new allies, the peace movement heavies who had shielded Dan Berrigan and were now shielding each other. They had heard reports that I had an FBI agent for a brother, and they labeled me as one not to be trusted. I was an informant, a provocateur. When I learned of this, I confronted the man most responsible — a "friend" — and demonstrated that there was no secret about my brother, or my father for that matter. I had written of both in poems and articles. I had wrecked myself at home, yet now I was accused of having maintained that first loyalty. I felt betrayed and angry beyond anything that man could understand. The rumors about me stopped.

But maybe FBI agents themselves had heard the rumors, because one day a pair made a visit to my office. I could have told them all we had in common, but I said nothing. Then I realized: they knew. They asked me about certain fugitives, a couple of whom I had known. I said nothing. Finally, exasperated by my refusal to answer their questions, one of the agents, a Jesuit-trained Irish Catholic who had no category for priest and nun resisters, blurted the question, "What kind of creatures are they, Father?"

"We're human beings," I answered.

To my knowledge, my father never learned of my Air Force arrest. It took place, Oedipally enough, at a protest at the main gate of Hanscom Air Force Base, outside Boston. Hanscom, a high-tech research center associated with MIT, was the development site of a program code-named Igloo White. It was a system of tiny electronic sensors that, when salted onto the fields and paddies of Vietnam, would pick up any movement and trigger air strikes by B-52s. Igloo White was an integral part of the Nixon-Kissinger escalation of the air war. The bombers would come when the triggering movement was of an infiltrating North Vietnamese soldier — or of a water buffalo or a rice-harvesting peasant. As a weapon that did not distinguish between combatant and civilian, Igloo White seemed the perfect emblem of the war's evil. I had no qualm about joining in the pointed protest against it. I remember the faces of the air policemen standing by as local police picked me up from the road after I, like my twenty or thirty comrades, went limp and refused to move. The APs were acne-ridden kids like those who'd saluted me as I drove my old man's car through the gate at Bolling. At the bus to which I was carried, and onto which I still refused to climb, a man in civilian clothes leaned over me, clipboard in hand. He warned me that if I did not cooperate, I could get hurt.

"You're with the OSI, right?" I said.

He was shocked that I knew of it.

I told him that my father was its first director. He stared hard at me, then said, "Your name is Carroll."

I nodded. Oddly, I felt a rush of pride that a decade and a half after my father had left OSI, the agent knew his name. And at last I didn't care if he told on me.

On March 8, 1971, something completely unexpected occurred — an event that drew even tighter the web in which Brian and I had become entangled. Unnamed members of the Catholic left, retaliating for FBI harassment, broke into the FBI resident agency in Media, Pennsylvania. They called themselves the Citizens' Commission to Investigate the FBI, and set about at once to publish the various documents they stole from the office. Never before had FBI files been revealed without authorization. The image of a rogue agency manipulating, infiltrating, and interfering not only with militant groups but with mainstream, even innocuous organizations like the phone company and the Boy Scouts was given substance by memos and reports that described such tactics in detail. For the first time in its history, the FBI was made to seem to the public at large simultaneously sinister and ridiculous.

I was part of the Boston effort to exploit the Media sources. I helped organize a "citizens' tribunal" that indicted J. Edgar Hoover himself. We convened in Boston's Faneuil Hall, and various activists, drawing on Media documents and other sources, "testified" to FBI abuses. Behind these "witnesses" were massive oil paintings and busts displaying the heroes of the Revolution. Faneuil Hall, famous as America's "Cradle of Liberty," was built by a merchant whose stock-in-trade was human beings, the slave trader Peter Faneuil.

Among the witnesses testifying that day was a Pentagon official, one of McNamara's whiz kids, whose insider description of the illegal conduct of the war was particularly riveting. This was his first public act of dissent, and I remember feeling sorry for him, he seemed so nervous. Like everyone, I was edified by his willingness to risk his career by joining us. His name meant nothing, although by June, only weeks later, everyone in America would know him, Daniel Ellsberg, as the person who leaked the Pentagon Papers. At the tribunal's conclusion, a dozen of us trekked over to the JFK Building, across Government Center, to the FBI field office on an upper floor, to deliver our verdict on J. Edgar Hoover. Guilty!

Sometime later, after Hoover died, Brian gave me a T-shirt bearing Hoover's picture above the words "J. Edgar Hoover is coming back, and is he pissed!" He was sure pissed that month. He suspended the head of the Media office without pay and launched a nationwide manhunt with his best agents to find those responsible for what in Bureau argot was immediately dubbed MEDBURG. A few Catholic pacifists had done what no gangster (not Roger Touhy) and no KGB operative (not Colonel Abel) had ever done before, and, by God, the director wanted them!

My father, meanwhile, was the chairman of a gala Washington dinner at which an association of former FBI agents was to honor Hoover. I received a phone call from Dad, the first I'd had directly from him since before I was ordained. He stunned me by asking if I would come to Washington and attend the dinner, so that I could offer the benediction. "Everyone knows my son is a priest," he said. "The director himself mentioned it."

"I thought I'd embarrassed you, Dad."

"Your mother tells me I shouldn't be asking you to do this. But it would mean a lot to me. It would mean a lot to Mr. Hoover. They still think of you as a former employee."

It was so easy to imagine what my friends would say: Do it. Turn it into an action. Throw blood on the table in front of him. Denounce Hoover to his face!

I heard the plaintive note in my father's voice. He was asking for far more than a few pious words from me at the beginning of a meal. He was trying to redeem my entire priesthood, to wrench it back within the sacred margins. He was also trying to redeem our relationship. If I did this, everything would be good between us again. How could I possibly explain that if I dutifully said yes, there was no way I could follow through with it, standing before a ballroom full of FBI men in black tie, blessing them, affirming what they believed, praying for what they did. And as for Hoover, he was as close to a personal enemy as I had. I would never throw blood, but if I went to the banquet, it could only be to denounce him.

Which I would never do to you, Dad, I wanted to say, and, This refusal is my act of love. Instead, I said only, "I can't, Dad."

He did not press. He hung up, and it was clear to me that he would not ask for anything from me again. I told no one in the movement of the chance I'd passed up. I was a traitor after all.

The only person on the left in whom I could have imagined confiding was Dennis, but by then he was in India, a draft exile. Amazingly, the person to whom I found it possible to turn, laying bare the outrageous and hilarious complexities of my situation, was Brian. His situation wasn't so simple either. I was close to his wife, Vicki, whom I had known since Wiesbaden. Their daughters were the nearest thing I had to children of my own, and I never missed their celebrations. When I visited their house in New Jersey that spring, it was to baptize their new baby, a big family event. Brian took me aside, and it was a relief to both of us that we could laugh about being on opposite sides. He invited me to go into work with him, which I did as a lark. He gave me a tour of the Philadelphia field office, introducing me around with the old wisecracking brio. At lunch I tried to tell him what a mistake the Bureau was making, but he didn't want to hear it, and I didn't push. He thought I was a naive fool.

I was relaxed about the Media burglary because, though we were exploiting the purloined files in Boston, I'd had nothing to do with the break-in itself. I had heard rumors that various

acquaintances of mine were involved, but few outsiders knew
anything for sure. It was a well-kept secret. No one in the Bureau, however, was relaxed about MEDBURG, not even Brian. In
relation to me, he was under pressure I did not know about. I
would later learn that I *was* a naive fool, not about the Berrigans,
as he thought, but about the Bureau. In Sanford J. Ungar's book
FBI, published in 1975, I came across this passage about Media:
those whom FBI investigators "felt they had identified as im-
plicated in the burglary were primarily affiliated with the Catholic Left, ironically including the sister of one agent assigned
to Philadelphia, and the priest brother of another. (The latter
agent invited his brother to the field office and pleaded with him
'to help us solve a crime.' The priest refused, and the agent reported back to his superiors that 'I can no longer understand my
brother.')"

I knew at once what bullshit this was. Brian had never asked
me to help solve a crime, and there was no question of his
"no longer" understanding me. He knew what my commitments
were, and accepted them. To Brian I was naive, perhaps, but
my allegiance was always clear, always strong. Our mutual dis-
agreement was out in the open, and so was our respect for each
other. Our Harrisburg compact held: "I won't tell my friends if
you don't tell yours." Obviously there were pressures on Brian
to try to turn me. Perhaps he pretended to, which would explain
why he'd put me on display at the office that day — and it
would account for the report Ungar had picked up. If Brian was
behaving slyly with anyone, it was not me. After I read the
Ungar passage, I sent a copy of the book to Brian. By then it was
five years after the fact. He called me up at once, alarmed at
what I might have thought and ready to explain. I told him he
didn't have to.

When the Bureau found that it could not prove that the
Catholics had pulled off the Media raid, it did the next best

thing. Using the services of an agent provocateur, the FBI set up some of the Media suspects, as well as numerous others, in a new burglary, this time of draft board offices in Camden, New Jersey. The action took place one night in August 1971, and several friends of mine from Boston participated. Because the Bureau had been tipped off from the start, dozens of agents, including Brian, had no trouble breaking in on the protesters, shoving the snouts of their shotguns under the chins of unarmed Catholic flower children. They arrested what came to be known as the Camden 28.

Brian told me later that he and his colleagues had waited to spring their trap in the embalming room of a mortuary across the street. But that was far from the worst insult to the Bureau's dignity, for when the case against the Camden 28 came to trial — I was there as a character witness for several defendants; Brian was standing by to testify for the government — the jury quickly voted to acquit. After the verdict, the judge lectured the FBI on entrapment. The Bureau, he said, had disgraced itself.

When I went to Washington the next year with about two dozen mainstream clergy and establishment liberals, the last thing I expected was to get arrested. This was an ecumenical group of clergy and lay leaders, not Catholic radicals. It happened that J. Edgar Hoover had died only days before, and much of Washington was in mourning. I refused to feel anything for him, although I couldn't help remembering my FBI summer job, my awed glimpses of the director, his meaning for my family. But that day I told the story to no one.

Our purpose was to visit the offices of congressmen and senators and urge the cut-off of funds for the war. In the strange dispensation of the era, such conventional lobbying had come to seem the audacious approach. To me it seemed radical to be wearing a black suit and Roman collar. My Paulist brother David Killian was with me, and we connected with another friend, Larry Kessler, head of the Thomas Merton Center in Pittsburgh.

After a day of making the rounds of congressional offices, we met up with the rest of our confreres in a vestibule beside the Capitol rotunda. In the rotunda itself, J. Edgar Hoover was lying in state, his flag-draped coffin flanked by an honor guard. We tried to pretend he was not there; our work against the war was the point. We had all been through like experiences, brushoffs and cold receptions even from antiwar politicians. Few were inclined to bring the war into the appropriations process. But in fact, if every senator and congressman who had claimed to be opposed to the war voted to cut off funding — this was nearly five years after Tip O'Neill had boldly rejected the war — they could have derailed it right there. But appropriations bills included the bacon for back home. Almost no one was prepared to risk losing his own line in the bill.

William Sloane Coffin, the Yale chaplain, himself a former CIA man and a former defendant in a famous draft resistance case, stood in our midst. In a fit of anger, he denounced the politicians. Business as usual was killing people! On the swell of his own passion, Coffin declared that we were not going to leave the Capitol until funds for the war were cut off. We all spontaneously assented. "If J. Edgar Hoover can spend the night in the U.S. Capitol," Coffin said, "why can't we?" And that is how it happened that I was sitting on the floor of the rotunda when, after closing hours, the police came for us. It consoled me to find myself in the same paddy wagon with Killian and Kessler. But when a fourth turned out to be Dr. Benjamin Spock, I began to think I was dreaming. Hoover dead? Dr. Spock arrested? Soon enough, it seemed a nightmare.

The D.C. cops were vicious. Those demonstrators who remained limp were carried up and down stairs at a backwards slanting angle so that their heads banged against the steps. Our fingers were bent out of joint by fingerprint technicians. We were roughly pushed into the D.C. lockup, a hellhole in the bowels of the courthouse on Pennsylvania Avenue. Other prisoners hooted and cursed as we were brought in.

The stench of disinfectant combined with sewage choked me. There was no air. It seemed like an oven. I was locked in a stinking two-man cell with another demonstrator. In the center of the cramped space was an unflushable metal toilet brimming with urine and feces, which had spilled onto the floor. Bolted to the wall were two narrow steel shelves, mattressless bunks. There was nothing to do but lie there and read the graffiti that covered every surface, trying to block out the fearful noises. I prayed to go to sleep, but never did.

By the middle of the night, my spirits had begun a free fall. Whatever sense of liberation I had felt on first joining the peace movement had long since evaporated. All the organizing and marching had come to seem futile as the war dragged on and on. Anarchy and nihilism seemed to mark not only the government but the movement too. And the Catholic wing of it was proving to be no more trustworthy than the SDS. The Berrigans, for example, had been staunch defenders of the way of life to which I'd given myself, making a special point of the new relevance of our vows, especially celibacy, which in an age of sexual exploitation marked us as the true radicals. So imagine the betrayal I'd felt at the recent news that Philip Berrigan and Elizabeth McAlister had secretly "married each other" at some point in the past. My heroes had been getting it on all this time, and what a fool that made me! It is impossible to describe fully the preciousness of the fragile bond we vowed celibates had shared, or the devastation we felt as, one by one, we saw it break. More and more of the priests I admired, and whose steadfast commitment was crucial if our vision of the new Church was to be realized, were leaving the priesthood. Literally thousands had resigned since I had become a priest, including some of the brightest lights of the Paulist Fathers. A joke of the time told of the note pinned to the rectory bulletin board: "Will the last one out please extinguish the sanctuary lamp."

It was far from a joke to me when Patrick Hughes took me to dinner one night at Jacob Wirth in Boston to tell me he was going to marry Marianne Murray. I knew her mainly as one of the Camden 28 supporters. She would become one of my dearest friends, the godmother of my first child, but at the time the news of Patrick's decision fell on me like a wall. No way was I saying "Go Patrick!" now. I had followed him out onto the thin ice of this crazy life, and he was leaving me here, like an old Eskimo. I was pissed off and hurt. Hadn't we made a deal with each other to stick it out? Weren't our challenges to the old ways promises to bring the new ones to completion? Hadn't we told each other that if we quit, the reforms of the Church, for one thing, would never take effect? And haven't events shown that intuition to have been the truth?

It was as if, that night in jail, I saw into the future, saw the coming collapse of the liberal Catholic impulse, the very thing I was trying to build a life around. But all around me, men were saying it wasn't worth it. Men I needed. And men I loved. It was as if I saw how Vietnam too would scar us all forever, how the dream of a new just, "great" society was falling in slow motion on a sword. In the D.C. lockup, the unclothed despair that I'd been fending off assaulted me like one of the sadistic guards. This was merely a single miserable night in the hoosegow, not the years' worth of prison that Dan and Phil and dozens of others were having to survive. Yet I fell into a pit of angst and fear that was also the old pit of my self-loathing.

Then, from the next cell, in the absolute middle of the night, in response perhaps to the sounds of a demonstrator's weeping, William Sloane Coffin began to sing. He had a rich baritone voice and a Protestant's command of music — although his father-in-law was the Jewish maestro Arthur Rubinstein. Gradually I began to listen to what he was singing. "Comfort ye, comfort ye, my people." It was a plaintive prayer set to the most familiar music ever to come from Dublin. "I know that my redeemer liveth . . . ," Coffin sang. And finally, bringing us all to our feet in our minds, "Hallelujah! For the Lord God omnipotent . . . shall reign for ever and ever. King of Kings, and Lord of Lords, Hallelujah."

Coffin was an epiphany of manliness, courage, and faith to me. I will never forget what his singing of passages from Handel's *Messiah* in that cellblock meant and did for me. He seemed to sing for hours. Some of the other inmates up and down the corridor joined in. Soon I was singing too. As those old words of the faith rolled over and out of me, I knew that I believed them to be true. My redeemer liveth, which meant I was where I was supposed to be. I was doing what I was supposed to be doing. Here I am, Lord. Send me.

When I got out of jail the next day, I was about to head back to Boston, but then I thought of Hoover, how his death would have saddened my parents. I called home. My mother answered. There was no question of lying to her, but neither had I any need to tell her what had brought me to town. I wanted only to connect. I said I was passing through.

She answered coldly, "We know what you're doing here."

"You do?"

"Your father is hurt this time. This time you've hurt him."

"Let me talk to him."

My mother went away from the phone, then came back. "He doesn't want to talk to you."

"I'll call from Boston."

"He doesn't want to talk to you *again!*" The pitch of her voice shot up. "I won't let you do this to him. Do you hear me? I won't permit it. Not you too."

In her tone I heard the fury of a warrior woman. Not my man, you don't! You don't do this to him! Those others might, but not you! Not you! Not to mine!

"Do you hear me?" she asked.

"Yes, ma'am."

"You've disgraced your father. He says he doesn't want to talk to you again, and I don't blame him."

"Can't he tell me himself, Mom?"

"No," she answered sharply. "He can't."

And that was that. I wrote a poem at the time that ends with these lines:

> I said to the general's son, "Get the hell
> out of my chair!" And he said to me,
> "You're lucky, war being what it is,
> all you lost is your Dad."

But by some miracle — no, that's wrong. By her doing, the war didn't cost me my mother. There were six men in her life. She loved us all. Her omnidirectional anger was proof of it. She loved her draft-dodger son and her FBI-agent son. She loved Kevin and Joe. She loved her husband. And she loved her son who'd become a thin-soup radical priest.

My father had built a life out of his response to her steadfast will. I found a way to salvage my life because, for all the ways I disappointed her, she continued, when she wasn't furious at me and perhaps because she could be, to convey her belief in me. I think now that I kept believing in myself because she did. Once when I was visiting home, while Daniel Berrigan was still underground, a fugitive, he was referred to on the evening news. Yet another Scarlet Pimpernel appearance, tweaking her beloved FBI. She turned to me and said, "I wish he'd come here."

Thinking of her old fondness for Hoover, her loyalty to Brian, I blurted bitterly, "So you could turn him in?"

An amused expression came into her face, and she said softly, "No, to hide him. They'd never look for him here. He'd be safe with me."

I was too surprised to speak. She explained herself by saying simply, "He's a priest, Jimmy. Isn't he a priest?"

And there it was. The primordial value. The family touch-stone. The soul of who we were to each other. My mother had spent the best energy of her life embracing a particular American ideal. Daniel Berrigan held it in contempt. But isn't he a priest? And aren't I?

I loved being a priest. The experience I'd had with a grief-struck Allen Tate foreshadowed the form my ministry would take — an effort to redeem the cruel myopia of the Counter-Reformation Church. My job was to accompany people on their versions of the journey I was taking. At Boston University, my main function as a priest was to discover and offer new images of what belief in Jesus Christ entailed. What happened to the little chapel I inherited there was the perfect symbol of my progression.

St. Jerome's Chapel occupied the first floor of a large old Back Bay mansion next door to Newman House. The building had been the residence of Cardinal O'Connell, Cardinal Cushing's predecessor. And the chapel, when I became its priest in 1969, reflected a rigid old view of the Church worthy of such a prove-nance. A rank of wooden pews offered seating for perhaps a hundred and fifty, a meager capacity considering that a third of BU's twenty thousand students were Catholics. But size didn't matter. The chapel looked more fit for an order of cloistered nuns than sixties college students. There were grim Stations of the Cross, dull smoked-glass windows at one end, and at the other a formal altar raised on a small pyramid of stairs. The pyramid was one sticking point, and the altar was another — symbols of the two main notes that the theology of the Vatican Council had rejected. The Church was not to be thought of as a mass of people at the bottom, a few cardinals near the top, capped by His Holiness the Pope. The Church was not a pyramid but a people, the people of God. And its main activity was not a sacrifice on an altar but a meal at a table. A table symbolizes fellowship, hospitality, and equality, which is why Jesus put tables at the center of his ministry and why, in its liturgical reforms, the Church had embraced it.

I took one look around St. Jerome's and thought, Here is where we start. In that first year, the pews went, and so did the altar, and so did the smoky glass. Students did the heavy work with me. Artists among them created new symbols for us: a beautiful mural instead of Stations, a modern set of stained-glass windows that reflected views of the street outside, hand-thrown pottery for the Eucharist. We put down a bright red carpet on which we could sit in a big circle until it was time to stand around the simple oak table a student had built. There was a rotation of banners, a riot of bright cushions, all made by the kids. By the time we celebrated the new St. Jerome's, we'd become a new people. After that, I could not go into the little place, whether for our Saturday midnight Masses or for my stolen hours of solitary prayer, without feeling the lift of my heart.

Students entrusted themselves to me there. In one corner was a confessional, twin booths for penitent and priest. The new theology encouraged a move away from the impersonal encounter in such dark corners and toward, for example, face-to-face meetings in an office. I made myself available in both ways, but some of the most moving moments of my priesthood occurred when people talked to me anonymously. Despite seven years of seminary, I was in no way prepared for the shock of having strangers place their complete trust in me, not because I was James Carroll, would-be poet, would-be prophet, general's son, hip young campus minister, but only because I was a priest. In the confessional, hearing stories of struggle, suffering, self-doubt, and despair; sensing that the very act of my listening was a consolation and that the sacred Word I spoke was healing — I remembered the words of Lacordaire that had once defined my dearest hope: "What a life! And it is yours, O priest of Jesus Christ!"

What I did best, and loved doing most, was relate the simple Gospel stories that repeated over and over again the one thing I'd been ordained to preach and the one thing my students needed to hear — that no matter who we are or what we do, God loves us. The more I said it to them, the closer I came to believing it myself. But in truth that faith continually eluded me.

My room at the Paulist Center on Beacon Hill looked out over Boston Common. Late one night I was awakened by sirens and the monster engines of fire trucks gunning up the hill. Then the noise passed, and I rolled over and went back to sleep. Almost immediately my phone rang. It was someone from BU, calling to tell me that St. Jerome's was on fire, along with the rest of the building, which housed archdiocesan offices. My caller told me that the huge building was engulfed in flames, which were visible all over the city. I went to the window, and sure enough the sky was glowing.

Minutes later I was there, standing across the street, numb. I saw the figures of two firefighters silhouetted against the sky, the men balanced on a blazing ledge high above, the building collapsing around them. First one, then the other plunged willingly into the fire — to die, I was certain, although they did not. I remember an overwhelming sense of awe and gratitude that strangers would do such a thing for me.

Their efforts kept the fire contained, but our building burned to the ground. Evidence of gasoline and rags was later found in the ruins, a case of arson, never solved. The same night, someone took a crowbar to the door of my office in the adjacent building, but was unable to get in. I asked the arson investigator if it could have been firefighters, but they'd never entered that building. Colleagues of mine later attributed the intrusion, and the arson, to Nixon's "plumbers," which, if I could have believed it, might have given that profoundly absurd experience some meaning. As I stood there that night, I did not explicitly see a metaphor for what was happening everywhere around me, but unconsciously, the burning of that chapel — symbol of all I'd brought to the priesthood and all I wanted from it — was surely decisive in my facing up to the truth of my situation. The vision of the new Church that I had first glimpsed in Pope John XXIII and in the writings of Hans Küng was already being repudiated right and left. Pope John was long dead, and Pope Paul VI was in the grip of a savage Catholic neurosis about sex. Küng, soon enough, would himself be officially repudiated, like everyone who agreed with him. To be a priest in the post–*Humanae Vitae* Catholic Church was to have such contradictions at the center of one's life. And notwithstanding the buckets of rhetoric about our priestly fraternity, none of which remotely addressed the hidden pain of ordinary men, to be a priest was also — here was what I could deny less and less — to live that contradicted life alone.

My brother Dennis decided to come in from the cold of his own contradicted life. He returned to the United States, and came at once to see me in Boston. He had learned that, after his refusal to report for induction, his draft board had referred his case to the

U.S. attorney. But because of the backlog of such cases, he had yet to be formally indicted. He had returned to America prepared to go to jail, but I encouraged the impulse he also had to apply for conscientious-objector status. He had refused to do that in the first place because, at the time, one could do so only by appealing to religious convictions, narrowly defined. Dennis would not pretend to be religious. To him, the war was wrong whether God existed or not.

Such restricted notions of "religious" had now loosened somewhat. I knew there were precedents for an appeal to "mere" ethical conviction as a basis for conscientious objection. If his application was rejected, he intended again to refuse to serve. This time he would go to jail. Without revealing his whereabouts, he contacted the Selective Service. He was told to report for a hearing in Washington, and advised to come accompanied by an attorney. An appeals board would decide whether to seek an indictment; if no indictment was called for, the board would reorder his induction or recommend him for CO status.

Meanwhile, I used my contacts to find a lawyer. That was when Dennis stunned me. He had not been in direct communication with our parents in nearly two years, yet he said that he intended to ask Dad to be his lawyer.

"You can't do that," I said. "Dad would never help you, and it would only be cruel to ask him." As it was cruel, I might have added, of Dad to ask me to offer a blessing at Hoover's dinner.

"He went to law school," Dennis said. "He was admitted to the bar. He's a lawyer."

"He's also ashamed of you. Believe me, I know. He hates what you've done."

Dennis shrugged, not answering with the question that hung above us both: But does he hate me?

I remember how angry I became at Dennis. His plan struck me as passive-aggressive, almost sadistic, guaranteed to escalate the insult and bad feelings between him and Dad. I knew so little. I have referred to my father in the period after his retirement as an almost entirely broken man. I used the word "almost" because something vital and courageous and large-hearted had remained intact in him. He drew on it in response to Dennis, agreeing to represent him before the appeals board.

He took the project very seriously. He studied the law and then met with Dennis, to advise him as he prepared his own statement. When the day of the Selective Service hearing arrived, Dad appeared wearing his uniform, one of the few times he did so in retirement. His three stars matched those of General Lewis Hershey, the infamous long-time Selective Service director. When Dad and Dennis entered the hearing room, the board members were seated on the far side of a long table. Our father introduced Dennis, but the chairman, struck by the uniform, wanted only to hear from the general. He asked Dennis to step outside. Dad looked at Dennis, then said, "My son has a statement to make."

With that, the board sat through Dennis's reading of his long, painstakingly composed declaration of conscience. I had read it, and found it to be a clear and forthright definition of the war's immorality and of a citizen's obligation to oppose it. When Dennis finished, the chairman asked him again to wait outside. Dennis left the room.

It was perhaps the next Christmas when I visited my parents, and we went to midnight Mass at St. Paul's College. By then I could not worship at the Bolling chapel. After Mass, I was sitting in the Paulist common room when an elderly priest asked my father about his defense of my brother. Unaware that I was listening, he described it. The chairman of the appeals board acknowledged that he knew who Dad was, and asked for his view. Citing the law, Dad explained why his son's position — not just then, but in the first place — was proper and legal. "The right to conscientious objection," he said, "is basic to the American idea." The board's task, as he saw it, was only to determine if the application for exemption from military service was authentically based on conscience. "I am here today," he went on, "not because I agree with what my son just said — obviously, wearing this uniform, I don't — but because I know with absolute certitude that his position is sincerely held, prudently arrived at, and an act, if I might add, of heroic integrity."

The chairman eyed his fellow board members, whose simple nods said it all. He gaveled the hearing to a close. Dennis was granted his CO status. He did a year's alternative service, as an orderly in a mental hospital.

The priest to whom my father told all this was a World War II combat veteran whose wounds had left the right side of his face frozen. His right eye would often fill up and overflow. Tears would stream down his one cheek without his being aware of it. That happened now. He said to my father, "General, I think it was big of you to support your son, but frankly, I don't think your boy's attitude does him much credit."

"I suppose I should agree with you," my father replied. "I share your instincts. I've spent my whole life defending our point of view. But I don't think you understand my son's position well enough to see the point he has. All I know for sure is this: if human beings don't drastically change the way they resolve their conflicts, we won't survive this century." Then, after a pause, still unaware of me, my father added, "My son Dennis certainly represents a drastic change from the way we were brought up. And that may be just the change we need."

There was a thin glistening on the priest's cheek as he listened to my father. I had to remind myself that his tears signified no particular emotion. Unlike mine. It wasn't only that I envied Dennis, confronting as I had to, yet again, how little I knew of my father's true capacity. It was also that I saw Dad, for the first time, as a "child-changed father," in the phrase Cordelia used of Lear. Dennis had touched him in that dark corner of the self on the walls of which his worst fear was scrawled.

And what was that but the fear of nuclear war? When Dad had first encountered the real risk of Armageddon, perhaps in meetings with our Bolling neighbor Curtis LeMay, perhaps in Wiesbaden while Nikita Khrushchev pawed at Berlin, or perhaps during the Cuban missile crisis when the Chiefs wanted to attack, how could that misfit general have ever imagined that a glimpse of the way out of this dead end would come from his lost-soul son?

It was as if the BU chapel fire had melted the ice onto which I had launched myself. Yet even as I felt the ice opening under me, I refused to contemplate a decision to quit the priesthood. I had taken a solemn vow. If that commitment could not hold — here was the fear — nothing of mine ever would. Abandoning my vocation had come to equal losing the faith. Being a priest had become my way of affirming the existence of God. And if I quit, God, whether He existed or not, would never forgive me.

But in January of 1973 — on the twenty-second, my thirtieth birthday, and the day Lyndon Johnson died — the last shots of the American war in Vietnam were fired. It would take another two years for the Communists to seal the victory, but the Nixon-Laird pullout of GIs was complete. Opposition to the war had formed the spine of my priesthood. What would define it once peace came? The question sparked panic and dread. With a certain desperation, I went that next June to Israel, for a summer-long retreat in the Holy Land. I firmly resolved to lay a new claim on my priestly vocation.

I lived at Tantur, a monastery halfway between Bethlehem

and Jerusalem. On most days I wandered alone in the West Bank towns and, especially, in Jerusalem. I haunted the places attached by the tradition to Jesus — the Holy Sepulcher, the Via Dolorosa, the Mount of Olives, Gethsemane. The shrines had a profound impact on me, although not in the way I expected. Most were tourist traps, insufferably commercial. The most sacred were presided over by smelly monks of various orders and denominations. Their open contempt for each other, and their slightly more implicit disdain for the Jews who policed the sites, repulsed me. The ancient corruptions of Jerusalem put the contemporary corruptions of my own church in a new and unsettling context. See how the Christians love one another? No. See how they vie for superiority and grub for cash. When I bent my head to enter the chamber in the Church of the Holy Sepulcher that enshrines the burial place of Jesus, I was shocked to find not the Empty Tomb but a toothless bearded Greek monk waiting to sell me a candle. "One dollar," he barked, a phrase he kept repeating while I, without a thought for the Resurrection, fled.

On the outskirts of Jerusalem, away from the crumbling Crusaders' churches, the Western Wall, the Muslim Dome of the Rock, and the noisy souk is a pristine enclosure called the Garden Tomb. Quiet and tidy, bordered by shrubs and benches, it claims to be the authentic site of the tomb Joseph of Arimathea made available to Jesus. The scene is like an illustration from a picture Bible, complete with a rolled-back boulder. The Garden Tomb was "discovered" in the nineteenth century, presumably by pilgrims who'd reacted to the more ancient shrine as I had. In the tranquil beauty of the garden one is supposed to bathe in the warmth of the old Resurrection faith — but it chilled my soul.

My visceral rejection of the neatly ordered tomb gave me part of what I'd come to Israel for: the sudden, sure knowledge that if the Incarnation means anything, it is that God comes to us in the mess of our conflict, confusion, and chaos. My conflict I saw at last. I returned to the crumbling, contentious Holy Sepulcher. A stone's throw from equally disordered Jewish and Islamic holy places, the church evokes the world's conflict. Before the scene had seemed blasphemous, but now I saw it differently: God is not aloof from any of this. When I reentered the foul-smelling chamber of Christ's "real" tomb, I found it possible to greet the monk and buy his candle. The miracle? Perhaps it lay in my having let go of the need myself to feel superior.

Later in the summer I was shown the holy places by Father Pierre Benoit, the aged French Dominican scholar who'd been a moving force behind the groundbreaking new translation of the Jerusalem Bible. Father Benoit had even more disdain for the commercialized pieties than I'd had. His commentary was laced with dismissive phrases — "It is said that . . ." and "Some fools believe . . ."

After a day of visiting sites tied to the beginning and end of Jesus' life, Father Benoit without explanation led me to the door of a Russian Orthodox convent. Some moments after his forceful knocking, the grill opened. At the sight of his face, a nun admitted us into the cloister. With his white robes flying, Father Benoit barreled along a corridor and down several flights of stairs. We entered an underground area undergoing excavation. By the light of swaying work lamps, he pointed to a pit, then waved me over. Adjusting one of the lamps, he showed me a simple horizontal slab of stone still wedged in the dirt. It was about two feet wide and six or seven feet long. Without a trace of his earlier cynicism he said, "This is the threshold stone of one of the ancient city gates. It was buried in the rubble of the Roman destruction in the year 70 and only recently is uncovered." The changed expression in his eyes drew me in. "It is certain that Jesus of Nazareth stepped on this stone on his way to Golgotha." He paused, then said again, "Certain."

Embedded in the floor of the great church in Bethlehem is a

marker that reads *"Hic Incarnatus Est."* In the Byzantine basilica it had not registered: *Hic.* Here the Word became flesh. But in this rough pit, the scandalous facticity of our faith hit me. *Here.* The infinite accepted limits. Why? So that a limited creature — me, for one — might accept limits too. With no awareness of doing such a thing, I knelt down in the dirt of that excavation, bent to the threshold stone and kissed it. The cold, clean surface against my lips — I feel it every time I think of the event. This was what I'd come for.

Touching the stone that had been touched by the feet of Jesus of Nazareth confirmed me in my faith — the faith I had been preaching to others but had failed to fully embrace myself. Jesus had crossed this stone for me, not because of my tidy life or my good behavior, not because I'd kept my vows, not because I was a general's son or even a priest. He had done so simply because I exist. God's love for me, manifest in this man, is a gift, not a reward. Grace, not salary.

Years before coming to Israel, I had gone as a literary pilgrim to Sewanee, Tennessee, hoping that Allen Tate's laying on of hands would take me out of the priesthood. The opposite had happened. Now I had come to the Holy Land clinging to the wreckage of my priestly identity. My brush with the sources of biblical faith changed the question entirely. It was not my commitment to God that mattered, but God's to me. And that commitment simply cannot be broken. The Holy Land would be forever holy to me because there I learned that believing in myself is not by definition the opposite of believing in God. I went to the Holy Land to ask Him what He wanted of me, thinking I already knew. But I heard nothing in the breeze off the desert. The question was no longer What does God want? but What do I want? The two questions were the same.

When I left Israel at the end of that summer, I knew I would serve out my assignment as chaplain at Boston University for another year. And I knew that I would preach the good news of Jesus Christ more pointedly than ever in what time remained to me in the pulpit. But I also knew finally that my days as a Paulist were numbered. It would be my deepest secret for a time yet, but I had made my decision to leave the priesthood.

About a year later, in 1974, I went to Washington to tell my parents. Observing the form required by my superiors, I would quietly resign from the campus ministry at BU and begin a twelve-month leave of absence before applying to Rome for "laicization." Even though this process involved several time-consuming steps, my mind was clear. The decision I'd come to in Israel had only been confirmed. As I approached my father's house, I was acutely aware that undergirding every aspect of the religious and political transformation I had been through was the war that had come between us. Later I would realize that my time as a Paulist — from John Kennedy to Gerald Ford, from the autumn of 1962 until the very week in the spring of 1975 when I sent my final letter to the pope — had coincided almost exactly with the time of America's war in Vietnam. For better and for worse, the war destroyed the thing in me that had made the priesthood possible.

I faced my parents across the kitchen counter. "I'm taking a leave of absence from the priesthood," I said. "I'm going to resign."

My mother exhaled. Only then did I realize that she had not taken a breath since I'd told them I had something serious to say. My father was staring at the cigarette clutched in the fingers of both his hands. His decidedly unconsecrated fingers.

Finally, pushing her chair away and standing, my mother said, "I expected this." She left the room without looking at me, or asking her question: Where is the place in heaven for the mother of a priest who quit?

When Dad raised his eyes the smoke clouded them, but even so, the depth of their cold rejection made me see what a puerile fantasy it had been of mine, that having found a place in his heart for Dennis, he could find one for me. But Dennis had called into question only his life's work, while I was reimposing a curse upon his soul.

"Can I tell you why?" I asked.

He only stared at me. Where was the man who had wept beneath my hands? He was as far from weeping now as it was possible to be. So was I. And why, since I had never seen hatred aimed at me before, did I think that's what I saw? What a devil's bargain had bound the two of us all these years. Why shouldn't he hate me, for my having been a party to it?

On the way here I had rehearsed a statement, foolishly thinking it might soothe him, and since I had nothing else to say, I recited it. "I'm leaving the priesthood, Dad, because I want to have a life like yours, with a loving wife and children."

"Children?" Now his eyes flashed. I glimpsed the full force of his feeling. Yes. Hatred, sure enough. "Why would you want children?" he said. "They would only grow up and break your heart."

I found it possible to stand and say, "I'm sorry that's the way you feel, Dad." And I left, admitting for the first time that I could not fill the void in him with anything I did or anything I was. The void was bottomless. He was on his own. So was I. Sad. Free.

11

THE LAST WORD

MY MOST INTIMATE times with Dad had been the two of us riding in automobiles. The green Studebaker on the way to early Mass at St. Mary's in Alexandria, me to be the altar boy, him to make a tee time. The Crown Victoria cruising along Mount Vernon Parkway, him whistling "Beautiful Dreamer," me cradling the football we would throw when we reached the fields at Fort Hunt. The Studebaker again, driving me on my paper route, if it was raining. The Air Force blue staff car, him and me in back, his driver at the wheel, bombing down the autobahn toward Frankfurt, where I would caddie for him. And the dried flowers of golf clubs and lentil soup would open for me ever after. That staff car was the one he leaned against, smoking, when he saw me score my touchdown on the hilltop field above Wiesbaden. Then the Lincoln in Washington, in the era of crises over Berlin, me finally at the wheel, him anointing me with his fear of the Bomb. My replying with a first promise to be a priest.

The last time I was in an automobile with my father at the wheel was in 1980, in his fat black Cadillac. I know the year because our daughter Lizzy was in the car seat next to me, not yet two. It was Easter morning, the occasion for our rare visit. Tension was still the norm. Next to Lizzy was Lexa, whom I had married in 1977. She is a novelist whom I had met because we shared a literary agent. As soon as I'd seen her, I knew that if my career as a writer never did anything for me except make our meeting possible, it would be more than enough. Lexa is a self-possessed, strong woman, the deepest person I know. She was riding silently now, a hand firmly on our baby's leg.

My mother was in front, next to Dad. We were doing sixty on the crowded Beltway south of Washington, on the way to visit Brian and his family near Quantico, Virginia. An Easter egg hunt was the idea, a holiday dinner, a stab at family happiness. Quantico is the site of the FBI Academy, where Brian was head of SWAT training at the time. I was sitting directly behind my father, who was seventy years old. I was excruciatingly aware of the fact that two times, then three, his head had drifted forward and down, then snapped up as he came awake again.

"Hey, Dad," I said, "why don't you pull over? Let me drive."

"I'm fine."

"You're sleepy, Dad. I can see you nodding."

"I'm fine."

"No, really. I'd like to drive."

"I said I'm *fine.*" In his anger, his foot went down on the accelerator. The car lurched up to seventy. I saw my mother slyly reach across for her seat belt and fasten it. I looked down at my snoozing baby girl. She was the new meaning of "Beautiful Dreamer" to me. I looked over at Lexa, who was glaring at me. My father had insulted her by refusing to come to our wedding, and since then he'd been barely civil to her. His reactions had been a mystery to her — she was not Catholic, had never known me as a priest. She could handle what to her could only seem my father's pettiness — she hadn't known him as a man of power either — but she could not handle his endangering our baby. Neither could I.

I reached forward and touched my father's shoulder. "Frankly, Dad, you're making me nervous."

"Well, you can *stay* nervous," he said.

And I did. It became physically dangerous to push him further. Here we were, driving south toward Richmond after all. But instead of Moscow threatening us, it was he.

Fortunately the rush of his anger woke him up, and we made it safely to Quantico. When we were out of the car, away from my father, I told Brian that we would not be driving back with him. Brian said he'd handle it. Ever the sleuth, he later filched my father's car keys and gave them to me. When it was time to go, Dad seemed to have forgotten that anything had happened, and he meekly got in on the passenger's side. I drove.

It was around that time that his doctors first spoke of Alzheimer's as a possible explanation for his behavior. They could never say for sure. Small strokes were cited as another explanation for what was, in any case, an onset of dementia. I began to read about Alzheimer's. Although it was first described at the beginning of this century by the German physician for whom it is named, it was only in the 1980s that symptoms long attributed to "normal" aging were recognized as consequences of this disease.

My mother fixed on Alzheimer's as an explanation for the transformation of her once loving husband into a restless and irritable narcissist. Now she encouraged me and Lexa to reevaluate his crude behavior toward us, especially his rudeness toward her. Lexa had been married and widowed before I knew her, but her love for her late husband, Tim Buxton, lived on in her abiding love for his family, particularly his mother, Helen, and his Aunt Lyd. Lexa's own father, Bill Marshall, and her stepmother, Betty, had opened their hearts wide to me. By comparison, my parents were stingy and rude. How could I explain to Lexa that their ill feeling wasn't aimed at her, but at me?

Still, I grasped at the straw of this new explanation too. In 1981 and 1982, I wrote what I intended to be a reconciling novel about a senior American intelligence official and his worshipful son. Called *Family Trade*, it is a romantic political thriller in which the son tracks through the labyrinth of Cold War deceit to discover that his long-disgraced father was in fact a patriot and hero. I dedicated the novel to my father, and sent him an early copy. He wrote back a respectful, almost affectionate letter in which he made it a point to say that I had handled espionage tradecraft convincingly. When I read his response, I gratefully began to believe that a recovery was possible. I wrote back, expressing such a hope. Then, out of the blue, came another letter from him, a savage critique of the "foul language" I'd used. This letter ended, "Never, repeat NEVER dedicate another novel to me! Never!" This second reaction made no sense. Was it the effect of Alzheimer's? Perhaps, but I later learned that what triggered this fresh rejection was the bad-taste headline of a *Washington Post* feature story about the novel and me: "Confessions of an Ex-Priest."

Indeed, in another context there was supposed to be such a confession, but I'd refused to make it. In leaving the priesthood I had been advised that my letter requesting dispensation, addressed to His Holiness, should acknowledge that the entire enterprise of my vocation had been a mistake — *my* mistake. It would help if I could confess to grievous violations — a secret promiscuity, say. Compulsive masturbation was good. Complaints about the negative personal impact of the rigors of the long years spent in training would help too. I should by all means describe my ministry as a failure. I should assert that my own mental health and moral state, as well as the good of the Church, would be served by my departure from the sacred fraternity of the priesthood.

I refused to do any such thing. Instead I wrote: "I enjoyed my life as a priest, and regard the training I received for it in the Paulist seminary as a privileged and rare experience. I love the Paulist community, and remember my years of service at Boston University as successful and happy."

By the time I wrote this letter, in 1975, I had landed a position as playwright-in-residence at the Berkshire Theater Festival in Stockbridge, Massachusetts. There, with the gracious support of a writing mentor, the playwright William Gibson, I had begun my career as a writer. I concluded my one and only letter to the pope, "In summary, my request for laicization rests chiefly on these two facts of my present life: that I am pursuing the work of writing and not pastoral ministry, and that I no longer choose to live as a celibate religious." Some confession. I would not meet the extraordinary Lexa Marshall for nearly another two years. "I solemnly swear that all of the statements I have made in these pages are true."

Attached to this letter in my files, I have found a letter written in support of my petition by David Killian, my Paulist friend and fellow jailbird. Reading Dave's letter now, I am deeply grateful at his refusal, too, to describe my priesthood as a failure. His letter, dated January 24, 1976, is addressed to the president of the Paulist Fathers. I quote it because its affirmation is so precious to me: "Jim, in my opinion, was a dedicated and faithful priest — charismatic and prophetic. His penchant for speaking the truth and his impatience with hypocrisy often might have disturbed others. Nevertheless, he also brought a love and gentleness to his ministry which was reconciling and healing . . . His sense of prophetic responsibility led him to criticize those in authority, whether bishop, university president or those in national government. He was especially outspoken against the war in Vietnam."

I imagine those Vatican monsignors, adding up the score, slapping a label on me: classic authority problem.

Not problem, Eminenza — solution.

His Holiness Paul VI, whose 1965 speech at the United Nations was part of what set me on this trajectory, did not reply to my request. He had his reasons. Perhaps those who'd advised a *mea maxima culpa* had been right. In any case, more than two years passed since my resignation from BU, and I heard nothing from Rome. Having met Lexa and fallen passionately in love with her, I chose not to wait any longer for permission to get on with my life. That I had still not been dispensed from my vows by our wedding day was the reason my father gave for his boycott.

Predictably, perhaps, I received the dispensation, embossed and in Latin, less than two months later, but by then I was, by the lights of the Roman Catholic Church, an excommunicant. That gave my father a sacred justification for continuing in what was by then a fundamental attitude. Once or twice, he asked me to understand: nothing personal to Lexa, mind you. Not personal, really, even to me. Just the law of God, a matter of right and wrong, the moral mandate of a lifetime. Such a tender fucking conscience, I thought. At last I found it possible to sympathize with Roger "Terrible" Touhy, who'd heard him as the "voice of doom." He'd become the voice of doom to me. But what my mother thought, and said behind his back, was that he was sick.

In truth, he was.

My family found itself reading about Alzheimer's effects just as they advanced in him. We read about irritability, and recognized the crux of the endless mixed signals and crossed wires that made even simple transactions dangerous. We read about "perseveration," the continuous repetition of a word or gesture, and thought of his odd new habit of saying "Oh boy" in every circumstance. We read about a patient's inability to handle distress in confusing situations — "catastrophic reaction" — and while my brothers thought of his outburst, say, checking into a hotel for Kevin's wedding, my mind went way back to my ordination in 1969. Were those once-in-a-lifetime wrenching sobs the start of this strange physical disease? Or were they symptoms of the old spiritual one with which I'd been so familiar?

Eventually there would be his versions of "hyperorality," the compulsion to put things into the mouth; of hoarding — he kept cartons of cigarettes under his bed even after he'd forgotten how to smoke; and of paranoid delusion. His last time at the wheel of an automobile, "Beautiful Dreamer" no more, was a mad midnight effort to drive from Ocean City, Maryland, to Washington, "because," as he told the trooper who tracked down his Cadillac on a back road of the Eastern Shore, "the president needs me."

Toward the end, he would seem to be consoled by a compulsive fondling of stuffed animals — "hypermetamorphosis." My children, who never knew my father as a figure of power and grace — how to convince them that once presidents did need him? — recognized him as a fellow lover of Kermit the Frog, which they chose as a special gift for him.

The most staggering consequence of the disease — to us, and I am sure to him — was the progressive difficulty in communication, the gradual loss of the ability to speak — "aphasia" — and of the ability to write — "agraphia." I believe now that my father's angry letters to me, increasingly halting and jerky, were what my mother insisted they were: symptoms of illness and markers on the road to the most terrible solitude. He was losing his mind, and the rest of my family was following me in losing him.

My mother was shattered. She remained a sharp and lively woman, yet unhesitatingly devoted herself to the restrictive regimen of taking care of him, first at home, then in a nearby nursing home where she visited twice a day. She was a guardian of his dignity, making sure he was properly cleaned and dressed. She insisted that aides call him "General," not "Joe," although behind her back they had taken to calling him "Oh Boy," before he stopped saying even that. For a time, mocking her, nursing home orderlies called him "General Diet," referring to the designation card that appeared on his dinner tray. My mother ignored the gibe, and eventually the staffers grew accustomed to my father's title, and used it unfailingly. If my mother had wanted them to salute, she'd have found a way to get them to do it. Her attitude was catching. In time they also took pride in what my father had been. My mother was his omnipresent protector. She took her meals with him. Without a hint of condescension, she fed him herself, as she had fed her babies years before. "Open wide," she'd say.

When I visited, I would feed him too, although what I said to get him to open up for the swooping spoon was "Airplane." I always thought of those B-52s. He stopped recognizing us, which was a shocking letdown for everyone in my family except me. For the first time in fifteen years, I did not sense his tensing when I arrived. I could sit with him for hours with no fear of bad feelings. I could shave him, clean his dentures, bathe him even. He gave himself over into my hands. I could even tell him my stories as I was writing them. While working on a novel inspired by his life, *Memorial Bridge*, I would hold his hand and relate whole passages, including my own presumptuous interpretations of his experiences in the Pentagon. He would listen as if nothing I wrote offended him. All because he did not know what I was saying, because he did not know it was me. It was the next best thing to being reconciled.

He would look at my mother, she said, as if she were a stranger. But what seemed even sadder to her — she showed me this by holding up a mirror — was that he no longer recognized himself. One day a bright young college graduate joined the nursing home staff as the new occupational therapist. She came upon my father in the hallway, sitting in his wheelchair beside my mother. The young woman spoke cheerfully to my father and, pulling a table over, put a fresh new pad of paper and a crayon down in front of him.

"He doesn't do that anymore, dear," my mother said. Her voice was pleasant, but she was determined to protect him from yet another failure. By then it had been three years since my father had written, more than a year since he had spoken intelligibly or recognized anyone. But while my mother explained this to the therapist, my father began to move the crayon across the paper. Both women watched his hand. Even scribbling would be an achievement.

The marks he made were not scribbling. In a sweeping, unsteady cursive scrawl, he was forming letters. My mother and the therapist leaned forward. Unmistakable letters. "M," the young woman said. "That's an M." My mother said nothing. She watched his hand move across the paper, the letters becoming visible individually, until a word was uncovered.

"Mary," the young woman read, and watched while my father wrote it again. And then again. The script was jerky, but legible. "Mary. Mary. Mary." Down the page. He did not stop. And he did not look up. "Mary."

The young woman looked at my mother, who said, "That's me."

The next day, my mother arrived at the nursing home with an entire box of crayons and a large pad of construction paper. She sat beside my otherwise uncomprehending father as he filled page after page with the one word "Mary." This went on for some days until, having forgotten again and once more in the grip of hyperorality, he put the crayon in his mouth. But my mother had her pages, his last word, the absolute treasure of her life.

Brian is now a seasoned FBI agent, assistant special agent in charge of the field office in Chicago. When I call him there, and am put on hold, a recording tells the story of the FBI's Windy City legends. A featured segment relates the tale of the capture, in 1942, of Roger "Terrible" Touhy. I am surely the only caller who, hearing the canned narration, ever wants to weep. "The FBI kid looked at me blankly," Touhy wrote, referring to my father. "That was it. The big escape was all done. The date was December 29th." Three weeks later I was born. And the rest is history. My history.

Just as I was leaving the priesthood in the fall of 1975, only a few years after Hoover's death, I became a volunteer bus monitor in Boston during the busing crisis. My job, as a delegate of the federal court, was to be an adult presence, supportive of the children and ready to report abuses. On the first morning of school, when I boarded a bus that was half full of black girls and boys about to run the gauntlet into all-white South Boston, one of the boys said, "You're an FBI man, right?"

The question shocked me. I recognized the child's awe as a version of what I had felt at his age. I asked him why he thought so. He eyed the plastic ID tag that was pinned to my lapel and replied, "Because the FBI are the only white folks on our side." And I thought of Bobby Kennedy, that day in the Justice Department auditorium, when he changed my mind about America.

Not long after that day in Justice, I met Patrick Hughes, who accompanied — and led — me on so much of this journey. He so endeared himself to my parents that at times their wariness about my embrace of this or that ritual of the new Church, or even my participation in some demonstration or other, would seem mitigated if I said Pat was there. The cold judgmentalism of the Catholic left was softened by my submission to it in Pat's company. Alone of nearly everyone I knew, he understood the division of my heart and the cowardly feelings I tried to hide. I had no secrets from Pat. His decision to leave the priesthood was a harbinger of my own. He and Marianne would be godparents to our Lizzy, and he would be the namesake of our own Pat.

Like some other ex-priests, Pat Hughes continued to celebrate the Mass despite his renegade status. We differed on that. I knew as I stood at the altar in Sacred Heart Chapel at the University of Notre Dame, where I was a visiting lecturer the summer after leaving BU, that I would never consecrate the bread and wine again. Except for Larry Kessler and Monsignor Jack Egan, to whom I'd confessed, no one in that vast church — a throng of Catholic lefties assembled for a summer institute on peace and justice — knew of my decision. They had no reason to understand why, as I fed them Communion, tears streamed down my face, or why, after I gave the last blessing, Larry and Jack came into the sanctuary to embrace me.

I would not preside at the Eucharist again, and for some years I refused even to think of preaching in a church. That was my way, I think, of making clear to myself, if to no one else, that I was not a priest. Being not a priest became more a note of my identity than its opposite had been. That changed when, on a shocking October day in 1980, Marianne asked me to preach the eulogy at Patrick's funeral. He had died of a heart attack. To preach for him meant standing at the pulpit of Boston's Paulist Center Chapel again, where I had lived and from where I had set out each morning as a priest. There was no question of refusing Marianne. When I'd taken my place in front of the grieving congregation and began to speak of Patrick, I knew exactly what to say. I told the story of his hurling himself out onto the thin ice at Mount Paul novitiate in 1962, and of my standing with my classmates on the shore, crying, "Go Patrick! Go Patrick!" I intended only to say that I'd recognized a man I wanted to be with, but — and this is what made it preaching — I now recognized in his story a reminder of that other One.

"Who is that, walking on the water?"

"Isn't that Jesus? The only one we loved?"

"Is that you, Lord?" Peter called.

And the Lord replied, "Come!"

And Peter went, right out onto the water, without a thought for consequence, or a nod to those who said it couldn't be done. And for a moment, he was walking on water too.

Once again I understood what Patrick had done, inviting me to stop worrying about being dry. To stop worrying about being worthy of his friendship, or of God's. It is an invitation creased, folded, carried near my heart which still puts me on my knees in gratitude. I concluded Patrick's eulogy by saying of him, "We were not worthy of his love until he gave it to us. And then weren't we worthy of all there is!"

Christian belief itself began with a eulogy, the one Peter preached of Jesus on Pentecost. That event revealed the structure of hope, which begins in despair. The followers of Jesus had disgraced themselves. In effect, they had all broken vows, they were all spoiled priests. "They all forsook Him," as Mark put it, "and fled." They went their separate ways. Only a miracle could have changed them from confused, inarticulate peasants into preachers who would ignite an empire. The miracle was that eulogy, delivered by a coward, of the only man he ever loved, the one whom he betrayed.

What I remembered in telling the story of Pat Hughes — this was his last gift to me — was that storytelling itself can be a priestly act. If there is something peculiarly "Catholic" stamped upon my soul, it is implied by this notion that the imagination itself is sacred. All of our greatest art, music, architecture, and poetry proclaim it as such, and so do the more modest efforts of ordinary writers. Patrick thought that what I wrote was sacred, long before I dared to. For a novelist imbued with this idea, the very act of storytelling, of arranging memory and invention according to the structure of narrative, is by definition holy. It is a version, however finite, of what the infinite God does. Telling our stories is what saves us; the story is enough.

And wasn't that just what my children taught? "Tell us a story, Dad" — their nightly refrain. And why shouldn't it have been? What the children have no way of knowing is how their stories bring resolution to ours. In addition to our daughter Lizzy and our son Patrick, Lexa and I are the parents of Jenny Marshall Carroll, who was born and died on the same day, April 24, 1986, a little more than a decade after I had left the priesthood. She was a perfect, beautiful little girl whom I believe God had sent as an unexpected miracle. She lived, as a miracle to me, nearly her entire life in our arms. She was born premature, but not so early that she wouldn't have done fine in any city hospital. But we were in the country. The small hospital to which we desperately went in the middle of a thunderstruck night had nothing our daughter needed. She was delivered by a terrified anesthesiologist. She lived for an hour and twenty minutes. Her eyes were open the whole time, and she looked at us. When I saw that she was going to die, I said to the nurse, "Bring me a glass of water."

The nurse said to her colleagues, with alarm, "He's going to faint!"

I said, "No. I'd just like some water, please."

Another nurse cried, "Get him a chair!"

I said, "I would just like to baptize our daughter, please."

"Oh," said the nurse. "You want baptism? We can have a real priest here in ten minutes."

No obstetrician, but a real priest.

And to my surprise at last, after Pope John, Hans Küng, Cardinal Spellman, Martin Luther King, Allen Tate, Daniel Berrigan, and Pope Paul VI, I thought: I am a real priest.

This was Jenny's gift to me. What I was never able to get from my father, or from the Church, or from my beloved Paulists — a sense of my first vocation as *mine* — I got from this perfect child with the large heart and the lungs that were just a little small. I *am* a real priest, if only to you. That is what I thought, but what I said, with water sealing my bond with her forever, was, "I baptize you, Jenny, in the name of the Father, and of the Son, and of the Holy Ghost."

From one scrubbed room to another. From my daughter's fiercely opened eyes to the eyes of my father, which are closed. The words of this story are inscribed in the air between me and the barely moving form under the sheet on the bed, six feet away from the chair in which I sit. "Dad" is the word. "Daddy." "Abba." This is his room at the Mount Vernon Nursing Home, two miles south of the house in which, even now, my mother is sleeping. It is the middle of the night. Otherwise, she would be here. My brothers and I are taking turns sitting with him around the clock, because he is dying.

A month ago, having come down with a debilitating pneumonia, he slipped into a coma. He has not opened his eyes since, but his breathing is slow and steady. His face is pink, and his hair is a soft and snowy white, angel's hair at last. He has a baby's skin. When I wash him, I use what I have learned in washing Lizzy and Pat.

A couple of days ago, the night nurse found that he had

moved enough in his unconsciousness to have pulled the feeding tube from his nose. He had been receiving nutriment through it for weeks. The nurse, as it happened, had hospice experience and knew not to simply reinsert the tube, as others had done. She called Mom and asked for a family decision. It was January 15, 1991, the birthday of Martin Luther King and the day by which Saddam Hussein was supposed to have removed his troops from Kuwait. When the phone rang, Dennis calling, I was watching the evening news. Only moments before, the night sky over Baghdad had begun to explode with the Roman candles of American bombs and Iraqi antiaircraft fire. When I heard Dennis's voice, I'd thought at once he was calling to share the grief that yet again our country was at war. But no. "Dad," he said. "It's Dad."

I flew to Washington at once. Dennis picked me and Kevin up at National Airport. Soon we were together with Mom in a small sitting room at the nursing home. The doctor had recommended an intubation, the surgical insertion of the feeding tube into Dad's abdomen. The procedure would enable him to live indefinitely, but in what state? Our mother's point of reference was the fate of Karen Ann Quinlan, who had lived with such a feeding tube for years, unconscious, while curled into a fetal knot. Once such a tube was inserted, who would order it removed?

Our parents had each enacted the living will years before. The Church taught that to prolong life by extraordinary means was not necessary, and in some cases not proper. In *this* case, we all firmly agreed. Dad's eyes had been closed for weeks, which we took as his signal. "He wants to go to God," Mom said, a simple statement of the truth. We called the doctor and told him not to reinsert the feeding tube. Then we began our vigil.

I am grateful to be here in the middle of the night. By now, the war in the Gulf is in fourth gear. During all other hours of the day and evening, television sets blare from every room on the corridor. The resounding noise of explosions, the clatter of armored vehicles, supersonic fighters, missiles — it all sickens me. The TV news people, in their safari jackets and shrapnel vests, convey the panic about gas attacks in Jerusalem. With deadpan neutrality, they report the barely veiled Israeli threats to use the nuclear bomb. The frantic search is on for Scud missile launch sites. The other residents of this wing of the nursing home must be deaf to have kept the volume turned so high. Throughout the day I was in a constant state of nausea, and kept my eye on all the buckets and sinks into which I could vomit. The feeling had been so old, so familiar, and so much a part of my memory of my father. America never more itself. America, in George Bush's terms, escaping at long last the emasculation of the Vietnam syndrome.

I watch Dad breathe, and I unfold my mind from around the primordial image of our relationship, that sepia photo of the brand-new general in his tan uniform, holding the hand of a stunned but eager cowboy. Now I am face-down in the dirt of the end zone, as the one truly glorious moment of my life takes shape. There he is, tall, smoking, perfect in his uniform at last, stars glinting, blue limousine behind. I blink and he is hunched over his putter, stroking the ball, while immediately above him the last of the B-52s hovers with Ah! Bright wings! That roar fades into the silence of our ride along South Capitol Street, the silence out of which spring the words I'd lived to hear and say. And bang, there he is throwing a crumpled linen napkin on his plate. Bang, his head is in my hands, the still point of a sobbing man I hardly know.

My eyes drop to the book in my hands. It is the blue, pocket-sized New Testament that an Air Force chaplain gave me years ago. He said, "I tell GIs, 'Carry it in your shirt pocket, at your heart. These books are known to stop bullets.'" Already lost, I thought he was joking. So I replied, "But can they stop a war?" The chaplain looked at me as if one of us were dead.

Dead? I feel a cold wind come into my father's room, and immediately I raise my eyes again. My eyes go right to his. My heart is the one that stops, because my father's eyes are open. For the first time in a month, his eyes are open, glaring furiously at me.

"You!" His voice jolts me. I jump in the chair. The one word, but in it I hear everything. You! Here I am dying, and they have left me with you!?

You! My last moments on the earth, and I am with you!?

You! You are starving me! My enemy! My betrayer! You! You are starving me!

I close my eyes, sure that when I open them again, his will be closed, as ever. This is a hallucination, a dream, a nightmare. I open my eyes. And he is still staring at me. His lips are firmly together. You? Did he say, "You"?

"Dad?"

I stand up. "Dad?"

I move closer. His eyes seem to follow me, like some mosaic Christ's. How is this possible? "Did you speak?" His eyes are wet, as if about to spill over. What I see in them is sadness, not anger. "Dad?"

I move around the bed to its other side. And still his eyes follow me. "Dad?"

I bolt from the room, and halfway down the dim corridor I come upon a stout black woman, an aide. "Would you help me?" The desperation in my voice conscripts her. She follows me as we race back to my father's room. I take the woman's hand and pull her to the foot of the bed. "Are his eyes open?" I ask. "Are they?"

"Lord, have mercy," she says, leaning toward him. She ca-
resses the protrusion of the sheet that is his foot. "Joe?"

Her use of his name startles me.

"Joe? Is that you, Joe?"

She moves around the bed, to his side. She takes his hand in
hers, tenderly. His eyes have not left her. "Joe, it *is* you." Spontaneously, she leans to his forehead and kisses him. "It *is* you!"

When she turns to me, she says, "It's a miracle."

A miracle? Who prayed for a miracle? I begin to back out of
the room. Jesus Christ. Instantly waves swamp me, first of regret
that he has come back, then of guilt that I should have such a
feeling. A moment later I am in the phone booth, talking to
Dennis. "He opened his eyes, Den. For a minute I thought he
spoke to me. But he opened his eyes. His eyes are open now.
He's still here!"

And Dennis — how I love him for this, how I envied him —
responded unhesitatingly, "Jim, that's great. Jesus, that is great!"

"Yeah," I said numbly. "And it means we should put the tube
back in. We have to feed him."

"Of course."

"So I'll order it, okay?"

"Should we ask Mom?"

"He's still here, Dennis. We can't starve him if he's still here.
There's no point in asking Mom."

"Right."

"I'll call the doctor now." And I do. He says, "As long as you
understand what this means. Your father may be alive for a long
time."

"I can't starve him if he's still here."

The next morning, I am preparing to leave, to go back to
Boston. Kevin is staying for another day, but I can't stand it anymore. He, Dennis, Mom, and I are crowded into Dad's room so I

can say goodbye. "I'll see you, Dad." The blank look he gives me seems entirely familiar. I almost ask him: Dad, did you speak to me? But I know he didn't. "You!" If anyone said that word aloud, it was me.

I kiss him on the forehead where his angel hair meets his pink skin. "I'll see you," I say again, thinking it is true.

Two nights later, just after midnight on January 20, 1991, at the age of eighty, with Dennis at his side — Dennis, who had refused to abandon the vigil, as years before he had refused to abandon the hope of a father's love — Dad died. It was clear by then that the Gulf War was a rout.

Robert E. Lee's greatness had been apparent to me as a freshman in high school, when I prankishly raised the Stars and Bars on his birthday. It had been apparent also to Abraham Lincoln, who offered Lee command of the Union Army. Lee declined and went back across the Potomac, to his great family mansion in Arlington. Though he had denounced slavery as a "moral and political evil," and though he had opposed Virginia's secession as "anarchy, nothing but revolution," he embraced the Confederacy. Lincoln regarded him as a traitor.

Union soldiers were beaten badly in the early battles that raged across the rolling hills on which, a century later, I would play games of "army" and "war." They hated Lee in particular. Beating retreats to Washington, Yankees fell like furies upon Lee's estate. They took it over, and with pointed contempt they dug up Nellie Custis Lee's rose garden and used it as a mass grave for their dead. An act of personal vengeance aimed at Lee led to the transformation of his estate into Arlington National Cemetery.

My mother's last gift to my father was the site of his grave. When, about a year before he died, she visited the cemetery superintendent, the man showed her the nearly full section that was designated for future burials. The plot he offered was in a remote corner among innocuous tombstones — not what Mary Carroll had in mind at all. The superintendent was an old man himself, and Mom asked if he would be interred in Arlington. When he said yes, she asked if he would show her the place he'd picked out for himself. He was delighted to do so. While they walked among the markers and door-shaped tablets, doors opened on their stories. The superintendent described his own career, and the general's wife described her husband's. By the time they stood together on the knoll just to the side of the Tomb of the Unknown Soldier, the most sacred hill of all, she was holding on to his arm. The man pointed out the nearby graves of General Thomas White, an Air Force chief of staff, of General Maxwell Taylor, and General Lewis B. Hershey. My mother told him related stories of "my Joe." The superintendent marked the end of their hour together by taking her to the highest point of that knoll, as close as one could get to the shrine of the Unknown, from which the entire city could be seen across the bridge that had linked Lee to Lincoln at last. And he offered her the spot for Dad.

The requiem took place at the pristine post chapel at adjacent Fort Meyer, a Mass offered by an old family friend. The chapel is a smaller version of the austere white-steepled church at Bolling Air Force Base, where this personal history began. My family assembled in the little church with a hundred others — friends, neighbors, a few of Dad's retired colleagues, former golfing partners, several dozen uniformed military officials, and an assistant director of the FBI. Lexa, Lizzy, and Pat sat together in the second row.

As the ceremony was about to start, I stood outside with my brothers under the chapel awning. It was a bitterly cold day. We were five six-footers, dressed alike in dark suits and topcoats. We were bareheaded, and the crystal cold displayed us to one another. When our eyes flicked over each other's faces, we saw how time had boiled our features down to what made us alike — the same knobby chin, our mother's nose, and our father's forehead. Each of us was losing his hair according to the same pattern, and it was turning gray.

Joe, now a senior psychology professor at the University of Puerto Rico, had made a career of caring for the disabled. At Boston's Perkins Institute for the Blind once, a doctor told me Joe was well known as an advocate for blind, deaf, and crippled students. Joe had named his two children for our parents. He was first in the pallbearers' line, partnered with me. He stood half straight, leaning on his cane.

Dennis's hair was long, well over the collar of his coat. On his lapel he wore a large button, a flowered portrait of a Hindu deity. After his CO days, he had gone on to be a permanent student until, lo and behold, he'd emerged from the academic cocoon with a Ph.D. in biochemistry. He had distinguished himself as a bench scientist at James Watson's laboratories. By now he was a senior USAID health official, overseeing efforts to combat tropical diseases like malaria and river blindness in the poorest nations of the world. With his wire-rim glasses he still looked like John Lennon.

Kevin was a social worker in Massachusetts. Beginning as an undergraduate volunteer working in an orphanage, he had spent his adult life rescuing children from abusive situations, trying to help stressed families find ways to stay together, and protecting vulnerable members when families broke apart. His open-hearted presence calmed fears, dampened conflict, put families back in touch with basic affection — all services he had performed, unsung, for us.

Brian was the baldest of us, and the best looking — our own Sean Connery. When an FBI agent retires, he turns in his gun and badge, which are then passed on to a new agent. Brian had tracked down Dad's badge, and traded for it. Now he carries that badge, doing the same work in Chicago that Dad had done. He was our father's dream son, and, amazingly for the age, our dream brother.

Standing with us, also as pallbearers, were a former FBI colleague of Dad's and two dignitaries: the current directors of DIA and OSI in their general's uniforms. We were lined up as if we would carry Dad's casket, although according to military protocol, only the young airmen of the honor guard would actually lift him. I had no idea whether that bothered anyone but me.

We huddled near the chapel doorway, puffs of breath at our mouths, while the Air Force Band, playing the funeral march, inched toward us. Behind the band came fifty members of an Air Force honor guard, ahead of a horse-drawn caisson on which Dad's casket rode. Next to the caisson, a stiff, marching handler led the riderless horse, an Army symbol of a fallen general, but which, for my generation, always evokes the memory of the dead John F. Kennedy.

"Excuse us, sirs!" Two captains in silver-edged dress uniforms suddenly appeared among us. They were addressing the generals. "Did anyone leave a black attaché case under the second pew?"

"What, Captain?"

"A briefcase, sir." He turned and pointed into the church. "Under the second pew."

I went inside and looked with the others. Unclaimed briefcase: ominous words, and despite the captains' rigid control, enough to set off alarms in each of us — a shrieking alarm in me. Then I saw it, the thin black box under the very pew in which my beloved Lexa, Lizzy, and Pat were sitting. I pictured the chapel being blown to smithereens — that devious fucker Saddam, what a brilliant stroke! I saw the bricks, the molding and lintels, the columns, the lumber of the pews, the needlepoint cushions, and the limbs of all those people tumbling in slow motion in the air, debris and blood, splinters, dust and shards of glass, the pure anarchy of attack.

The DIA general had read our reactions. "No, Captain, the briefcase is not ours."

Of the two honor guard officers, one went to halt the caisson, the other went into the chapel. He walked down the center aisle, leaned into the second pew, genuflecting neatly. Without a break in his posture, he had the briefcase in his hands, in front of his face as if it were the Word of God. He walked into the sanctuary and disappeared through the door from which the priest was about to come.

My brothers and I, the generals, and the former FBI man had all watched the captain until he and the briefcase were gone. Then we exchanged glances, the secret of our relief.

"You can *stay* nervous," my father had said. Dutiful son to the end, I did.

After the Mass, the honor guard put his casket back on the caisson. My brothers and I, with the generals, fell into rank behind the horses. Brian had the proper bearing of an agent. Dennis, with his hair brushing the collar of his overcoat, a distinguished scientist now, but still a hippie. Kevin, his face tear-streaked, broken by grief, working to keep his shoulders still. Because of his limp, Joe could not stay with us for the walk behind the caisson. As I watched him climb into the first car, I wanted to call out to him with what I suddenly recognized as my oldest wish: Carry me, Joe! Carry me!

The muffled drums began, and we marched like soldiers

through the snow-covered hills of the cemetery. Dad was the one who'd died, so why was I the one whose life flashed before his eyes? The life I have reported here. From the hills of Arlington, one can see the spire of the National Shrine of the Immaculate Conception, where I'd sung as a seminarian; the tower of the National Cathedral, where I heard Martin Luther King preach the week before he died; the swath of Pennsylvania Avenue on which I'd stood for eight inaugurations and a funeral; the Pentagon, to which I'd driven the Lincoln and to which I'd marched; and the Lincoln Memorial, which broods above the black wall of the war. And one can see to the distant hills of Maryland, site of Andrews Air Force Base where, in November 1995, as I am finishing this book, the United States Air Force would name the OSI building in honor of my father.

The reason I felt so relieved to reach his grave was that at last I could rejoin Lexa and Lizzy and Pat. They held me, just in time. Once the priest finished the traditional words, which I confess had never seemed so empty, the freezing air above us split with the sound of guns. *Boom,* bolt action, *boom,* bolt action, *boom!* The twenty-one-gun salute. Patrick clung to me, afraid. Afraid like me.

Afraid, for another thing, of what my once beloved airplanes were raining down on the heads of men, women, and children in the streets of Baghdad. On that very afternoon, January 25, 1991 — the Feast of the Conversion of Saint Paul — thousands of peace demonstrators were heading for Washington, below this hill. The only sizable protest of the Gulf War, seventy thousand strong, was to take place on the Mall the next day. Weeks before, I had helped begin to organize the Boston contingent. But now, it never crossed my mind to stay. As soon as the funeral was over, Lexa, Pat, Lizzy, and I were going home.

The earth had opened under me, my personal abyss. I was

staring in. Yes, I saw the bombs. Yes, I saw the war-induced end of the world. Yes, I saw the doom of history. I saw it all in the death of my father. War had come down to war between us. I saw the lesson of it clear: we both lost. Every ounce of abstraction has been purged from what war means to me, what war does, what it is. No one wins. Victory is impossible. Victory is meaningless. Victory is a lie. Victory is another name for murder. And that is why, as a citizen of a nation still hell-bent on achieving victory, I am and always will be nervous, afraid — a desperate father, a permanent pacifist. The broadly political is always personal for me. And always religious. Doubt is at the heart of my faith, as objection is at the heart of my loyalty. Such is the structure of my patrimony, my curse and blessing both. But it is a patrimony I wish I could have given him: a father and a son at war — but at last this way to see us not at war. I have this story to tell about the two of us, and he never did. The story is a victory over the need to be victorious. These have been my words, but it was his life that gave me mine. At last I have this belief from him: in despair is the beginning of hope, not the end, which is why this particular war was holy, and why this story is sacred.

My father was dead. A fallible man. A noble man. I loved him. And because I was so much like him, though appearing not to be, I had broken his heart. And the final truth was — oh, how the skill of ending with uplift yet eludes me — he had broken mine.

ACKNOWLEDGMENTS

I want to acknowledge editors who have helped bring this story into focus. I first wrote of my history with the FBI for Padraig O'Malley of *The New England Journal of Public Policy*, and of my childhood connection to the Pentagon for Steve Pearlstein of *The Boston Observer*. I wrote of my first sermon for David Rosenberg, editor of *Communion*, published by Anchor/Doubleday. A version of that essay is reprinted here with permission. Some aspects of this story inspired my novel *Memorial Bridge*, which Joseph Kanon edited. Jack Beatty of *The Atlantic Monthly* expertly drew segments of this book together for excerpting in that magazine. Over nearly four years I have told small parts of this story in my weekly column for the *Boston Globe*, where my editors have been Kirk Scharfenberg, Loretta McLaughlin, H.D.S. Greenway, and Marjorie Pritchard. My friend and agent Don Cutler, as always, gave me crucial support. The manuscript editor Larry Cooper helped improve the text. Friends who read early drafts were Tom Kennedy, Bernard Avishai, Tom Winship, Howard Zinn, David Killian, Paul Lannan, John Kirvan, Sissela Bok, and Bob Baer. My brothers Joe, Brian, Dennis, and Kevin were the first to read this book, and the first to affirm it. My editor Wendy Strothman made my work possible at the beginning and at the end. My wife, Lexa Marshall, enabled me to write this book, and our children, Lizzy and Pat, gave me a compelling reason to do so. From the bottom of my heart, I thank you all.